Naihanchi (Tekki) Kata:
The Seed of Shuri Karate

"Exploring the essence of traditional karate through the study of a single form"

Volume Two – Combative Application

By Chris Denwood

Naihanchi (Tekki) Kata: *The Seed of Shuri Karate*

Volume Two – Combative Application

Published by:	Lingwood Publishing
	P.O. Box 105
	Whitehaven
	Cumbria
	CA28 0BF
ISBN:	978-0-9927139-3-5
First Edition:	June 2019
Cover Design by:	Jenny Ling

Disclaimer

http://www.chrisdenwood.com

DEDICATION

This book is dedicated to my beautiful wife, Jenny, and to our two amazing children, Jayden and Isabelle. Each morning, I wake up feeling blessed to have so much unconditional love around me, plus unwavering support, encouragement and belief in my endeavours. Without them I simply wouldn't be the person I am today.

Practicing Naihanchi Kata on the Hojo-Bashi Bridge over Enganchu Pond at the Bezaitendo Shrine and Enkakuji Temple (the temple of the Royal Family) on the grounds of Shuri Castle.

ACKNOWLEDGEMENTS

Similar to my previous work, there are so many people around me who have in some way or another, helped to lay the groundwork for what you will come to read over the following pages and although it would be impossible to mention everyone, my heartfelt acknowledgement goes to all the important people in my life. My family, friends, teachers, students and supporters, who have all provided inspiration for me to continue pushing boundaries and grow on a daily basis. If it wasn't for these fine people in my life, then this book would simply not exist.

To my dear wife, *Jenny*, and children, *Jayden* and *Isabelle*, for their unconditional love, support and encouragement, despite the strain my work can sometimes cause.

To my parents, *John* and *Mary*, for simply being proud of me. This provides me with more energy than they will ever know.

To my students, *Dave*, *John*, *Lewis*, *Garet*, *David* and *Stuart*, for helping with photo shoots and reviewing the final manuscript to make sure that the words I've put to paper accurately reflect what I'm trying to convey. Your help has been invaluable.

Special acknowledgement to *Doug James Sensei*, for sharing his wealth of experience with me and laying such a strong foundation for my *karate*. His exacting standards and encouragement over the years have been pivotal in developing what has become a lifelong passion for martial arts.

Sincere thank you also to *Minoru Higa Sensei* for allowing me the opportunity to study at his historic dojo, to learn from his extensive knowledge and to experience the warm camaraderie offered by members of the *Kyudokan* family.

Finally, my gratitude to *Katsuhiko Shinzato Sensei* for his valued friendship and willingness to share insight into his fascinating approach to *karate*. An incredible teacher and living example of the continual and ego-less refinement of budo that I aspire to.

Looking in awe across the stunning Fukushuen Chinese style garden in Naha. This is a great place to come after a hard day's training to simply sit, relax and reflect.

CONTENTS

Meditating in Seiza at the Okinawa City Budokan. Reflecting on the morning's training and preparing my mind to absorb more study over the afternoon.

"A restricted mind results in restricted movement."

~ Katsuhiko Shinzato

PREFACE

Upon the release of the first volume of this three book series back in October 2013, I was both surprised and honoured to have received such positive feedback and words of encouragement from fellow *karate* practitioners around the globe, who were all kind enough not only to purchase a copy, but to also make time to let me know how much they found it of use. For something that originally began life as a means to personally record my own study, I'm extremely happy to see it grow into something more valuable to others who share a similar passion.

Since then, having been literally overwhelmed by endorsements and kind words, I feel it only appropriate that the first couple of paragraphs of this second volume should be used to express my sincere and heartfelt gratitude to everyone for their amazing support. Indeed, the '*karate* camaraderie' displayed by our global fraternity is a very special quality that is accessible to all who endeavour to consistently drive themselves along the path of *budo* and although these personal journeys may differ radically on the surface, we should always remember that we belong to one family.

Needless to say, my enthusiasm to share more of my approach has been high and even more so since the reception of *Volume One*, but my increasing work schedule and growing family commitments have delayed this second volume somewhat. However, I have endeavoured to immerse myself with any hours I could find into putting together what I hope you will find to be valuable chapters for this next instalment. A project that has proven significantly more challenging to write than initially expected. I knew long before I began to draft ideas that I would be in for many more sleepless nights, consuming copious cups of coffee, during some of the more 'inhuman' hours of the day. But as I always preach to my students, if it was easy then it simply wouldn't be worth it. So appreciating that it's been a rather long wait, I trust you'll come to find this second volume a worthy addition to your martial arts library.

I always find my writing to be most productive either very early in the morning or late at night when everyone else is asleep. Not the ideal routine to support the physical aspects of my training, but there is indeed something very 'pure' about these hours of the day. They seem to offer a sense of clarity and focus that 'standard' hours tend to lack, shining a potential path through all those jumbled up ideas, sparking intermittent flashes of inspiration in my mind. Inspiration that has allowed me to record my exploration of *Naihanchi Kata* down on paper. By far the hardest part of this volume was my efforts to articulate a principle-based approach to *kata bunkai* into words that readers may not only understand, but may also use as a guide towards development of their own approach. I suppose only time will tell whether or not I've actually managed to achieve this.

After the last instalment, which focused almost entirely on a number of fundamental structural and dynamic components found in *Naihanchi Kata*, this second volume draws attention to the combative analysis of the form for the express purpose of civilian self-protection. Rather than taking what seems to have become the stereotypical routine of presenting a collection of discrete applications for each technique or sequence of movements, I would instead like to offer an alternative and what I feel is a more holistic approach. An approach that proposes a cohesive principle-based learning platform given by the form's solo choreography. As such, the pages that follow present what I consider and teach to be some of the most important ideas concerning the practical application methodologies of *Naihanchi Kata*, derived from my continuing study of the form and supported by many other experiences/influences along the way.

Before we get into any detail, I think it would first be useful to review the five stages of analysis I originally presented in *Volume One* and then recapping some of the most important points for consideration. If you already own a copy of *Volume One*, then I would recommend that you quickly re-familiarise yourself with its contents before embarking on this next instalment, as it will certainly help you appreciate the bigger picture. Having said that, it is not necessary to own a copy in order to make full use of the principles covered within the following pages. I have been conscious to write each volume so that they may be used in part, but ideally collaborated together in order to offer a more comprehensive understanding. The choice is entirely with you.

I've made sure to add a pictorial walk-through of the *Naihanchi Kata* choreography I currently practice and teach at my *dojo*. Although we also practice variations to this version and since many stylistic differences exist across the art, this should be used only as a reference guide for the application concepts to follow and as such, perhaps may offer a level of insight into how these may be adapted to best suit your own approach. This is especially useful if you do not yet own a copy of *Volume One*, which of course covers the solo form in greater depth.

The chapters within this volume also include some thought-provoking quotes from pioneering teachers of our past. Specifically, words that have provided me with a source of inspiration for the information I've presented within. I think it's important that in the true spirit of *On-Ko-Chi-Shin* (to learn from the old is to understand the new), we must aim to enthusiastically stand on the shoulders of these giants and like a phoenix rising from the ashes, aspire to evolve as our experience allows, from those insights generously left behind.

I sincerely hope you enjoy the read and my very best wishes.

Chris Denwood

May 2019

INTRODUCTION

The *karate* form known as *Naihanchi Kata* (*Tekki Kata* in *Shotokan Karate*) is a unique pattern, featuring side to side stepping with strange 'crab-like' footwork and is found in almost all *karate* styles derived from the original *Shuri-te* lineage on *Okinawa*. It is a relatively short *kata*, the physical movements are pretty easy to pick up (from a superficial point of view that is) and due to its lack of visual aesthetics, it is rarely a good choice for winning *karate* competitions. In fact, it used to be common to hear modern-day practitioners refer to this *kata* as being boring, lacking in any substance and only worth learning in order to pass grade examinations!

Despite its somewhat insignificant appearance, the movements of *Naihanchi Kata* actually contain a large amount of information and specifically for me, a series of vital lessons, which together aim to provide an understanding of *karate's* fundamental strategies. This essential curriculum is often hidden to practitioners by the apparent simplicity of the form, but those of us who actively choose to scratch below the surface will reveal a *kata* that is immeasurably deep and just like an acorn, holds the blueprint for something much bigger.

There is an old saying, which proclaims that *'kata is the heart of karate'*. It is also supposedly said that one's training should begin and end with *Naihanchi Kata'*. And with such a deceptively rich form, every performance of *Naihanchi Kata*, either knowingly or unknowingly, strives to connect each practitioner to the very core of their art. From tradition, we know that the form was considered to be fundamental by many of the pioneering masters and as such, demanded many years of intense and no doubt explorative practice.

If early *karate* teachers insisted on such levels of study, then I think it's also important for modern-day practitioners to consider *Naihanchi Kata* as being of real significance. Thus, it is essential to approach the form without the 'post war' *karate* filter (those that gave rise to the long range punch/block/kick approach), to generate a more plausible explanation as to why this form may have been so revered by the early generations of *karate* exponents.

Traditionally, the art of *karate* can be split up into three principal components that when stitched together can allow for both a holistic and functional expression of the art. The first of these components is *kata* or 'form', which represents the manifestation of the root principles through physical movement of the human body. Generally speaking, any physical technique can be regarded as *kata*, whether it be a single punch or a fifty movement pattern. Essentially, *kata* defines the art's principles in action.

The second component is *oyo* or 'application' and this covers the combative function of *kata* through the study of *bunkai* (analysis) in accordance with the original aims and objectives of the art. So in other words, in addition to expressing the root principles, we also need to understand the reasons to do so. Originally, combative application (*oyo*) would have always preceded its representative physical template (*kata*), but the loss of knowledge regarding this process means that modern-day practitioners are forced to conduct a method of analysis that consists of reverse-engineering, built around what little historical data we have plus educated judgement, contextual-based assumptions, best fit investigations and common sense.

The third and final component is *hojo undo* or 'supplementary exercises', which sits almost like an umbrella over the other two components and is used to help support and develop the key functional attributes associated with the effective application (*oyo*) of the physical form (*kata*), which in turn expresses the universal principles of the art. In short, everything should fit together like a jigsaw puzzle and if it doesn't then we should ask ourselves why.

Rather than a linear (or academic) arrangement of study where there exists a defined order of things, the three components of traditional *karate* as described above, although being individually unique, are intended to be studied in harmony with one another so that a more spherical (and creative) learning process may be followed. It is imperative that to attain effectiveness, all three components are developed, as omitting any one of these would fail to provide a complete picture. It's also important to make sure that our overall training protocol accommodates for the inevitable compromises we routinely need to make within various elements of practical training in the name of safety.

In my opinion, *kata* should be viewed as a process of learning, rather than a physical entity, with the solo choreography and performance representing only a single element (template) for more comprehensive study. To help demonstrate this idea, the three volumes of this project offers five distinct layers of analysis, which collaborate to provide a more holistic viewpoint. These layers have been divided such that like an onion, each can sit neatly over the former, coming together to surround a central core (i.e. the form itself). They are as follows:

- *Bunkai Shodan* (first level analysis) aims to develop a degree of self-awareness through proper structure, alignment and dynamics of the specific *kata* techniques.

- *Bunkai Nidan* (second level analysis) covers the direct combative application of the form aligned to an overarching strategy for self-protection and a series of guidelines essential to a thorough analysis of *kata*.

- *Bunkai Sandan* (third level analysis) looks at what I call 'breaking the mould' and includes a series of two-person pre-arranged and semi-spontaneous combat drills that amalgamate some of the key principles found within the *kata*. This allows for a more free-flowing approach, helping to bridge the gap between form and function.

- *Bunkai Yondan* (fourth level analysis) looks at the subject of live drilling and explains how the combative lessons associated with *Naihanchi Kata* may be practiced with varying degrees of compliance for specific skill development and more realistic practice.

- *Bunkai Godan* (fifth level analysis) focuses on supplementary training, both physical and mental, detailing also the use of a number of both traditional and more contemporary tools for effective attribute development.

Volume One covered the foundations of the form itself, the outer choreography plus some of the generic structure and dynamic components associated with *Bunkai Shodan*. *Volume Two* (this volume) will continue with the specifics of functional combative application, covering both *Bunkai Nidan* and *Bunkai Sandan* respectively. *Volume Three* will then help to bring the previous two volumes together by detailing a series of practical training methodologies for both *Bunkai Yondan* (live drilling) and *Bunkai Godan* (supplementary training). It is my intention for all three volumes to combine and present a comprehensive training method for *Naihanchi Kata*, providing readers with a solid platform to work from and integrate into their own *karate* studies.

Over the course of the forthcoming chapters, it is my intention to refrain from following the typical "here's a movement and here's the application" type of script and instead try to express what I feel may be found under the surface of *Naihanchi Kata*. Of course, I will still be using direct examples from the form, but these will be predominantly given with the aim of highlighting some of the key conceptual lessons I believe may be communicated through the choreography.

The real potential of this *kata* does not come from the movements themselves, but more so from the principles on which those movements are based, so it is no coincidence that the combative strategies discussed here may be found in pretty much every other effective self-protection system on the planet. Their contextual characteristics are based on simplicity, gross motor action and versatility, so if you expect to find complex applications and advanced training methods herein then I'm afraid you'll have to look elsewhere. Apart from the most gifted martial artists among us, these simply do not function consistently well within the realm of non-consensual conflict. Not only due to the time it takes to acquire such skill, but also the physical/cognitive processes required to deploy them under stress and pressure. In light of this, *Naihanchi Kata* may be viewed as a revealing approach to basics. The core vehicle by which traditional *Shuri*-based *karate* systems transmit their essential combative framework, before progressing onto classical application forms and seeking more progressive and comparatively 'intricate' practices.

The guiding framework presented in this book, which is used to organise and prioritise its essential combative lessons from the *kata* was stumbled upon by chance one evening, during an impromptu training session years ago in my garden *dojo* with a couple of students. To me, the notion of *Naihanchi Kata* incorporating a unified combative strategy based on its sequenced choreography has always made perfect sense, but until that day I was unable to join the dots. As usual, the answer had never been too far away, only requiring a slight shift in my thought process and a hearty dose of *Shoshin* (beginner's mind) before I was able to expose a more complete picture without the distorted mess that my hindering assumptions and former conditioning had already created. Since that day I've been refining this framework and will no doubt continue to refine it further as time goes by.

My study of *Naihanchi Kata* is constantly evolving. My understanding of this form has changed dramatically over the past few years and even as I write these words, new doors are being opened for me to explore. Therefore, please consider this book (and the others in this series) as nothing more than a record of my progress to date and in no way the conclusive outcome of my work. You may have to come back in forty years or so for me to consider proposing something like that!

I would also like to highlight the fact that in no way do I claim to present the original meaning of *Naihanchi Kata*. This is just an interpretation that makes the most sense to me and that has proved most valuable to my training. I share this with open arms simply so that others may also find some value. With each new inspiration I gain new insight from the *kata*. With each new insight I gain a deeper sense of gratitude and more often than not, even more questions to deliberate. Thus, I consider myself to be on the first rung of a very long ladder where *Naihanchi Kata* or indeed *karate* is concerned and I would urge readers not to acknowledge the information detailed here as anything other than work in progress.

Any errors are entirely my own and please read all picture sequences within this book from left to right and from top to bottom.

OK…let's make a start!

NAIHANCHI SOLO CHOREOGRAPHY

"When you perform kata, the most important thing is your mental attitude"

~ Gogen Yamaguchi

There are numerous versions of *Naihanchi Kata* across *karate* styles and so in order to provide a common point of reference for the application concepts to follow, I'd like to share below the solo choreography I currently practice and teach at my *dojo*.

For step by step details on each movement of the form, plus key structural and dynamic components, I kindly encourage you to consult *Volume One*.

One characteristic of *Naihanchi Kata* that separates it somewhat from the majority of *karate's* classical application forms is that the second half of the choreography is essentially a mirror image of the first. We can assume from this that all lessons derived from the *kata* should be practiced equally on both sides of the body. This makes sense within the context of self-protection, as even though we should prioritise what may be probable (i.e. most people are right-handed thus it is more likely to be attacked and develop retainable skill with the dominant side), we must also accept the fact that self-protection is both chaotic and unpredictable. There are no guarantees as to how a situation may present itself or indeed, what opportunities are (or aren't) available at any given time. Therefore, it is ambidextrous skill in fundamental concepts such as those expressed within *Naihanchi Kata* that is most desirable.

Another observation to note is that the longer opening salutation featured within this version of the solo form has been derived from my background in *Wado Ryu*, which is where I received my first exposure to *Naihanchi Kata*. Although not typically part of the versions practiced on *Okinawa*, I was always very much intrigued by its addition, especially since (1) it is akin to the opening salutation from *Kushanku Kata* and (2), the side to side head movements seem to have been derived from Choki Motobu's influence. After learning more about *Otsuka Sensei's* training, his view of classical *kata* from the writings he left behind, plus finding valuable use in its application myself, I have chosen to retain it. You will come to see within the following chapters how this opening salutation may be applied to become an integral part of the *Naihanchi Kata* combative strategy.

BUNKAI NIDAN

PART ONE: CONTEXTUAL STRATEGY

CHAPTER 1

FROM LITTLE ACORNS GROW

"Karate-Do is a lifetime study"

~ Kenwa Mabuni

There are many ways in which one may apply the movements of *kata*. On one hand we may propose that the classical forms once held (and still do hold) definitive meaning, and any stray from that original understanding would simply not be 'true' *karate*. On the other hand, we may argue that the whole essence of *karate* is to develop an individual expression and to 'best fit' what suits our own body, lifestyle, requirements and/or aspirations. A contentious third hand may also suggest that *kata* was never even intended to be combative and instead, prioritizes other potential benefits.

Indeed, the history of *karate* has left modern-day practitioners with mere snippets of evidence scattered throughout what has become an abundance of varied conjecture. This, combined with the many stylistic adaptations during the course of the art's popularization means that to claim any irrefutable answers would be naive at best. Based on individual viewpoints gained through varied training and cultural conditioning, five people could meet in a room and explain the nature of *kata* in five different ways. Who would be 'right' and who would be 'wrong'? Who would have the ultimate authority to claim what is 'right' or 'wrong'? And I suppose more importantly, does it really matter?

Given the way *karate* has been passed down since its initial evolution on Okinawa and the numerous ways it has been interpreted even at its own birthplace, I would suggest that all we can do as honest practitioners of this art is to make use of the information that has been kindly presented to us, value the training we've received to date, trust our rational thought processes and aim to derive logical outcomes that may 'best fit' where we are today on our martial journey. If those viewpoints happen to change during the course of time and experience, then it would be more positive to consider this is a sign of progressive development and that the 'process of *karate*' left by the pioneering master of our past is working as it should be.

I was told many years ago by one of my teachers that the most virtuous *karate-ka* gain admiration from others not through ranks or titles, nor through claims or judgements, but rather, through progressive study and mutual respect for others who are on a similar journey, just following different routes. It is with this sentiment that I always feel very grateful to have the opportunity to learn how and why other practitioners explore their art, especially if their particular methodology turns out to be at odds with my own current understanding. I either find new ways of approaching my daily practice or come to acknowledge those viewpoints that at this moment in time, simply aren't for me. Both of these outcomes offer huge value and help to highlight forthcoming steps along my *karate* journey. It is with a similar open-minded viewpoint that I'd like you to consider the contents of this book. Please take from it what you find most valuable, put to one side that which doesn't suit you and maybe come back to it from time to time to see if anything new comes to light as you continue to grow.

The evolution of *kata* is not unique to *karate* or indeed, the Asian fighting arts. Indeed, examples of *kata* exist in systems of physical expression (combative or otherwise) throughout the world and across thousands of years. In terms of expressing human movement, there is no better means of encapsulating key principles, recording important information, teaching integrated strategies, passing on past experience and offering a distinctive learning platform than *kata*. This is why the notion of *kata* is absolutely central to the practice of *traditional karate* and why as practitioners of this art, we must aspire to understand more about its fruition.

The *kanji* associated with the word '*kata*' are numerous, but the most common used by *Japanese* martial arts is 型 (mould, template or model) and 形 (shape, form or style). In fact, *Japanese* people use the notion of *kata* to express many types of 'correct behaviour' within their society. In terms of *karate*, we may understand *kata* to be a choreographed method of movement that records information and serves as a physical textbook in order to conduct a continual process of skill development. In other words, the acorn that within it holds key elements of the '*karate blueprint*'.

It's interesting to note the *kanji* that *Hironori Otsuka Sensei* selected to write '*kata*' for his *Wado Ryu* was different than other styles of *karate*. The character 型 may also be referred to as *igata*, meaning 'standardised mould, non-transformable and not changing'. *Otsuka Sensei* instead believed that *kata* should be alive and able to conform and change as situations demand. Therefore, he preferred the character 形, which carries a more 'flexible' connotation. He compared the two terms *igata* 型 and *kata* 形 - the former being 'dead' and the latter being 'alive', stressing that the most important aspect of *karate kata* is that it is in fact 'alive'. I think this is an excellent way of looking at *kata* as a malleable process of learning, rather than a stagnant or immovable item.

To give an example of the above idea, I'd like to draw from my experience in learning to play blues guitar. In order to be able to freely improvise solos, it is important to first become comfortable with pentatonic scales. For instance, the minor pentatonic scale has five distinct shapes (or *kata*) that may be joined together end to end and provide the ability to play notes across the whole guitar neck. These were most probably created from past experience and in an attempt to organise essential learning. However, simply running through these in sequence to a backing track would never provide a stimulating solo. The idea of the five shapes is that they may then be transposed into any key, broken up into chunks, combined in different orders and expressed in an infinite number of ways with a variety of techniques. By becoming comfortable with these scale shapes and conforming to some simple rules associated with blues music (a defined context), the door quickly opens up for the ability to perform improvised solos. *Karate kata* I feel is no different to this and by treating *kata* in this way, you open the door to more free-flowing application. Thus, *Naihanchi Kata* choreography may be regarded as being a collection of the fundamental scale shapes of *Shuri*-based *karate*. It is up to us to become competent enough to create our own improvised solos and bring these scale shapes to life.

Another aspect of *kata* to understand is that they are essentially a product of the experiential processes used to create them. As such, were most likely never meant to be the starting place for analysis, but rather to culminate and record the essential findings from those processes. Yet modern-day practitioners have only the *kata* and limited historical resources to work from, so the process of reverse engineering undertaken after learning the solo form is far from ideal. And although I am an enthusiastic supporter of *kata* study, I also appreciate the reality that the solo choreography of *kata* are by no means essential in order to learn effective self-protection skills. That being said, there is no doubt that *kata* is an integral part of the art we call *karate* and in order to study *karate* for self-protection, it is sensible that we aspire to make contextual use of those 'recorded findings' that have been carefully passed down to us from bygone days.

Although maybe not as originally intended, studying *kata* 'back to front' does offer some additional advantages. One of the most significant being that it promotes an open-minded approach in order to analyse the solo choreography and demands that one looks at *kata* with eyes that always seek the potential to see more. This makes the study of *kata* a very explorative process; it allows practitioners to be mindful of many possibilities, investigate numerous avenues, absorb other viewpoints and come towards an understanding that suits them best. Whether or not any of my findings within these pages are akin to the original purpose of *Naihanchi Kata* are for me irrelevant. If this book is to highlight any one aspect of *kata* study then I hope it will be the potential within the process and how this valuable blueprint may be used throughout all *karate* practice.

Indeed, my approach to *Naihanchi Kata* is certainly different now to what it was a couple of years ago and almost indistinguishable from ten years ago. And in my effort to refrain from stagnancy, I fully expect my approach to keep evolving well into the future. However, although it's certainly important that *kata* analysis possesses scope for continual development, I also think that such a challenge requires a robust contextual framework (seed) to grow from. So what I've termed in this book as *Bunkai Nidan* represents what I have found to be a very useful basis for the practical combative application of *Naihanchi Kata*. A starting point if you will and a generic outline from where future advancements may then be made to suit individual pathways.

Where in *Volume One*, *Bunkai Shodan* laid the foundation for foundational structure and dynamics, *Bunkai Nidan* aims to set the scene for practical application, from which those universal structure and dynamic principles may be combatively expressed. It is about emphasising the important characteristics of functional analysis through a series of logical, progressive and conceptual-based lessons aligned to a clear objective – civilian self-protection. This contextual basis highlights the crucial requirements of minimalistic, gross motor actions with high levels of redundancy, all delivered via a dominant mind-set to succeed at all costs. As some of the classical teachings left to us from past masters suggest, the movements that make-up *Naihanchi Kata* are considered to provide core capability for *Shuri*-based *karate*, paving the way for more meticulous and advanced interpretation thereafter.

In later chapters we will also see how the essential strategies conveyed through *Bunkai Nidan* may be further cultivated by a process I refer to as 'breaking the mould', to develop a deeper understanding of the form that is free from the binds of not only its specific choreography, but also our prior examination. This makes up the third level of analysis (*Bunkai Sandan*) and is undertaken to help expand knowledge and to create a more free-flowing expression of *kata* as a process for further learning. Of course, the vastness of *Bunkai Sandan* cannot be defined in its entirety within this book, so I will offer only a few examples based on specific lessons given by the *kata*, which you may then use as a starting point for your own exploration.

So for now and as suggested, in order for *Bunkai Nidan* to take shape we must have a starting point and an applicable agenda by which to base our combative analysis. It's important therefore that we adequately understand the context of our aims, which is king in any human endeavour. Lack of perspective at this early stage would be like setting off on a long journey without a destination, map or means of navigation – in other words, it would almost certainly lead to failure. Consequently, the next chapter centres on the idea of understanding 'context' as our main driving force and sets the scene for the core framework by which we will later develop our *kata* analysis.

CHAPTER II

CONSIDERATIONS FOR PRACTICAL APPLICATION

"The time to strike is when the opportunity presents itself"

~ Tatsuo Shimabuku

From the relatively little-known island of *Okinawa*, the fascinating system of *karate* has spread like wildfire and today, has secured itself in the history books as one of the most prevalent and widely practiced martial arts to date. Inevitably, with such popularity comes adaptation as the methods of practice pass through many different bodies and many different minds, in many different ways.

I consider myself very privileged to have had the opportunity to give up my day job as an engineer and turn my life's passion for *karate* into a professional career. Although not the best financial decision I've ever made, I nevertheless feel far richer for having done so. Although some traditionalists would suggest that making a living from teaching *karate* is counter-productive to the way in which it was originally transmitted, I nevertheless feel much more connected to my art and the way in which I practice, teach and share its benefits since becoming 'full-time' has only been enriched. So much so that every reader of this book will hopefully enjoy a product of this life decision. I think the key is to learn how to strike the right balance, so that tradition may find its rightful place in today's society and thrive, rather than shrivel – it's all down to those well-known and universal complementary opposites we know comfortably as Yin (In) Yang (Yo).

In an effort to maintain such balance, we currently hold both 'open' and 'closed' classes at my *dojo* group here in the UK. Our open classes are for everyone and our closed classes are by invitation only and available to a small selection of members who have shown passion to take their exploration of *karate* to a more advanced level. Although the curriculum structure is essentially the same for all, the depth of study within that curriculum is very different and regardless of rank or experience, all our members have access to the same opportunities. The benefit for me is that I can share my approach to *karate* freely and at the appropriate level for each class. The advantage for members is that they have the opportunity to enjoy what they want from the art – whether that's a once-per-week escape from family ties, a way to relieve some work-place stress, a weekly activity to do alongside their kids, a means of confidence building through challenging activities or for the predictable minority, a more thorough and life-long cultivation of *koryu* (old-school) *karate* methods. In terms of contemporary practice, we consider all of the above (and so many more) as valid reasons for training. Everyone has their reason.

Since adopting the above *dojo* framework, I've gained great fulfilment in teaching *karate* for the betterment of others, regardless of what their individual aspirations for training may be. Over this time, I've been very fortunate to have had the opportunity to teach (and equally learn from) bullied school kids, rape victims, overweight and disabled men and women lacking in the self-confidence needed to get up and pursue their life goals, bouncers, security and police officers, newcomers to the area looking for a challenge or fresh group of friends, autistic children who have responded well to *karate's* methodical and disciplined curriculum, pensioners looking for a new lease in life, highly strung business men desperate for an activity to help relieve workplace stress and dysfunctional relatives who have come to the *dojo* in order to develop a stronger family bond. I've come to accept the fact that the role of a modern-day martial arts teacher can be just as diverse as it is rewarding. It has led me to realise just how very special the art of *karate* is, as a multi-cultural gift to help support practitioners of all types, within the ever-changing world around us.

The term *Practical Karate* (or *Applied Karate*) has been used extensively in recent years, most notably by those practitioners who align themselves to the combative application of the art for the aim of civilian self-protection. Nevertheless, since the word 'practical' is used to imply the actual doing of something, as opposed to being overly concerned with mere theory, this label may justifiably be used to describe any expression of *karate* that is 'in use'. For example, a sport-based practitioner who is focussed solely on developing advanced sparring techniques or aesthetic *kata* performance to earn success in competition could be considered just as practical in their field as one who is working hard to develop skills for personal safety, to help keep a nightclub door safe, to protect friends and family whilst on holiday or maybe even to embrace the more philosophical teachings of *budo* after having recently lost their way in life. All of these applications of *karate* (and more) may be deemed practical depending on individual circumstance.

Of course, the *karate* we practice today has evolved into an art that carries with it numerous benefits and based on personal viewpoint, each of which may be no more or less valuable than the next. So I suppose it would be more accurate to think about the term practical *karate* as being a measure of whether or not your investment in the *dojo* serves to adequately meet the specific goal(s) you aspire to. Unfortunately, it is very easy to fall into the trap of blindly following your training for the sake of conformity and accepting the esoteric premise that one day the 'clouds will part' and your answers will be magically revealed. Furthermore, you may feel indisputably satisfied in the *dojo* but then if asked, would struggle to put your finger on the exact reason(s) as to why you're training.

I've been in the above predicaments more than once during what has now been almost thirty years in *karate* and I suspect like many, found myself looking up from my efforts only to feel like I'm drifting around with no set course ahead. An inevitable part of the process I guess and an interesting dynamic of growth that offers us a valuable sense of breadth. However, it would undoubtedly benefit us all to be mindful during our training in order to take active responsibility and critically assess whether or not what we're doing in the *dojo* is serving to take us positively towards our objectives.

In light of the above, I would suggest that the very first step in making your *karate* practical would be to clearly identify your own specific requirements for training, which may well change over time of course, in order to make sure that the boat you're devotedly rowing week in week out isn't being inadvertently steered away from its intended destination.

My own definition of *practical* karate aligns first and foremost to its use as a system of self-protection and this is the perspective I'll be aligning to within this book. Like most, I have other goals for training too, but more often than not I've found that these tend to grow from this principal objective.

Just to be clear, when I talk about 'self-protection', I'm referring to this in a holistic sense and not simply the combative components of training. For me, the protection of 'self' also covers challenges such as managing physical health and well-being for longevity, controlling a nourishing palate, attaining stability of mind, body and spirit, effectively handling relationships, plus experiencing a sense of gratification for life and all the opportunities it has to offer.

On balance, the most problematic threats we are likely to face on a daily basis (stress, obesity, anxiety, depression etc.) are to be found much closer to home than the stereotypical knife-wielding street thug or serial killer. Very cliché I know, but unless you operate your daily life within a particularly risky environment, then the ancillary aspects alluded to above will generally prove more applicable.

Certainly, the self-protection aspects of martial arts such as *karate* may be used as an effective pathway for more rounded development and I think it's important to think this way. But as pragmatists, we must also be sure to stay aligned to their principal combative objective. As such, this book deals with the core combative elements of self-protection and in this chapter I would like to offer my view on what I believe are the most essential aspects to consider for the study of *karate* as a means to protect oneself against the threat of civilian violence and the consequent exploration of classical *kata* to meet that aim.

A particular viewpoint of *karate* held in one *dojo* may be poles apart from another, and indeed, the original aims and objectives that the founding masters aspired to meet. Additionally, the lack of substance concerning the documented history of *karate* has led to a degree of ambiguity, whereby much of its deeper exploration requires considerable reliance on common-sense based assumptions and calculated reverse-engineering. In addition, the reasons we enjoy practicing *karate* today plus their associated training methods can (and I suppose should) vary somewhat in contrast to what may have been considered the norm in 18th or 19th Century practice. Indeed, change is an inevitable law of nature and there is no place for stagnation in the preservation of applied martial arts practices. Although the evolution of physical human form remains consistent in terms of our application of *kata*, it's clear that as the world changes around us, so too must our practice and understanding of holistic self-protection.

For most pursuits in life and certainly in the case of *karate*, context is king. And one of the main problems associated with modern-day practice is not so much the differing goals to which practitioners strive for, but rather thinking that certain aspects of training may develop skill towards what may well be conflicting attributes. This misunderstanding concerning the relevance of training practices and the context to which they best serve is probably one of the principal motives behind why, like many martial arts, *karate* can receive the highest praise in some circles and at the same time be doused with derogatory opinions and attitudes in others.

As touched on earlier, working without a defined context would be like trying to traverse a vast ocean in a sailing boat without a pre-determined route nor means of navigation. You may of course get lucky, but it's more likely that you'll get lost. Generally speaking, there are three main motives for why people choose to practice *karate*. These are, 1: for self-protection (non-consensual confrontation), 2: for success in sporting competition (consensual confrontation), or 3: for personal development (be it physical, emotional, mental and/or spiritual). Throughout these also exists numerous crossovers, which can of course help to encourage a more rounded understanding of the art. The practice of *kata* for example may be used to help develop physical health, as a method of moving meditation to reduce stress, to excel in the field of sport or as I believe it was originally intended, to study and develop effective self-protection skills. However, in terms of understanding context more accurately, we have to focus not simply on what we consider being 'right' or 'wrong', but more so on where these areas tend to differ and in particular, where they may clash. The reason being that what may function extremely well in one environment, may prove catastrophic in another.

For instance, it could be argued that applying the principle of physical restraint and/or pain compliance may be appropriate in professional situations where the security guard, bouncer or police officer is being employed to uphold the law, maintain order, make arrests if required and ultimately, keep the peace. Conversely, such tactics may be risky for a member of the public who for instance has suddenly been forced to face multiple enraged attackers on route home from work, or has become the target of a vicious rape attempt, since execution requires close proximity to the threat for an extended period of time. Instead, it would be more prudent to place emphasis on doing what is necessary to increase distance and escape the situation as quickly as possible. A strategy, which may be in direct contrast to what the professional is being employed to do.

Another example regarding context would be to consider the distinction between martial arts for sport and martial arts for self-protection, again looking at the stark contrasts between these two types of confrontation. Although crossovers do exist, the prime objectives, ranges, techniques and tactics for a consensual bout are worlds apart from what is necessary for civilian safety and vice versa, perhaps becoming either 'trophy' or 'life' threatening if inadvertently mixed up. A strong and well-placed kick to an assailant's knee joint may be deemed both reasonable and necessary in order to facilitate escape from a violent mugging attempt. However, the same technique applied in the sporting arena would promptly (and rightly so) have you disqualified. Similarly, a purposeful takedown and follow up on the ground that seeks to exploit a trained response may well be a winning strategy in a tactical MMA bout, but to actively seek intricate submission manoeuvres within a rule-less altercation out on 'the cobbles' could become extremely hazardous, where pavements and uneven floor surfaces, confined spaces, broken glass and other rubbish, concealed weapons, multiple assailants and no immediate medical assistance are all very real and dangerous possibilities.

Strategies such as blocking and technical defence tactics using visual cues and/or rule based expectations, non-telegraphing strikes, set ups, feints, testing the opponent's reaction, management of numerous ranges, intricate combination delivery and counters to style specific techniques etc. may be necessary to master for competence in a skilled vs skilled contest. Yet, they are for the most part invalid in self-protection, where the purpose, ranges, environment, risk, consequences, levels of violence, intensity and laws surrounding such scenarios are very different indeed. Because of this, it is important that we don't simply succumb to the assumption that the training we undertake in the *dojo* will automatically meet all of our training objectives. It is simply not the case.

Thus, the proper application of context in *karate* is about working to understand and accept the benefits, limitations and potential crossovers that the various elements of your training possesses. It is also about using good judgment to study in a way that is most applicable to your goal(s). So if you aspire to be the next world *kumite* champion, then devoting the majority of your time to close-range limb control or grappling skills would not be very productive to that particular goal. Likewise, a self-protection practitioner prioritising the development of perfectly controlled long-range reverse punches, head-height kicks or aesthetic *kata* performance may well need to re-think their game plan and hierarchy of training investment. In isolation, none of these approaches are necessarily right or wrong and of course, there's nothing stopping an individual from training for more than one goal so long as they understand where each training practice sits, plus its inherent value and limitation(s). It is all a matter of context.

Prioritise Simplicity

Due to the significantly stressful, chaotic and unruly nature of physical self-protection, priority in training should be given to developing simplistic gross motor application methodologies that incorporate high levels of redundancy and with the ability to easily adapt to changing circumstances without the need to alter base technical requirements. It is no coincidence that classical *karate kata*, especially fundamental *kihon* forms such as *Naihanchi*, *Sanchin* and *Seisan*, strive to develop such attributes within their repetitive choreography. In fact, I would go as far to say that *karate*, as a systematic approach, is ultimately based on becoming adept at only a select number of core movement pathways that may be suitable to use within a plethora of application scenarios.

For instance, the dynamic application of *choku-zuki* (straight thrust), which is one of the first techniques taught in traditional *karate dojo*, actually imparts less about punching and more about how to efficiently (and effectively) drive the arms out from and back towards the core simultaneously within the sagittal plane using the whole body as an integrated unit. So whether or not that movement pathway is used as a strike, joint attack, body manipulation, neck wrench, elbow strike from behind, a simple push away or even an extension of the arm to gain a tactile index to work from (all potential applications of *choku-zuki*) depends entirely on circumstance. And although there may be specific training methods to help develop certain attributes, such as pad work for impact, resistance band or grip training for pulling strength etc., the core movement mechanics are common to all interpretations and as such, it is those mechanics that we should highlight in our study.

As another example, the concept of using your feet to stomp a felled assailant before making good your escape could be seen as an effective tactic for civilian based self-protection. Your feet are the closest weapon to employ in such a situation and compared with leaning over to strike with the hands or dropping to seek a submission, there's much less chance of being gripped, over-balanced and pulled to the ground. Depending on the level of threat, this stomp could be adjusted from a superficial ankle smash in order to help prevent chase, to something more significant should the situation become desperate or life-threatening. However, the gross motor body mechanics and attributes associated with stomping remain the same. Only the target changes.

Due to the effects of adrenaline, both weapons and targets should be prioritised based on a high level of redundancy and although specific weak areas of the human anatomy should be aimed for, these should not replace the ability to generate maximum impact. Accuracy is a quality that must never be assumed nor depended upon. So in the case of a very simple application for *age-uke* (rising receipt) against being gripped by the opponent, then rather than using a single knuckle strike to attack say the LI-10 or LU-5 points (traditional *Chinese* medicine nomenclature), we should instead use the whole forearm like a baseball bat and strike hard within the vicinity of the radial nerve. If we manage to hit specific points then we should consider that an added bonus. Ultimately though, we're aiming to ensure that if all else fails, the sheer force and high redundancy level of our attack would still cause sufficient trauma, flex the assailant's elbow, shift the opposite side away and bring their head sharply forward and onto our oncoming *age-uke* 'strike'.

Even primary targets such as the head should be generalised for simplicity as the reality of self-protection demands that you think about generic 'zones' that are rich in target areas. In terms of the upper-level, this would comprise of anywhere above the collar bone, 360 degrees around the body. Directing strikes to much larger areas and focussing on developing impact with attitude over accuracy will help to increase the chances of success under pressure. A good example would be the natural 'funnels' crated by the opponent's head and shoulders, to which many applications from *Naihanchi Kata* focus on directing percussive impact and effective control capabilities.

In terms of technical ability, practical *karate* should prioritise training methods that offer effective functionality for comparatively little investment. For instance, it is relatively easy to quickly teach someone the fundamentals of generating power using gross motor body mechanics. But some of the intricacies associated with this fascinating subject can take a great deal longer to develop. *Karate* does not make it mandatory to go into such depth for functional effectiveness, but offers an added extra for those who elect to delve deeper.

As a comparable to the above, culinary enthusiasts will know that adding even a pinch of a certain ingredient can make a meal taste very different, even though both versions may be equally appetising to a hungry person. So in terms of satisfying appetite, the pinch is not necessary. In the same way, those who choose to take up practical *karate* should be able to come away with some rudimentary and effective self-protection skills after their very first class.

Seek Objective Function over Subjective Aesthetics

Karate that looks nice is not necessarily the same as *karate* that works nice and for practicality within the context of self-protection, we need to make sure that our measure of success in the *dojo* is centred on objective function, rather than subjective aesthetics. In fact, I would suggest that the bench mark for *karate* aesthetics should be born from its function. In this way, we can learn to seek a specific technical appearance during solo practice that will help us reinforce some of the functional attributes required in application.

As a comparison, we can look at the difference between figure skaters and speed skaters. Whilst both of these disciplines require the use of skates and the ability to manoeuvre on ice, the former emphasises subjective aesthetics (it has to look appealing to a panel of judges) and the latter emphasises objective function (it is measured against time where the fastest wins). Nevertheless, whilst seeking aesthetics in isolation will not necessarily result in a faster performance, speed skaters will still look graceful in their application and very similar to each other too, since this is also a by-product of continually refining function.

Using the example above, much of the *karate* practiced today seems to be a combination of speed skating and figure skating, to be found in various blends across styles, teachers and *dojo*. However, for practical function, it is imperative that we lean more towards objective measures of success that are relevant to our particular goals. For instance, no matter how visually appealing a strike may be to onlookers, the measure of success should be based on its ability to cause percussive trauma. As such, even the specific solo choreography of *karate kata* and how they are performed should be derived from objective function. The effortlessness and gracefulness displayed by a speed skater still comes from their practical ability and in the same way, the aesthetics of *karate* should come from the bottom up (pure function), not the top down (visual preference).

Advocates of practical *kata bunkai* for self-protection purposes should ensure that the classical solo form mnemonics are studied for function in a dynamic, not fixed sense. Although it is very common to see applications being derived from the distinctive snap shot shapes within various *kata* (whether aesthetically pleasing or not), comparatively less focus is placed on what is far more valuable – the transitional movement between those shapes. It is those movement pathways that give life to the choreography and as such, where our measure of objective function should be placed. In a nutshell, it is about the ability to use the teachings of *kata* in order to transition efficiently, since even a collection of one thousand applications are of little use unless they are expressed with effective structural alignment and movement mechanics. This makes study of the solo form much more meaningful than simply a series of static templates combined together.

To explain this idea further, I'd like to refer to what I call the Multi-Tool Principle. A multi-tool can be purchased from hardware stores and is a great option for tradespeople or DIY enthusiasts. Through the use of what is essentially a single electrical spinning motor attached to a handle, a variety of tasks may be accomplished by simply changing the accessory on the end. They can screw, drill, sand, route, cut, clean, engrave and more. However, it relies on the motor being both powerful and durable, otherwise none of the accessories in the tool box would work. As such in *karate*, we must also be mindful not to invest our time collecting a multitude of techniques (accessories) unless we can successfully apply those in our tool box with effective movement pathways (a strong motor and drive shaft). Therefore for the pragmatist, function should always be at the forefront of our minds when training so that objective success is prioritised whether or not we use a particular movement to strike, lock, throw, seize, clinch, pull or choke etc.

Emphasise Impact with Attitude

The numerous application methodologies found within the choreography of classical *kata* and the universal principles from which they are derived reveals to pragmatists a holistic curriculum that aligns well to the context of civilian self-protection. Thus, we find that *karate* is first and foremost a close-range percussive system, which also seeks to control limbs and incorporates a number of contingency grappling methods, should this primary strategy fall short of the mark. So the requirement to deliver impact with asymmetrical attitude (not a back and forth interaction) is central to the arts function and should thus be prioritised when studying for this purpose.

A pre-emptive stun and run approach employed under the veil of artifice is typically the most clinical way of dealing with a physical threat and is the only engagement tactic that may be considered 'unattached', as by definition, grappling based support options demand some form of grip or connection to the opponent, which may hinder your chances of making a clean escape. It is no accident that *karate* places a heavy emphasis on striking and in the majority of cases, even its secondary strategies are geared towards resuming percussive impact where possible, detaching and/or fleeing to safety. You don't need to look very far in classical *kata* to see this very effective methodology frequently at work and you should also incorporate tactics that make use of deception to help capitalise on your response and subsequent escape.

Hitting a focus mitt hard in the *dojo* is not the same as hitting an aggressor determined to hurt you and exercising self-protection in reality will almost certainly have you scared and partially capitulated. Although you may elevate the level of your training to be as realistic as possible, the very nature of it being 'training' means that it will never look, sound, smell, taste or feel exactly like the real thing. With all safety nets neatly tucked away in the *dojo*, the rawness of self-protection will sicken most level-headed people to the core. It is therefore vital that you aim to cultivate an emotional mind-set that will help fuel your physical attributes under dire circumstances. Thus, training for impact also needs to be backed up with an attitude that is fully committed to the notion that it IS NOT ACCEPTABLE for another person to pose a significant threat to your safety. A mental shift needs to take place away from a passive (victim-type) state to one of assertive intent so that you can maximise the chances of making it back home safely to your loved ones. This emotion needs to be harnessed, controlled and funnelled in order to inject determined energy into your technique. When cultivated to a rapid-fire on/off capability, that mental energy when triggered ensures that your physical response may be raised to its optimum effect when needed most.

Finally, the work you undertake in the *dojo* to meet the goal of self-protection needs to incorporate an 'asymmetrical' bias, which means it should refrain from displaying the back and forth exchange dynamic that is more prevalent in competitive skill-vs-skill consensual confrontation. Instead, the mind-set should be that of it's always 'your go' and favour a relentless effort to maintain dominance. Even useful and time-efficient two-person flow drills that feature smooth transitions between one application and another need to be practiced under the caution that if you're flowing, then by definition you're losing, since it assumes that your previous attempt to end the confrontation has been countered. Although valuable, it's important that these drills are also backed up with associated 'break-outs' that aim to sever what can easily become a rather addictive habit to implement flow.

So your main strategy in the *dojo* for physical self-protection should be built around delivering concussive impact with attitude under the veil of artifice, with an asymmetrical mind-set that is determined to either end the confrontation as swiftly as possible in order to make good your escape or employ grappling-based support options should they become necessary. It just so happens that the teachings given within the choreography of classical *kata* such as *Naihanchi* serve to fit this model accurately.

Consider Environmental Factors

Karate practice in the *dojo* is a far cry from the environment you'd be expected to operate within in order to manage a self-protection situation, so this stark contrast needs to be considered and prepared for. Normally, *karate* classes are conducted in open spaces that are pre-prepared, well lit, adequately ventilated and free from significant risk, all controlled via a group of like-minded people with similar agendas. However, when facing a real threat that requires the application of your *karate*, you'd be extremely lucky to encounter the same luxuries. For self-protection, you need to take into account the following:

- Area: Street, bar, toilet, stairwell, elevator, shopping centre or underpass.

- Composition: concrete, grass, carpet, mud, soil, gravel, snow, ice or water.

- Objects: walls, tables, chairs, ash trays, trees, cars, other obstructions.

- Lighting: dim, bright, day, night, sun, power cut, street lamps or torch.

- Climate: hot, cold, rain, snow, ice, wind and weather appropriate attire.

- People: multiples or third-parties, family, friends, witnesses and public.

- Exits: standard, emergency, escape routes, restrictions and alternatives.

Some of these factors above may be reasonably simulated within the *dojo* for training purposes. Others may require scenario drills held within various environments in order to gain experience. Even then, a number of specific variables may never be accurately replicated, so holding supplementary discussions on potential strategies in different scenarios may also help to fill gaps. There are also useful habits you can develop in everyday life that will help address some environmental factors, such as checking for escape routes in new buildings, scoping for potential weapons of opportunity within your location and taking extra care when in confined spaces or crowded areas etc.

Adopt a Holistic and Principle-Based Game Plan

Simply practicing the physical combative aspects of *karate* does not represent 'practicality' in the specific context of holistic self-protection. This is especially true if all you focus on are typical reactive technique-based applications against a variety of possible attacks. Even if these attacks you practice countering are away from the long-range skill-vs-skill scenarios and lean more towards realistic close-range acts of violence, there still exists a substantial gap in the self-protection game plan. Not only does this limited way of training miss the wider picture, but it also sets to root three potentially dangerous problems.

Firstly, by only practicing reactive applications, you're essentially conditioning yourself to being attacked first. Regardless of how adept you become, the mind-set of waiting to be physically attacked before responding is severely flawed in self-protection, where it is pretty much impossible to visually react in time over and above a non-cognitive flinch-based cover. At distances at or inside arms-length (typical conversation range), it's imperative that you also take into account pre-emptive action and in-fight counter responses should your initial plan fall short of the mark. Even the pioneering masters of our past explain in their writings that the famous maxim of *Karate-Ni-Sente-Nashi* (there is no first attack in *karate*) refers to the initiation of violent threat, not the physical act itself. So long as you are not the instigator of confrontation and you honestly deem it both reasonable and necessary to protect yourself, then it would be unwise to wait until physically attacked before retaliating. This notion is also acknowledged by U.K. Law, which serves to underline its good sense in one's personal safety game plan.

Secondly, it's scientifically proven that equating a large tool box of technical responses against a variety of attacks is less likely to be successful in the heat of the moment, as you will never have the reaction time nor clarity of mind to sift through options and make a suitable selection. Hick's Law tells us that increasing the number of choices for a particular event will increase the decision time exponentially. So it is far more productive to develop a core principle-based framework and emphasise a small number of combative strategies that are versatile enough to adapt to a wide variety of situations. So for example, rather than collecting a series of technical defences against each different type of 'grab', it's much better to hone an initial single direct response that could be employed effectively against a variety of grabs. This idea is heavily supported in core *karate kata*, where the same movement pathways are used to meet a variety of common acts of violence or are equally valuable in a pre-emptive sense. Of course, the uncertainty of self-protection means that it's impossible to achieve this principle exclusively, and we are fortunate to have been left with a host of *kata* to draw from, but minimising the inherent mental log-jam associated with 'technique collection' should always be at the forefront of our mind when training for practicality.

Thirdly, if you only ever practice the physical combative aspects of training then you're missing a huge part of the personal safety game plan. It's like neglecting to teach your child how to safely cross a road and instead instruct them only on what to do if they get knocked down by a car. Or failing to adopt an avoidance-based fire safety plan in your workplace and instead only practice what to do if a fire breaks out. In all aspects of personal safety, prevention is always better than protection and *karate* training should also follow this way of thinking. Thus, if you fail to develop such aspects as a strong awareness protocol to include threat recognition, avoidance and subsequent escape, verbal dissuasion tactics and situational control, environmental considerations, plus at least a rudimentary knowledge of self-protection law, statistics and post-conflict management, then you'll never have any other option other than a poorly constructed reactive protection protocol, which in terms of personal protection is the most risky and least favourable outcome.

As a final point, we must also take into consideration the four main risks that are of serious concern in self-protection, but are often poorly addressed in traditional *karate dojo*. These are (1) environment, (2) dealing with multiples, (3) weapons and (4) being knocked to the ground. Practicing *kata* applications with a partner in a nicely lit modern sports hall with protective matting and a nearby first aid kit to hand just in case is worlds apart from facing two armed muggers in a dark car park or having to deal with being caught unawares and knocked to the floor in a dingy night club toilet, having already cracked your head open via the sink on the way down. Therefore, it's valuable in training to consider and simulate where possible aspects such as confined spaces and restricted escape routes, bystanders, lighting, climate, surface, surrounding objects, the management of more than one opponent, the protection of family or friends, survival strategies against common weapon attack and ground skills that prioritise regaining your feet if downed.

No matter how realistic your self-protection training methods become, there will always exist specific flaws to save everyone from being carried out on stretchers after each class. The very fact that we can walk out of the *dojo* on our own two feet and go back home to our family means that our training is not real, and rightly so. It is not only unsafe and unproductive to train in an environment that poses significant harm to one another, it is also unnecessary too, as we can aspire to adopt an interconnected and overlapping framework that helps us to construct a more complete jigsaw puzzle in relation to our practical goals.

Let's take the development of a palm heel strike for example. Practicing in thin air through *kihon* or *kata* will allow you to develop generic skill in technique and in particular, the launch phase along with attitude. However, only working in thin air will not help develop impact. Therefore we need to also work with focus mitts, *makiwara*, heavy bag or similar tools to gain experience in striking against an actual target. But even with the above in place, we are still lacking in human target acquisition and specifically, the application (and timing) of such a strike in self-protection. This is where partner drills and scenario training with protective equipment comes into play, which may incorporate varying levels of compliance, stress inoculation, barriers, verbal dialogue, artifice, strategy and subsequent escape. Additional to this may be a series of supplementary exercises (*hojo undo*) with traditional and /or modern implements to help develop the physical attributes associated with enhancing the technique's functionality. The idea is that the inherent safety and/or development flaws in one method of training are considered in another, so that in collaboration they form a comprehensive framework for holistic progression.

I think it's important to reiterate the fact that if what you are doing in the *dojo* is serving you well and steering you purposefully towards your personal goals, then your *karate* may be considered practical for you. However, for the specific context of civilian self-protection, I believe that like me, you may get the most out of your training by aligning to the aspects given above. In short, it is about embracing a simplistic and versatile principle-based framework for the contextual analysis and application of *karate kata*, which is then included within a holistic game plan, comprehensively exercised through an overlapping training methodology that aims to minimise the impact of inherent flaws whilst developing the essential attributes to help maximise objective function.

The main barrier many practitioners are faced with when applying *kata* is that they tend to look at the choreography with off beam eyes for self-protection. Eyes that may have been prior conditioned with more contemporary viewpoints, potentially at odds with those expressed by the founding masters of our past and indeed, the original intent of the form's structure.

Once you come to understand the key requirements of non-consensual confrontation then with a little contextual based exploration, you'll come find that the *kata* do a pretty reasonable job of speaking for themselves. Such is the brutal beauty of *karate*.

CHAPTER III

SELF-PROTECTION GAME PLAN

"The techniques of kata have their limits and were never intended to be used against an opponent in an arena or on a battlefield."

~ Choki Motobu

Due to the lack of detailed information or indeed, definitive teachings surrounding the original application of classical *karate kata*, the modern pragmatists among us face a challenging task of trying to reverse engineer a sufficient understanding based on the historical material available, logical theories, like-minded research and common-sense assumptions. Thus, we can propose that the phenomenon known in *karate* as *kata*, is essentially the product of attempts to record essential combative teachings into a number of digestible solo representations, which as we all know, have already been subject to varying degrees of adaptation through the development of numerous styles since their initial creation.

So, to begin a contextually driven exploration of *Naihanchi Kata* in terms of its combative function, it would be prudent to first start with the presumptions that:

1. The primary reason for *karate* practice was to avoid, manage and protect against non-consensual threats of violence,

2. *Naihanchi Kata* was regarded as a fundamental training template,

3. The choreography of *Naihanchi Kata* represents a series of logical and systematic teachings,

4. Application methodologies given by the choreography of *Naihanchi Kata* are contextually fitting.

If these presumptions are accurate or at least reasonable then it stands to reason that the specific movements that make up *Naihanchi Kata* may well represent key lessons in order to meet them. So with this idea in mind, the first step would not be to dive directly toward the application themselves, which is often the most common way to approach *bunkai*, but rather to first fathom a suitable game plan that may be used as a guide so that we may holistically explore the *kata* choreography and make better sense of the reverse engineering analysis we then choose to undertake.

From the previous chapter, we have already discussed some of the key aspects to consider in *karate* for self-protection. Rather than subjective aesthetics, we should care more about objective function. Rather than complexity we should care more about efficiency. Rather than winning, we should care more about not losing. Rather than captivating an audience, we should care more about maximising safety. And rather than exercising the ego, we should care more about exercising effectiveness. Thus the process of *Bunkai Nidan* presented in this book aims to reveal that by applying the *Naihanchi Kata* choreography, we are at the most essential level, reinforcing the most crucial skills required for self-protection. And it is from within this seed, the basis for the rest of the art may then be realised. It is at this stage that we can now begin to identify some important parameters for our game plan to sit within. To recap…

- Soft skills such as situational awareness, threat recognition, avoidance, diffusion and escape tactics should make up the bedrock of one's self-protection strategy.

- Where possible aim to 'avoid' before 'diffuse' and 'diffuse' before 'engage'.

- Always look to exploit distance and time in order to maximise safety.

- Make use of artifice (deception) in order to create the initiative.

- Combative training should prioritise a gross-motor 'stun and run' strategy based on delivering pre-emptive percussive impact with a dominating attitude.

- A reactive strategy should also be honed for genuine ambush attacks or when the pre-emptive strategy falls short of the mark and contingency options are required.

- All strategies should favour simplistic principle-based movement patterns that incorporate high levels of redundancy and avoid unnecessary complexity.

- Prioritise a small toolbox of multifaceted techniques and tactics that are effective against common acts of physical violence.

- Once the initiative has been created, maintain assertive dominance until capitulation and/or escape can safely be made.

- Defensive strategies should be built around the use of natural and evolutionary flinch-based reactions.

- Aim to support constant physical readiness through functional health and fitness.

- Always assume the likelihood of multiple assailants and weapons being present.

- Avoid going to the ground wherever possible, but nevertheless prepare for that possibility.

- If taken to ground, employ strategies that emphasise the requirement to regain a standing position as soon as possible.

- Consider environmental factors that may affect application such as terrain, space, weather conditions, temperature, lighting and escape routes etc.

- Follow up any actions taken as a responsible and upstanding member of society and aim to ensure that they fall within the self-protection law upheld within one's locality.

By having the above perspective to work from and by continually auditing subsequent findings, it is possible to begin exploring the movements of the *kata* with a contextually driven set of eyes. Moreover, it highlights the possibility that *Naihanchi Kata* is not simply a bunch of outdated techniques illogically stuck together for the sake of aesthetics, but in fact presents a well-structured, functional and systematic approach to sharing some of the most important lessons associated with civilian self-protection; *Karate* lessons that have collaborative purpose across an integrated and principle-based approach towards common goals.

I think it's important to reiterate once again the fact that *kata* (as a solo mnemonic) originally came about as a product of its function and as such, the contemporary reverse engineering undertaken may sometimes prove to be a little disorganised. So without a fit for purpose and contextual-based connection between solo technique and its corresponding application, it is entirely understandable why some practical *karate-ka* choose to abandon the repetition of *kata* altogether. Personally, I find this rather unfortunate, as I see the solo form as being far more than a specific aid-memoire and we have the opportunity to make well-informed and impartial judgments about the combative meaning of *kata*, using the information available about the origins of the art and its subsequent development.

Despite the varying reasons that one may study *karate* today, the writings left behind by the masters of our past point very strongly to the fact that the primary intention of the classical forms were to record functionally effective combative principles, techniques and tactics that have been proven successful to protect against non-consensual acts of violence. These historical signposts help us to derive a starting point and provide impetus to further explore what may be hiding below the surface of the art's choreographed movements – hence the subject of this book. However, playing devil's advocate, I suppose it is also entirely possible that this was never the original intention of *Naihanchi Kata*, or indeed *karate*.

Indeed, this whole book series is based on the possibility that *Naihanchi Kata* provides a multi-layered learning tool, offering the necessary information and skills in order to gain an understanding of the most essential methodologies of old-style *Shuri*-based *Karate*. But, could it be that this model I've chosen to write is historically incorrect? Well, with little chronological evidence available to confirm without doubt the original meaning of *Naihanchi Kata*, I suppose this will always be a query for deliberation and as such, it would be foolish to pretend that this possibility doesn't exist.

I suppose a more useful question based on the above would be whether or not it actually matters if the model presented here is historically correct? You see, it may be that the traditional movements handed down were never even intended for use in civilian self-protection. It may be that the *kata* is simply an impractical antique loosely preserved and revered for posterity's sake from a bygone age. It may be that the form was originally designed for use with a weapon in hand, for calisthenics, to record the sequence of a two-person mutually interactive dance-like performance or even an ancient spiritual exercise for connecting mind with body. But does this really matter in terms of the contents presented within these pages?

Certainly from a historical perspective, we could argue that it is vital that we strive to uncover the true meaning of *Naihanchi Kata*. From a functional perspective however, I would suggest that the priority should lie instead with what makes the most practical sense. So, if someone turns to *karate* in order to gain effective self-protection skills and find that *Naihanchi Kata* provides a useful template to catalogue essential lessons in order to develop such skills, then it would make perfect sense to acknowledge and embrace these. Even if historically we later find this notion to be way off the mark. Of course there will always be some controversy to the way in which *kata* may be interpreted, but I'm sure that like-minded pragmatists will come to agree that any functional explanation for *Naihanchi Kata* has got to be better than the old 'fighting in a paddy field', 'against a wall' or on a 'long thin boat' theories!

So now that we have gained an appreciation as to the significance of context in *Traditional Karate* as being the basis for our exploration, the next stage would be to use this perspective gained in order to extract a useable structure that we may use to help guide our analysis. For me, it wasn't until I had achieved this within my own study that more 'conceptual' lessons within the *kata* choreography became apparent.

I always make use of a core game plan for the self-protection aspects of the *karate* practiced in our *dojo*, which is based on strategies employed generically throughout any good reality-based system. If it is true that *Naihanchi Kata* provides a central skill-set for *Shuri*-based systems and if it is true that *karate* was originally designed for civilian self-protection, then I believe it is also logical to propose that the movements presented within the form may strive to propagate skills and tactics to fit somewhere within the following structure:

Self-Protection Game Plan…

- Legal Considerations

    (Knowledge and understanding of self-defence law)

- Situational Awareness

    (Peripheral attentiveness, threat recognition and evaluation)

- Risk Mitigation

    (Behaviour, attitude, posture and effective barriers)

- Threat Avoidance & Escape

    (Removing yourself away from the potential hazard)

- Situational Management

    (Distance, time and place within the environment)

- De-Escalation

    (Verbal dissuasion, posturing or other means to scale-down the situation)

- Primary Physical Strategy

    (Percussive impact delivery, ambush reaction and supporting skills)

- Secondary Physical Strategy

    (Dealing with common acts of violence, counter-grappling and felling techniques)

- Tertiary Physical Strategy

  (Manipulations, restrictions and restraint)

- Post Altercation Management

  (Maximising safety, gauging further action and managing the aftermath)

Due to changes in period, culture, environment and opportunities, we can argue that legal requirements, personal security measures, de-escalation tactics and post-altercation management may vary to some degree. However, the strategies covered within the *Naihanchi Kata* application framework as presented in this book i.e. situational awareness, threat control and core physical combatives will for the most part remain the same. Of course, specific skills may vary, but the lessons they aim to impart should be comparable to almost all human-to-human interactions. We are all essentially still built the same as when *karate* was first developed on *Okinawa*. So for example, it would matter little whether you seize hold of your enemy's top-knot, pony tail or beard. The principle of exploiting hair growth to manipulate the head and create a combative advantage remains constant.

So before we move on to the application framework of *Naihanchi Kata*, let's first take a closer look at each of the components that make up the self-protection game plan:

Legal Considerations

It is imperative (not to mention common sense) that any *karate* practitioner who trains for self-protection has sufficient understanding about the laws in their region pertaining to such aims. The reason for this is simple – convictions in courts around the world are won and lost every day based not always on what crimes may or may not have actually been committed, but rather, what was or was not stated after the event. Therefore, an understanding of self-protection law will not only help you to remain within the legal boundaries, but it will also help you better articulate details of the situation to others, should your actions go before judge and jury.

My knowledge of self-defence law has been gained through a combination of personal research and correspondence with a number of subject matter experts. I'd like to make it clear that I have no formal qualifications in this subject so please regard the following as being for information only, as it does not constitute any form of legal advice.

Please also be aware that the information below is based on UK law and therefore may differ from your own locality. Generally speaking though, legal systems normally weigh very strongly in favour of the victim, regardless of what often tends to be presented in the media, which can often distort the public perception of self-protection.

In the UK, self-defence law considers it legal for a person to use reasonable force in order to defend themselves, another person or their property from threat should it be deemed necessary. The two key words here are 'reasonable' and 'necessary', which both must be admissible under the circumstances. In other words, an action that may be reasonable and necessary in one scenario, may not be reasonable or necessary in another. Thus, if you ever decide to claim self-defence as legal justification then based on the 'innocent until proven guilty' mandate, it will be up to the prosecution to prove that the force you used was excessive before you may be charged with a criminal offence.

To put the above into perspective, if a situation presented itself with an opportunity to escape and you chose not to take it, then it could be argued that any physical response thereafter was not 'necessary' and therefore may be considered assault. In contrast, if you were unable to escape, maybe due to environmental factors, the enemy has restricted your movement or if there are others that need protecting (family members for instance), then so long as you held the honest belief that imminent danger existed, a physical response may be judged necessary.

In terms of your actions being 'reasonable', then consideration must be given as to whether or not those actions succeeded to nullify the threat and no further. Therefore, continuing the use of force after the threat has been eliminated or after an opportunity to escape has become available may be ruled excessive and consequently, not an act of self-defence. Consideration must also be given to whether it was 'reasonable' to perceive the threat in the way you did. If you were voluntarily intoxicated for example, then this may cloud your judgment.

Of course, the specific details of self-defence law and how it may relate to martial arts would satisfy a manual in itself, so to best satisfy the requirements of this particular book, here are a few key points worth considering:

- Due to the stresses experienced in a violent confrontation, the law does not expect you to calculate the 'exact' amount of force required, so long as you honestly and instinctively thought that it was necessary. Furthermore, if you happened to make a genuine error about the existence of a threat in the heat of the moment, then you are still entitled to your response as acting in self-defence.

- The law does not state anywhere that you must wait until physically attacked before retaliating and in actual fact, considers pre-emptive action a valid form of self-defence. Again, this is based on the honest belief that an imminent threat is present and the use of force was necessary.

- If you voluntarily engage in physical conflict then those actions by definition would not be seen as self-defence. This is an important consideration as human ego coupled with our conditioned belief system tends to be the root cause of most physical conflicts, both small and large scale.

- If you carry an object that was made, adapted or intended for the purpose of causing injury (even if only for self-protection) then this would be classed as an offensive weapon and as such, a criminal offence. This includes purposefully placed items, such as a baseball bat under your bed. However, everyday objects on your person or at hand within the immediate environment may be used against an attacker for self-defence purposes. These 'weapons of opportunity' or 'equalisers' may include such items as a pen, set of keys, handful of coins, mobile phone, umbrella, chair, water bottle, item of clothing, rolled up magazine etc.

Simply put, if you are training in any form of martial art that is based on building skills for self-protection, then you should make it a priority to learn about basic legal aspects and consider how this may affect or influence the specifics of your game plan. Personal safety should always supersede any apprehension about the aftermath. Although these concerns may not have been so imperative for *karate* practitioners in the past, they are today whether we like it or not and thus, any application of your art will be automatically governed by law.

Situational Awareness

If you are not aware of your surroundings, the people within your vicinity, or indeed the changing situations and interactions within your immediate environment, then any subsequent self-protection strategy can only ever involve a physical response to imminent danger. This places you by default into the 'victim state'. As such, the development of situational awareness, along with associated threat recognition and evaluation skills are critical for any kind of personal security protocol.

Situational awareness aims to help make the most of distance and time, which are the two key components directly related to the main objective in self-protection - to maintain safety at all times. Developing a daily baseline of cognizance that may help you recognise and evaluate potential threats within your environment as early as possible offers greater opportunity to consider alternative strategies to either eliminate or minimise risk to an acceptable level without being forced to physically engage.

As you will come to see, the application basis for *Naihanchi Kata* as presented in this book covers conceptual lessons on developing situational awareness from the outset, indicating its importance for self-protection. Further detail on this particular aspect of the game plan will be offered within the relevant chapter.

Risk Mitigation

Risk mitigation involves the implementation of various methods, tactics, behaviours and body language that all come together to form an everyday personal security strategy that aims to reduce the chances of being chosen as a victim. Risk mitigation is successful because it makes those who want to harm us work much harder in order to carry out their plans. Of course, it doesn't guarantee safety, but building behaviours and tactics into a simple strategy that covers most aspects of your daily life may have a huge impact on the likelihood of facing violence.

Most elements of risk mitigation are actually based on common sense principles, with the procedures and precautions that make up your strategy being simple to employ in daily life in order to make them habitual. There is no need to be overly paranoid or consider large investments of time or money in order to increase your levels of general safety and what works best for one situation, may not be effective or sufficient for another. The key is to make informed decisions about what is most appropriate for you, your family and your lifestyle.

Before you can plan an effective risk mitigation strategy, you must first consider the dynamics of what you're trying to protect against. You need to identify what sorts of threat could potentially exist within your locality, what specific goals and aims such threats may have, what information may be gathered to fuel a potential threat on your person and any emerging patterns or historic instances of threat that may require extra focus. Understanding the capabilities of potential threats will allow you to evaluate your vulnerability for which your subsequent mitigation tactics should then aim to strengthen.

There are literally thousands of ways in which you could exercise risk mitigation, from simple habits such as making sure that all your windows and doors are locked before going to bed at night to more elaborate protection systems and expensive mechanisms designed more specifically for 'high value' targets. For most people, the aim is to employ a number of easy, low cost and habitual methods into everyday life. Even the simple act of walking tall with your head up monitoring the environment can make a real difference when it comes to whether or not you are 'chosen' to be a victim of violence.

Those members of society who resort to physical violence through deliberate thought processes may want to first feel confident that their actions will have the desired effect. Therefore, any significant doubt or barriers presented that would make gaining the outcome more challenging (either consciously or subconsciously) will usually result in no attack taking place, as there are usually plenty more victims for the unsavoury minority to choose from. As such, gaining positive results from risk mitigation is one of the highest forms of self-protection, not to mention one of the safest.

To illustrate the concept of risk mitigation in practice, below are a few examples of simple tactics that you may choose to employ throughout your daily activities. I would encourage you to use those that best fit your lifestyle and then consider filling any gaps with suitable examples of your own. To strike a sensible balance, it would also be worth considering the effect of higher and more obvious protection measures on the appearance to a perpetrator that you may have something worth taking or indeed, a vulnerability you may be compensating for. So if you're living in the only house on the street with an expensive high-tech security camera installed, then this may stand out as being attractive to potential burglars despite what items you may or may not have to steal inside.

- In general, be alert, aware of your surroundings and walk with a confident gait. Body language is a major deterrent due to the sheer amount of subliminal information it can send out to others around you. Not only will you be more likely to spot a potential threat, but you'll also be less likely to meet one. That's a win-win situation in anyone's book!

- Always be mindful that intoxication can have a significant effect on ego, coordination, sight, balance, reaction and judgment etc. When socialising, be extra vigilant of those around you and follow your instincts. Don't visit places or areas that are notorious for trouble. Simply go and enjoy your evening elsewhere. If something feels wrong then it probably is. Don't ignore those feelings that modern society often ignores or ridicules. These are likely based on primeval behaviours that were essential to the survival and advancement of our species. So it pays to acknowledge, embrace, and develop them as part of your self-protection skill-set.

- Consider what you have on show such as jewellery, wallet, mobile phone or other expensive tech gadgets. A valuable item placed on the passenger seat of your car may well be asking for the window to be smashed. Choosing to have your Rolex or diamond necklace on proud view in a dubious environment could be asking for trouble. Posting on social media about you and your family being on a great beach holiday may be advertising for your home to be broken into. It's not about being overly paranoid, but more so to openly reflect upon the potential consequences of the actions you take in daily life.

- Your mobile phone can be a great asset, so long as you don't keep your face stuck to it! Ensure it's always charged when you go out and have at least one important number on speed dial should an emergency arise. Leave it near your bedside in case you happen to be woken by noise or movement elsewhere in your property during the night. The technology within mobiles phones also puts a host of information features, navigation, tracking etc. at your fingertips. Plus with many designs carved from a single block of aluminium, in the worst case scenario it may also be used as a weapon of opportunity.

- Be cautious when using public transport. Don't get into a taxi that isn't clearly licenced, try to sit close to the exits and driver when on a bus (especially on late night routes) and resist the temptation to sit in an empty train carriage. For obvious reasons, falling asleep on public transport is also chancy. Especially if you completely miss your stop!

- Ensure your car always has at least a quarter tank of fuel. Carry a basic first aid and tool kit in the boot. Make it a habit to look inside the car and over your shoulder before getting in and be sure to scope the immediate environment before exiting you vehicle, as these are the most vulnerable times for being attacked. When in slow moving traffic, always leave a sufficient gap in front so that you can quickly escape the queue if necessary. For the same reason, it pays to reverse into parking bays. When driving in built up areas and with multiple traffic light stops, you may also want to consider locking your doors.

- When in any building (particularly an unfamiliar one), always make it a habit to check for emergency and potential exit routes. This is especially important when staying in hotels or spending time in densely populated venues such as a bar, sports arena or concert hall.

- If you like to go walking or jogging then ensure that you regularly change your route. If travelling on your own then always inform someone of your plans and expected return. Don't be tempted to take the dimly lit short cut and be extra cautious at cash machines. If you insist on listening to music through headphones, then keep the volume low or consider only wearing one.

- When at home, try to ensure you have the facility to see a caller before answering the door. This could be as simple as installing a viewing hole or using a security chain. Only allow those people into your home that you trust or can produce sufficient identification and never disclose that you're on your own. As you arrive at home and before you put your key in the front door, become accustomed to quickly checking for signs of forced entry and always take a moment to look over your shoulder. A cursory glance may only take a second, but it can appear to anyone who may be watching that you're 'switched on'. Consider installing a home security system or if finances won't stretch to that then you can simply fit a fake alarm unit on the outside wall as a deterrent.

All the above are simple and effective habits that can have a positive effect on your personal security. The list isn't exhaustive and you should review your own personal circumstances to suit. Also, be aware that when 'engineered' protection measures sit alongside 'people-based' protection measures, there is a risk of dependence and reduction of our own efforts as we automatically expect the engineering to do its job. An example of this may be having a very secure home and then becoming less personally vigilant as a result. Again, there is a sensible balance to strike but in all cases, risk mitigation is an extension of the general awareness protocol that governs a solid self-protection strategy. This awareness protocol is alluded to within the opening movements of *Naihanchi Kata*.

Threat Avoidance & Escape

Exactly what it says on the tin – threat avoidance and escape is the best way of employing self-protection by circumventing the need to go physical. If you're able to see and then avoid a potential problem before it escalates, then this would be an ideal strategy by maximising safety (the main goal) with minimum risk. Plus as we've already discussed, from a legal perspective, avoidance or escape is always desirable for self-defence if the option to safely remove yourself from the situation becomes available.

Maintaining good situational awareness is key to this, by making the best use of distance and time to identify a potential threat and opportunity to evade.

Naihanchi Kata establishes the concept of situational awareness early on within the form's choreography. Threat avoidance and escape also combines the control of ego and non-consensual mind-set. The whole premise is based around the intention of going through life without ever having to exercise violence. But with the caveat that if violence is ever forced upon you, then to have developed sufficient skill, vehemence and tenacity to do whatever it takes to get back home safely to your family or indeed, protect the ones you love.

Escaping the situation is often suggested in self-protection, but the specific skills associated with this tactic and indeed whether or not it may be possible/practical to accomplish are less frequently taken into account. If you need to run away, then how is it best to go about doing so? Where would you run to and what would you do when you got there? Are you physically able to run? In which circumstances may attempting to run away be more dangerous? Are you in a situation whereby escaping the scene would put other people you care about at risk? When would be the best times to run away; before, during and after an altercation? Like all other tactics in self-protection, escape is a physical skill that requires mindful consideration and practice.

Situational Control

Since most human interactions take place at around arms-length (a typical conversation) and given the fact that action will always beat reaction at this range, it's vital that situational control is employed to create both a physical and psychological barrier in order to maintain distance from a potential threat. The hallmarks of situational control are to employ a combination of unassuming movement, positioning and interaction that offers the best opportunity to manage the possible threat and minimise subsequent risk.

It's important that you adopt a staggered base with emphasis over the front leg so that you can't be easily knocked back off-balance, but still maximise movement potential. It's also vital that both hands are up in front so that they're 'in the game' should the situation take a turn for the worst. If you can positon offside slightly (rather than directly in front of the potential antagonist) then that would be most desirable. All of this should be backed up with dialogue at the appropriate level, constant awareness of potential threat and environment, plus any triggers to indicate that you may need to either engage, shift focus or escape.

Good situational control puts you in a more advantageous position, where pre-emptive action may be launched if the situation deteriorates to a point where violence is unavoidable. Plus if the worst happens and you are attacked without perceived warning, then you can adopt a defensive position much quicker, hopefully buying valuable time to regain the initiative.

De-Escalation

Whilst not covered in detail within this book and often underrated, de-escalation is nevertheless a valuable component within the self-protection game plan, as it focuses on non-violent resolution. If the opportunity to de-escalate is available then it should always be the first tool to use once situational control has been established. Most brewing confrontations will normally include some form of dialogue, whether used to assert, probe or distract. This means that verbal dissuasion and reasoning may be used to manage the situation. Again, these skills require you to swallow your ego and depending on the specifics, require the ability to choose between different tactics to assure the best possible chance of maximising safety.

De-escalation or 'verbal *karate*' as we call it, is an art in itself and requires plenty of real life experience and/or extensive role playing in order for it to become most natural. However, it is still possible to put into action a few simplistic principles that may help you if dialogue starts to become progressively heated. When combined with good awareness, threat recognition and avoidance skills, de-escalation helps to push the 'physical response' further down the options list where it should be. The problem is that many *karate* practitioners ONLY concern themselves with the physical aspects of their art and fail to incorporate these ancillary strategies into a more holistic arsenal. Ironically, this will then only leave the physical response to rely on, which by definition goes against the principal objective that they claim to strive for (never to engage in conflict). Catch 22.

For de-escalation to work well, you have to come across as being genuinely interested in your antagonist's gripe and display a sense of empathy in dialogue, facial expression and body language, whilst being ready to switch to a physical response swiftly with good situational control always in place. Attachment to ego is probably the largest contributing factor for verbal disputes to deteriorate unnecessarily and turn physical. So for de-escalation to become useful, your 'opponent' has to feel that his or her views are being received and understood, even if you have absolutely no intention of conforming to their needs or demands.

It is incredibly uncomfortable to be around someone who is angry and on the verge of becoming violent and of course, the level and type of de-escalation employed needs to match each situation. For some it may only serve to 'fan the flames' and for others, the option may not even be on the table. Having said that, in many circumstances, the following strategy of three key elements may help scale down escalating disputes to a more peaceful resolution.

1. *Acknowledge feelings* – people have a right to feel how they choose to feel, whether angry, sad or otherwise. However, what people feel and what they do as a result of those feelings are often dependent on how the situation and dialogue unfolds. By acknowledging and empathising with the other persons feelings, they no longer have a 'platform' to intensify their emotions upon. Something as simple as, "Hey, you seem pretty angry…let's talk about this and maybe I can help".

2. *Explore alternatives* – helping to explore other options, as opposed to settling for what the other person may think is becoming increasingly inevitable may help to widen their scope of vison towards settling on a more peaceful resolution. These may be as straightforward as buying each other a drink, giving up a parking place or simply apologising if you've been perceived to have caused an issue.

3. *Offer choice* – Ultimately, people want to feel as though they have freedom of choice and a potential restriction against this may cause a situation to escalate. By giving freedom of choice (or seeming to), you tick two boxes on the path towards de-escalation. Firstly, you remove any restriction they may feel about the way forward. Secondly, you pass on a sense of responsibility that whatever consequences occur from this point forward, come directly as a result of their choice. This also serves to morally empower you should the situation degrade and a physical response becomes necessary.

Unless the person you're dealing with has already made a firm decision to go physical and is merely using dialogue as some sort of pre-conflict interview to gain enough confidence or exercise deception (something you need to be aware of), then many will find it very difficult to escalate a situation where their feelings have been genuinely acknowledged, other rational options have been explored and their freedom of choice has been respected. In this way, de-escalation works to nullify the fight or flight response that grows from the apparent necessity to compete for a positon of dominance within the micro-social hierarchy created by the verbal exchange. This is why the management of ego plays a huge part in self-protection.

As previously mentioned, your level of situational control needs to be sufficient to enable a physical response should it be required. Either pre-emptive based on pre-threat cues etc., or a reactive counter attack depending on the intelligence you may receive.

Primary Physical Strategy

The primary physical strategy is based on delivering pre-emptive gross motor percussive impact along with simplistic limb control where necessary in order to switch off the threat, stun and run or maintain continued dominant assault until such a point that the opponent capitulates and/or effective escape can be made. This is recognised by most authorities on self-defence as being the most clinical way of dealing with a threat of violence that is both unavoidable and inevitable.

It's important that you can recognise potential pre-threat cues that may indicate that an attack is imminent. These could include the likes of aggressive body language, deteriorating speech to single syllables, dedicated weight shifts, grooming gestures, hands disappearing from view, or eyes scanning immediate environment for potential witnesses etc. The ideal would be to act pre-emptively under the veil of artifice, but if an attack is forced upon you, then an equally simplistic flinch-based default cover and pressing counter-response that interconnects to the above should also be practiced and honed for primary protection.

Apart from the underlying development of attributes such as impact, deception, asymmetrical mind-set and attitude, the primary physical strategy encompasses little more than a core principle-based approach to delivering tactical unattached strikes, or barrage of strikes incorporating dominant tactile attachment (index), plus the ability to negotiate obstructions in order to overwhelm the aggressor and therefore produce an opportunity to escape as soon as possible.

Although tactics may require some minor adaptation depending on each specific scenario, the single core premise for our primary physical strategy including the 'soft skills' that preceded it should be applicable throughout.

Secondary Physical Strategy

As the old saying goes, 'even monkeys fall from trees'. Thus the self-protection game plan must also incorporate a set of secondary tactics that aim to deal with potential problems that may likely come your way and consequently limit your ability to regain the primary strategy. Although they are designed to malleably integrate, keeping the two strategies separate within the game plan minimises any unnecessary complication whilst adding a valuable back-up layer of skills should they be required.

Although by its nature the secondary strategy is a little more comprehensive, it should still be heavily based on gross-motor mechanics and simplistic principle-based methodologies, with the main aim of allowing swift recommencement of the primary strategy whenever possible.

The secondary strategy should also cover problems that occur not only through active delivery of the primary strategy, but also through information gained via awareness of the changing environment. Multiple assailants, weapon attack, third-party protection, being knocked to the ground or a combination of these are good examples of where the secondary strategy may quickly need to be accessed. As such, the application concepts expressed within the *Naihanchi Kata* choreography are adaptable to suit various common acts of violence.

Tertiary Physical Strategy

The tertiary strategy is made up of auxiliary enhancement skills such as joint manipulations, vital point striking, blood and air restrictions, pain compliance, control and restraint etc. Skills that require more complex motor mechanics, greater investment in training or non-essential tactics that although may be applicable for certain situations, typically keep you in close proximity to a threat for an extended period of time.

Tertiary skills should be considered the 'garnishes' of our combative protocol, where investment in primary and secondary skills should always take priority. Although not crucial, certain tactics may also be valuably employed as 'enhancers' in order to help maximise the overall effect of your response to a given situation.

I think it's interesting to note that the curriculum of *koryu karate*, regardless of style, quite often matches the physical strategy framework as described above and also the generic importance that should be placed on each element. Originally being a holistic system that covers a number of combative aspects such as tegumi (grappling), kansetsu-waza (joint attacks) and tuite (seizing), shime-waza (chokes and strangles), nage-waza (throwing) etc., emphasis is appropriately given to the delivery of successive percussive impact along with simplistic methods of controlling limbs in order to clear strike paths, reduce potential for the enemy to gain dominant attachment and/or actively detach from grips should they become imposed. It is my opinion that the classical application *kata*, despite containing the variety of combative aspects given above, also accentuate their natural priority for civilian self-protection.

Post Altercation Management

Rarely considered to be a part of self-protection, post altercation management is in fact a very significant aspect of the game plan. The steps you take immediately after a non-consensual violent confrontation and even in the days, weeks and months post event can have a serious impact on not only any judicial outcome, but also on your personal serenity. Depending on the type of person you are, being forced to act in self-protection may influence numerous aspects of your life. Every experience we encounter has the ability to subconsciously mould us if we do not take action to bring any issues to the surface and deal with them.

We hear stories all the time of people who have been adversely affected by conflict. It can change the way you look at the world and others around you, your body language, social interactions, levels of trust and self-esteem. It's not uncommon to read about victims of robbery who can't bring themselves to step outside their front door without being accompanied. Victims of bullying or harassment who come to the tragic conclusion that the only way out is to end their life. Victims of rape who spend the rest of their life alone and in fear because they can't get close to anyone without dredging up all those hurtful memories. Victims of family abuse who end up turning to vice and repeating the same behaviour to the next generation. Post-traumatic stress can affect us all and it's tragic that some victims never recover from the emotional scars that remain long after the physical wounds have healed.

Post altercation management is about making an attempt to anticipate some of the possible issues should we be dealt a bad hand and in doing so, help to empower the rest of our game plan by offering a degree of assurance that there's light at the end of the tunnel. It's about installing a positive frame of mind such that we are better equipped to deal with the aftermath and be ready for some of the potential repercussions. 'Knowledge is Power' is a very apt phrase here.

Not being a medical professional, it would be inappropriate for me to try and describe how we may best cope with these emotional issues, but having experienced some of these in the past (albeit to a lesser degree), I know first-hand how debilitating they can be. Here are some points to think about concerning post altercation management:

- It is NEVER acceptable for you to endure violence so whether you can run or are forced to fight, as long as you have lawfully acted in self-protection then your actions should never be considered inappropriate. Trying to rationalise your actions or perceived inadequacy in performance is a road not worth walking down.

- Always make safety your overriding priority and again, don't apologise to yourself for doing so. Maximising safety is THE ultimate aim for self-protection and even if you are feeling somewhat guilty about thinking that way, you can guarantee that your attacker won't.

- If you act as a responsible citizen post altercation then there is a greater chance of the law being firmly on your side. Extra kicks to the cranium just because you can or a failure to report the incident will never look good if things go to court. You may also want to consider calling for help or the emergency services if you feel that your attacker may have been badly injured as a result of your actions.

- Don't forget to care for your injuries. The adrenal dump experienced during an altercation will make you more resistant to pain and shock. The upshot of this is that your injuries after the event may well be far worse than you initially presume. It's been known for victims of knife attack to not even realise they've been stabbed until after the event and for unfortunate individuals to die hours or even days after an attack, due to latent injuries. It's better to be safe than sorry, so visit casualty and obtain a professional assessment of your condition.

- In the unfortunate event of being involved in a violent altercation, it may be prudent to refrain from providing a statement to the police immediately, as the adrenal effects of an altercation can cause memory distortion. The emotions you'll be feeling may cause you to say things in the heat of the moment that aren't accurate and thus, may weaken your case. It's always good practice to sleep on it and if local law will allow, make a more focussed statement the following day using legal representation if required. This will give you some time to process your thoughts. However, it's also important to note that each 'playback' in your head (especially a traumatic event) has the potential of becoming a new 'memory', which may also distort your concluding recollection to law enforcement.

- It's also good practice to document the event as soon as you can and in as much detail as possible. Write down a list of facts about the altercation, times, places, who was involved, things you noticed and any descriptions or profiles about your assailant(s). Take photo evidence if you can. If you rely solely on your memory then you may forget a crucial piece of information key to your legal defence or leading to a successful arrest. Remember that memory isn't a sequential recording like video. Recall is often influenced by prior or subsequent thoughts, events, experiences and ego. Thus, as time elapses, the potential for distortion and loss of key facts becomes more likely.

- Never feel afraid to seek support for any emotional issues that come up post event. Everyone is different and none of us are invincible. There is absolutely no requirement to deal with the aftermath all on your own and there are plenty of support networks, therapists, counsellors and the like, who will be able to provide advice, guidance and treatment to help you cope with whatever problems may arise.

Risk Evaluation Model for Self-Protection Game Plan

During industrial risk assessment processes, an evaluation model is often used as a visual tool to portray hazards for a particular task or scenario, providing an opportunity to identify and assess the key barriers and mitigating factors that may either already be in place or lacking between a safe or unsafe outcome. In this case, the 'event' is situated in the middle of the model, where pre-emptive (left-hand side) and reactive (right-hand side) measures are put in place.

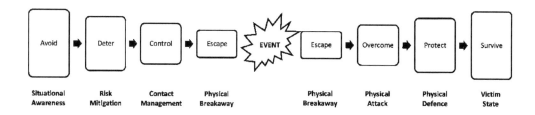

Risk Evaluation Model for Civilian Self-Protection.

Since effective civilian self-protection training is based on a proactive risk assessment process, it is possible to use a similar model to represent our core game plan and arranged to make best use of the two critical components of distance and time. The left-hand side of the model represents what barriers may be put in place before the event (attack) takes place and the right-hand side represents reactive measures after the event has been realised.

As the model above shows, the safest we can be is at the extreme left-hand side, where good situational awareness and subsequent threat recognition/negation skills would allow for either the event to be avoided completely, or for the potential threat not to choose you as a victim. The worst possible place we can be is at the extreme right-hand side, where the event has already taken place and due to either a lack of preventative skills or facing a genuine ambush attack, you are now fighting to survive.

In an ideal world we can preach to never be at the right-hand side of the model, but in reality there are so many variables that make such a claim preposterous. The classic example, which has certainly become more prevalent in recent years here in the U.K. is that one should always run away from a knife attack and that any strategy to protect against a knife wielding enemy will possess inherent weaknesses. However, what about those times when you can't simply run away and where escape is unfortunately not an option. Therefore, the best way to use this model is to help identify how our self-protection training may be best prioritised and also to recognise some of the 'far from ideal' aspects we still need to consider for more holistic coverage. Taking the Importance of priority into account, we can amend the standard model as follows.

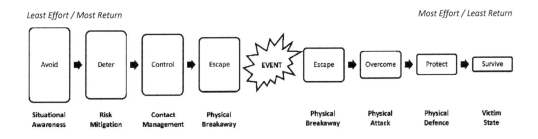

Adapted Risk Evaluation Model for Civilian Self-Protection including importance of priority.

The adapted model above integrates the law of diminishing returns. The extreme left-hand side takes comparatively little effort and yields the greater returns than the extreme right-hand side, which requires much greater effort and produces far less in terms of a return. This means that *karate dojo* that promote the 'self-defence' aspects of the art and tend to operate their classes only within the 'physical defence' portion of this model (someone punches, so you do this etc.) are missing crucial parts of the game-plan that are arguably far more important.

So in summary, we have now taken some time to consider the core self-protection game plan for use as an applicable basis for our contextual driven study of *Naihanchi Kata* and outlined its main components. The following chapter will move on to present the proposed application framework for *Bunkai Nidan*, which aims to interconnect the form's choreography into a more integrated and functional methodology.

CHAPTER IV

APPLICATION FRAMEWORK

"Karate is a method of avoiding injury should one ever be confronted by a villain or ruffian."

~ Anko Itosu

It is said that as *Sanchin* is for *Naha Karate*, so *Naihanchi* is for *Shuri Karate* and it is within these fundamental *kata* that we may find the foundation of our art. So if we were to think of *karate* as being a rocket ship, then the forms of *Sanchin* and *Naihanchi* would represent the main control system – that which makes all the mechanisms work together in order to deliver the mission. The various other application forms within the style would then act as the ancillary components used to help make space travel as safe, efficient and effective as possible. However, without that main control system, then all those ancillary components (no matter how impressive their design or application) would become inherently redundant. In a similar way, the fundamental *kata* of *karate* are regarded as being the driving force that serves to connect and integrate the other forms. And if this notion is accurate, then in terms of combative application, they should provide the most fundamental strategies by which we may achieve baseline skill and from which we may then develop.

So far throughout this book we've taken some time to build a generic understanding of civilian self-protection as a contextually driven model and looked at a holistic game plan that may be used in order to meet the essential objective(s) associated with putting such a model into action. This preliminary work has been undertaken to help ensure that our combative analysis of *Naihanchi Kata* may serve to fit the two base theories that (1) *karate* is first and foremost a culmination of effective self-protection based practices and that (2) *Naihanchi Kata* is the fundamental form associated with *Shuri*-based systems.

As a result of the information contained within previous chapters, we are now in a strong position to bring our attention to the physical mechanics of *Naihanchi Kata* and explore a series of combative lessons that may be given by its specifically prescribed choreography. Thus, the conceptual application framework offered here in this chapter is a logical result of the prerequisites already covered and a 'map' that we may use to navigate the *Naihanchi* form and investigate what the traditional teachings have alluded to with a goal focussed mind.

Just as we make an educated assumption that the discrete movements of *Naihanchi Kata* have fundamental combative relevance, then it stands to reason that so too must their specific arrangement and as such, we will also look at how body movements, stance transitions, stepping patterns, angle changes, lines of performance (*embusen*) and of course, the order of techniques within the form may all contribute to an integrated practical analysis of principles that align directly to our application framework.

Despite the numerous stylistic differences found within classical *kata*, most are not so significant that their essential make-up is drastically altered and it is usually found that even those in the minority that may be considered substantial, tend to offer variations on common themes once sufficiently explored. I have found this also to be true with *Naihanchi Kata*, having studied and compared a number of alternative choreographies from various styles and naturally settling on a version that suits my current understanding.

So whilst the specific techniques from *kata* plus the transitions between them aim to impart important combative principles, we should also be able to accept that the choreography has something equally important to teach. For *Naihanchi Kata*, I believe this to be an expression of the essential strategy one may follow in order to effectively apply the combative lessons given by the form. Based on my own study and taking into account the learning I've gained from various teachers along the way, I have found that on a fundamental level, the choreography of *Naihanchi Kata* serves to deliver an order of application concepts that aim to address (to varying degrees) the following framework critical to effective self-protection:

Naihanchi Application Framework	*Mapped to Self-Protection Game Plan*
1. *Situational Awareness*	*Situational Awareness*
2. *Combative Range*	*Situational Control*
3. *Framework & Movement*	*Situational Control*
4. *Positional Advantage*	*Situational Control*
5. *Reactive Tactics*	*Primary Physical Strategy*
6. *Percussive Impact*	*Primary Physical Strategy*
7. *Negotiating Obstacles*	*Primary Physical Strategy*

8. *Counter Grappling*	*Secondary Physical Strategy*
9. *Felling Options*	*Secondary Physical Strategy*

Table showing Naihanchi Application Framework mapped to the core self-protection game plan.

As you can see, the above are given in order of distance, time and importance, with the most peripheral strategy being dealt with first and then leading to secondary contingencies and closer attached strategies should things not go to plan. All of these are designed to connect seamlessly and on a physical level, culminate with your opponent capitulated on the ground thus offering you the chance to escape.

It's no coincidence that this specific order happens to be reflected within the form's composition, strengthening the idea that *Naihanchi Kata* may serve as an essential curriculum for self-protection. This breaks away somewhat from the conventional way of thinking and instead of a collection of discrete and unrelated applications, offers a more integrated model for consideration and inclusion in *dojo* training from day one. It also places *Naihanchi Kata* firmly back at the root of the *Shuri* based styles and allows the learning from this form to disseminate effectively in order to augment the other supporting *kata* within each system.

Multiple Applications

Of course, we can't be certain whether historically, the choreographed techniques of *karate kata* each had only a single purpose in mind, or were chosen as examples to represent more generic combative themes. As such, contemporary analysis of these movements using varying contextual scenarios and by different practitioners with individual skill/experiences will naturally yield multiple possibilities.

Now you may argue that the above only adds more uncertainty to the pot, or you can instead see this explorative process as being holistically more valuable than if we were to have already been passed on the irrefutable answers by the pioneering teachers of our past. Indeed, we do have some guidance to make use of, but the very fact that we are required to search for ourselves inherently makes us all better martial artists.

The way I like to look at the notion of multiple applications for a particular movement (or series of movements) is two-fold. Firstly, as above, we simply can't be certain. So for me it pays dividends to keep an open mind. Secondly, the very nature of self-protection requires the ability for one's physical response to be based on multiple functions for fundamental movement pathways in order to prevent against *Hicks Law* and natural adrenal responses from having a debilitating effect. However, we have to also appreciate that these combative functions must be integrated into simplistic and useable strategies, otherwise we only add to the 'log-jam' problem. In other words, knowing three or four applications for every movement in the *kata* is practically useless over and above what is a mere academic accomplishment.

CHAPTER V

PEOPLE SKILLS & MENTALITY

"When your temper rises, lower your fists. When your fists rise, lower your temper."

~ Chojun Miyagi

In the case of civilian self-protection, the way we interact with people is always far more important than the development of physical attributes. Of course, trouble can come your way regardless of how you may act, but recognising that your actions can have significant impact on how a situation may develop or even be realised, means that managing the risk of an altercation is always best served on the basis of first and foremost being a decent human being within society. With respect and courtesy being the cornerstones of traditional martial arts such as *karate*, I'd like to draw your attention in this brief chapter to some important considerations on the topics of effective people skills and mentality for the holistic application of self-protection within everyday life.

People Skills

Many interactions that grow to become violent do so due to escalated disputes and our ego certainly has a lot to answer for in terms of getting us into trouble. Therefore, in self-protection, it's important to develop our strength of character in tandem with our ability to physically protect ourselves. The idea is to have a long enough fuse to refrain from escalating violence, but with a large enough explosion to deal with violence should it ever become necessary. Just as Patrick Swayze's character Dalton explains so eloquently in the film Roadhouse, "Be nice…until it's time…to not be nice!"

The ability to empathize with other people's point of view, whether it is genuine or not, can go a long way to de-escalate potential problems before they become real threats. Oftentimes, swallowing a little pride or simply choosing to ignore words spoken in an attempt to anger us can have a profound effect on the final outcome. This shows far greater strength than elevated ego-based confrontation ever could.

One of the biggest ironies in traditional *karate* is that practitioners are conditioned to spend many years polishing mind, body and spirit within the 'conduit of combat', whilst at the same time, developing a strong will to resist using such skills unless absolutely necessary. Although this disparity can bring up other issues surrounding what may or may not be considered 'effective' in self-protection and has no doubt caused certain training methodologies to lose their potency, the realization still stands that physical protection against a potential threat is always best avoided than managed.

Karate has always incorporated into its teachings the development of a virtuous character. Often mystified and revered against a lifetime of training, I agree that although the character may be polished through a martial arts journey, I think it first requires the foundation of a considerate human being to build upon. Thus, transmitting any form of combat training to individuals with malicious or dishonest tendencies may be a risky endeavour. I remember once when a local MMA fighter bragged to me during a conversation that the main reason he entered the cage was so he could beat people up without the risk of being arrested! Indeed, people of poor character or with malicious intent can find their way into any martial art.

The above example is typical of why *karate* teachers of old would initially decline the requests of hopeful students and even upon acceptance, would challenge them with the completion of menial tasks in order to test their character. This is also why the monotonous repetition of fundamentals serves so well not only to build a solid foundation, but also to reveal any flaws in persistence, separate the wheat from the chaff and help weed out those individuals who may have 'insincere reasons' for training.

So in short, it must be remembered that any good self-protection strategy should always aim to prioritize people skills over physical skills, soft skills over hard skills and avoidance over situational control. There is no place for inflated ego in any of its forms, including misplaced honour or pride and developing the ability to de-escalate a potential situation well before it becomes a physical threat represents outstanding aptitude in self-protection.

Now of course, it may not always be possible to exercise an adequate level of self-protection with only soft-skills and in some instances, a physical response may become necessary. In these situations, it's important that one's mind-set be adjusted within the blink of an eye to help support this more assertive strategy. After all, application without proper mind-set is like trying to bake a cake without any heat!

Mentality

Physical prowess, knowledge and experience means absolutely nothing if we don't apply the proper attitude by which to act in the pursuit of our personal safety. This mind-set needs to be with us at all times, cultivated through training and be ready to access at a moment's notice. The hampering ethical or cultural-based dilemmas in your head should have already been ironed out through deep introspective deliberation, so that you can employ physical skills with full resolve in order to better the chances of maximising your safety with minimum harm.

Remember that for self-protection to be effective, the physical component requires sufficient back-up by an attitude that is fully committed to the task at hand. I remember teaching this idea of developing what *Bruce Lee* famously called 'emotional content' to a rather frail-looking lady, who came to me looking for self-defence classes. A while ago she had been the victim of rape and in recent months was finding it almost impossible to come to terms with her recollection of the fact that she (in her words) "allowed the altercation to take place" without fighting back. Reaching out to learn self-defence was in sheer desperation to take a step towards exorcising the demons that had taken up residence in her head. Those demons had so far wreaked havoc on her career, her marriage and her sanity.

Naturally, I first persuaded the lady to seek some professional counselling, which turned out to help a great deal in managing the aftermath of her ordeal. She slowly began to develop more self-esteem and her life started to get back on track. But in terms of her self-defence training, she was having a really difficult time being able to access any form of intensity to accentuate her physical ability. Witnessing her striking focus mitts was like watching a baby trying to break through a paving slab. That was until I shifted her 'contemplation' away from her and towards her young daughter.

Once I had her visualise her daughter being at risk from harm, her attitude changed instantly. The pads she was previously 'tapping' were now at risk from literally being torn apart! My hands throbbed inside them and the energy driving hard towards me was that of absolute rage. I had changed nothing about her physical technique, only her mind-set. The result spoke for itself as she finally flicked the switch, changed gear and transformed her demeanour from resembling a kind-hearted domestic Tabby into a hungry and infuriated Wildcat.

We all have the ability to access our survival mechanisms and indeed, the instinct to help keep us alive in dire circumstances, whatever the specific trigger may be. We've all heard reports of eight stone women lifting cars to save loved ones trapped underneath, small children dragging unconscious parents from burning houses and frail pensioners fighting off determined attackers a third their age. But by the same token, we've also heard plenty of stories to the contrary. It is not so much the physicality that separates these incidents, but the energy gleaned from their associated mentalities.

As part of your holistic *karate* training for civilian self-protection, it is worth finding and learning to access your personal 'trigger' point, which may be used to instantly switch modes from kind-hearted diffusion to that of controlled aggression. You must spend time bathing in this energy and learn how to fine-tune it to your advantage so that it doesn't overwhelm you. Practice switching into this mode every time you strike pads, break objects or engage in reality-based application/simulation training. Acquire the ability to employ vehemence at a moment's notice to support your physical response and this will serve you well.

In terms of *Naihanchi Kata*, you may use your performance of the form to build mindfulness, mentality and intent through visualisation. The very fact that we don't cripple each other in the *dojo* every week means that we're constantly compromising our practice in the name of safety, and rightly so. Thus, the solo performance of *kata* gives us the opportunity to run through techniques of the choreography with full resolve and to practice flicking that internal switch using varying cadences. Obviously this is not a replacement for live drilling with a training partner or impact development against pads etc., but strong visualisation during movement has proven its worth across a multitude of physical disciplines and martial arts is no different. For me, this is one of the most important aspects of solo *kata* performance.

In adrenaline fuelled situations it's not uncommon to hear about people fighting on even after withstanding broken bones, stabbings and shootings. However, it's impossible for an enemy to fight back after being knocked unconscious, which makes the effort of 'switching off' the threat a top priority. Having said that, knocking an adversary out is not always as easy or as clean as what some may have you believe, so if escape is not an option, then the ability to deliver successive impact with intent until capitulation is the most appropriate plan for physical self-protection against violence. Due to this, it is critical that you follow a conceptual methodology that will enable you to scale force accordingly.

Levels of Force

Obviously, the action you should take against someone attempting to end your life would be at the extreme end of the scale when compared to the action you should take against an angered drunken relative at a family barbecue. Also given the fact that you will be in no state to accurately assess the situation or sift through a wide selection of applications, the platform for you to instantly and appropriately scale the level of force required must be built into the same conceptual application methodologies.

In terms of developing the appropriate mentality, it is always best to practice with varying levels of threat in mind. On one hand it may be more prudent to practice dealing with higher levels of violence and never need to rely on it, than to practice for lower levels of confrontation and find yourself in a situation that requires something more. On the other hand, we need to also consider that whatever we regularly rehearse may affect our perception of and attention towards a potential situation, increasing the risk of overreacting. At worst and under pressure, we could create an imagined threat simply by expecting it. Thus, rehearsing a continuum of threat levels would help develop more flexibility in response. However, due to the requirement to maintain an appropriate level of safety in training, it is near impossible to accurately replicate the same feelings/emotions/actions you'd experience for real. This idea of gauging force in live drilling and how to develop associated attributes will be covered in more depth within Vol.3 and the *Bunkai Yondan/Godan* layers of analysis.

So in summary, I think it's important to reiterate the fact that along with the physical skills required to help aid personal protection, these need to be backed up with proper mentality, integrated with the ability to scale force appropriately and placed behind the development of good people skills that refuse to let ego get in the way of dealing with a situation peacefully. Good traditional martial arts training should provide many of these attributes and especially so, the motivation to become an exemplary member of society.

CHAPTER VI

THAT'S NOT KARATE...IS IT?

"In karate, hitting, thrusting and kicking are not the only methods, throwing techniques and pressure against joints are also included."

~ Gichin Funakoshi

The popularity of mixed martial arts has clearly identified the need to be adept at combat within multiple ranges and across various skill-sets. The same is true for non-consensual conflict, where striking (although key) forms only part of the whole jigsaw. Whereas much of contemporary *karate* has chosen to determinedly omit these multiple ranges to focus and excel within a long-range sporting context, it's clear from the writings of past masters that this was not always the case and indeed, self-protection based *karate* must by its very meaning, exhibit adaptable characteristics in order to cope with what is a chaotic, unregulated, distressing, and constantly changing environment.

Recent attempts to bring *karate* back to its traditional roots has led to an assumption that certain ranges and skills-sets have been added via the study of other martial arts. Some hold the belief that *karate's* throwing techniques must have been taken from arts like *Judo*, its limb control from systems like *Wing Chun*, *Silat* or *Kali* and its clinch fighting from wrestling styles. If that logic was applied, then I guess it would also mean that its punching came from *Western Boxing*! In truth of course, this is not the case and although study of these 'specialist arts' would no doubt help to add valuable experience to these combative tactics, *karate* has always possessed mixed-range skills. Writings of past masters, traditional teachings and not to mention a realistic study of *kata* clearly support this.

I think it is important to consider the fact that all martial arts are essentially based on providing solutions to problems. In the case of *karate*, evidence points to the fact that the primary issue was that of experiencing a violent encounter. And although other auxiliary problems (and solutions) may have been added over time to develop the very versatile art we have today, the fact remains that the foundation of classical *karate kata* fundamentally aims to disseminate solutions to address this original cause for concern. And as it is the problem that drives the urge to find a suitable solution, it stands to reason that the practical application of *karate* contains the necessity to work within a variety of combative ranges, albeit to varying levels of proficiency as the problem specifically demands.

The above reasoning is why you may not find certain boxing methods, throws, joint attacks, limb control strategies and grappling tactics in *karate* compared to what other 'specialist arts' may include within their curriculum. However, it is also one of the reasons why you will see similarities that to the uneducated may appear to have been nothing more than contemporary add-ons from other martial arts knowledge. The reality though is that given its combative perspective for self-protection, a holistic methodology is certainly prevalent within the choreography of classical *karate kata*.

If certain problems exist in more than one martial art then it doesn't take much rational thought to realise the possibility of similar (if not identical) solutions being developed separately from each other and this certainly seems to be the case for *karate*. Across history we've seen the same process occur in the likes of weaponry, clothing, shelter, medicine, engineering and many other advancements throughout the course of human development. Thus, I would suggest that it's not the case of a *judo* throw, *wing chun* trap or *muay thai* elbow being used in *karate*, but more likely that early practitioners of various martial arts, whilst having no contact and being many miles/years apart have simply happened to find very comparable solutions to help solve common problems. And since the principles of combat are universal, it should be of no surprise that certain techniques born out of these tactics will show resemblance to each other.

Another assumption often made is that study of multiple ranges/skills creates a jack of all trades and a master of none. Again, I believe that it is not the range of skills that should be in question here, but more so the ability to exercise these according to specific context that the objective demands. Sticking with the comparison above, it's obvious that even a highly skilled *karate-ka* will never match the throwing capabilities of a seasoned *judo* exponent. Yet, the level of throwing skill required for each art is purposefully disparate, not to mention the priority given to such skills in order to meet the specific objectives of the art.

Those who have even a rudimentary knowledge of trapping/grappling ranges will clearly recognise such applications throughout the classical *karate* forms. What's important for practitioners is to be mindful of how these skills may best fit to serve the solution(s) to the particular problem(s) that those choreographed sequences were created to record. With respect to civilian self-protection, this naturally made traditional *karate* a 'mixed' system demanding varying levels of skill from different ranges as required.

It also makes sense that the range of skills identified as being *karate* may have been intentionally limited during its transition from Okinawa to mainland Japan in the early 20th Century. With ancient warrior arts already well developed and weaved into modern martial ways, the Japanese had no prevailing need for throwing (*judo*), weaponry (*kendo*, *naginatado*, *kyudo* etc.) or joint locking (*ju-jutsu*) skills. However, with the lack of a new and completely dedicated striking art, an 'adapted' version of *karate* may well have served to fill that gap and importantly, without stepping on any toes.

By the time the art re-emerged in Japan after the *Second World War* through popularisation by pioneering and 'conforming' teachers such as *Gichin Funakoshi*, *karate* began to take on a whole new appearance and over the space of only a few years, significantly reviewed and altered its modus operandi. Whether or not the transition into what we would call modern-day *karate* was of benefit and in what capacity will always be a matter of personal opinion. However, the fact remains that change has occurred and has naturally continued to transform over recent generations. In all walks of life evolutionary adaptation is often a necessary requirement for survival and/or success. This was certainly the case for *karate* and numerous other martial arts that may have drifted, either deliberately or accidently away from their original intent.

The key to *karate's* practical application for self-protection lies within the contextual understanding of *kata* against its originally perceived aims and although it is impossible to ascertain whether or not a particular approach is 100% accurate, it is relatively clear that with careful analysis, the classical mnemonics handed down to us reveal an art that's both diverse and innovative, plus equally as fluid as those arts who's practitioners often judge *karate* as being overly rigid and stale. Blinkered views that stem from gaining only superficial experience into *Okinawa's* mixed non-consensual based system of self-protection.

The conceptual lessons presented in this Volume for *Bunkai Nidan* focus entirely on the core combative teachings of *Naihanchi Kata* as aligned to the fundamental self-protection game plan. This however is not the only way in which the choreography of the form may be viewed and there are additional strategies from other classical application *kata* to consider also. If you're looking for advanced concepts, intricate details and high level technical skills then by their very definition, you won't find them part of a fundamental self-protection strategy. So the following pages detail what I believe to be an essential methodology that may help gain a solid and time-efficient grounding from which to then progress further and develop from.

BUNKAI NIDAN

PART TWO: PRINCIPLE-BASED ANALYSIS

CHAPTER VII

LESSON 1: SITUATIONAL AWARENESS

"The mind must be calm and alert. Use your peripheral vision and look for that, which is not easily seen."

~ The Bubishi

Commencing our analysis of the key conceptual lessons from *Naihanchi Kata* for civilian-based self-protection, is the emphasis on developing everyday awareness skills. Simply put, if we fail to maintain an adequate degree of situational awareness during our everyday life then our ability to recognise and evaluate levels of risk becomes dangerously limited and as such, any potential threat to personal safety will most probably go unperceived until it's too late and a physical reactionary response then becomes necessary.

The above is why any training in self-protection should always emphasise the requirement for effective awareness, threat recognition and avoidance skills. And given the assumption that *Okinawan Karate* was developed to protect against non-consensual violence, then it stands to reason that the same skills should be cultivated in the *dojo*, and may well be present within the teachings passed on to us through the choreographed movements of classical *kata*. If practicing *karate* for self-protection then physical protection methods against such acts of violence should make up only part of a holistic game plan for personal safety. Given the context, then skills for 'prevention' should always take priority over skills for 'protection'.

Apart from contingency anti-ambush tactics that aim to cater for genuine surprise attacks, the main core strategies in self-protection are constructed around having an appropriate level of situational awareness. If you can develop and naturally employ effective awareness skills then in nine times out of ten, you'll be able to avoid trouble well in advance of having to resort to a physical response. Given that the dictionary meaning for awareness is 'knowledge or perception of a situation or fact', then by definition, we must make efforts to not only learn what a potential threat looks like, but also to acknowledge and manage its presence. All the awareness in the world is rendered useless if we are unable to recognize the hazard for what it is or as is often the case in self-protection, understand the veil of deception the may be used to hide it.

Situational awareness essentially begins with the five physical senses of sight (ophthalmoception), hearing (audioception), smell (olfacoception or olfacception), touch (tactioception) and taste (gustaoception). These act as human tentacles that reach out and delve into the outside world, for without them we would be virtually imprisoned within the darkness and silence of our own body.

Our five physical senses have evolved primarily to keep us safe from harm. Here are a few simple examples of how they work to achieve this:

- *Sight:* On admiring the beautiful view from upon a high sea cliff, you become visually aware of how close the edge is and as a result, take extra care.

- *Hearing:* You're upstairs and hear the smoke alarm go off in the kitchen, causing you to take swift action.

- *Smell:* Returning back home, you open the front door and instantly smell the strong odour that alerts you to a gas leak.

- *Taste:* Sinking your teeth into a juicy looking piece of fruit, you taste that it's rotten inside and quickly spit it out before ingesting it.

- *Touch:* Suddenly the lights go out in the room, requiring you to carefully feel around for the nearest exit route whilst negotiating obstacles.

The ability to detect stimuli beyond those governed by the five 'traditional' senses also exists, however the definition of what actually constitutes a 'sense' is still very much under scrutiny, as well as the accurate responses to specific stimuli. This for the most part is extraneous for martial artists who are more interested in the practical utilisation of their senses, rather than how they may be defined. These extra 'senses' include thermoception (temperature), proprioception (relative position), nociception (pain), equilibrioception (balance) and mechanoreception (vibration).

With adequate experience, our human senses (acting as detection elements) help us develop a 360 degree range of peripheral awareness. When combined with a thorough understanding of common attack rituals, pre-threat cues, behavioural escalators and the ability for one to quickly evaluate a potential situation for level of risk, then we have a very strong foundation for personal protection.

Whilst the movements of *Naihanchi Kata* are understandably incapable of directly teaching a comprehensive lesson on personal awareness in self-protection, it nevertheless succeeds to express a number of key teachings that are designed to inspire the practitioner to delve deeper into this subject, spend time developing these 'soft skills' and build a solid basis for the more 'physical' applications to follow.

As situational awareness is an intangible component, some *karate* practitioners may believe that the development of this aspect cannot exist within the corporeal movements of *kata*. In my view, it is not so much the movements of *kata* themselves, but rather the mind-set sought when performing those movements that really counts. As the saying goes, "what we think, so shall we become" and this is just as relevant when aiming to develop our awareness to the point it becomes a more natural and intuitive life-skill.

The concept of awareness in *kata* is generally emphasised through the application of *zanshin* (remaining mind) when performing techniques in sequence. When moving in different directions around the *dojo* floor, we must always be attentive to our surroundings. Where are you in relation to everything else? Where is *Sensei* standing? Where are all the other students situated? What sounds can you hear? What does the air smell like? What tastes do you experience? Aim to feel the air as it moves around your body and the pressure that your feet make with the ground as you transition smoothly through the various postures.

The most effective way to tune in to your senses is to relax, become more attentive of their actual existence and learn how to really 'absorb' the stimuli encountered, rather than simply trying to force those feelings upon your mind. It should not feel like 'you' and 'them', but rather a single integrated whole (or self). Although this may sound a little *'Zen-like'* when applied to the subject of personal safety, it is this absorption of our senses that will condition our awareness to work on auto-pilot.

But how do we know if we are becoming more aware and how do we gauge levels of awareness to help in more practical application? Well, an incremental expression of awareness may be better understood through the use of *Cooper's Colour Codes*.

Cooper's Colour Codes

This system was originally developed by Jeff Cooper, a US combat pistol instructor who stated in his book, *Principles of Personal Defense* that:

> *"The most important means of surviving a lethal confrontation is neither the weapon nor the martial skills. The primary tool is that of combat mind-set."*

In the study of self-protection, we often make use of colour codes to help set a series of mental flag posts for increasing levels of awareness and associated combat mind-set.

The colour code system originally introduced by Cooper was centred on one's state of mind, as opposed to specific tactical responses to incremental alert levels. It essentially allows you to move from one mind-set to another and enables the acknowledgement of handling a particular situation or set of circumstances.

Although Cooper did not claim to have invented anything new, he is generally regarded as being the first to document such a system as an indication of mental state. Nowadays, the system is adapted and used in many fields such as security, advanced driving, hospitals plus of course, personal safety.

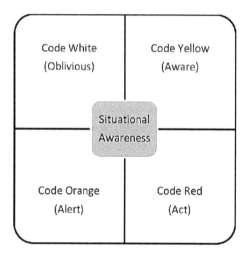

Above is the colour code system as it is commonly used in self-protection with a short description below of what each colour represents. When you read over each component, try to relate to a particular feeling or mind-set that each suggests. This is where the real value of the model lies:

- *White (Oblivious):* This represents a state of being unaware and therefore, unprepared. Code White is often coined 'The Victim State' because this mind-set is often what assailants either consciously or subconsciously look for before moving in to execute their plans. If attacked whilst in Code White, then by definition, the only strategy that may be employed would be a reactive response. Thus, living your life in Code White instantly denies you of many personal safety strategies that help to keep you safe from harm. Unless very skilled (or lucky), it is only really the inadequacy or ineptitude of the aggressor that may save you. An individual walking along the pavement with earphones in listening to music whilst writing a text to a friend on their mobile phone is a classic example of what would constitute as being in Code White.

- *Yellow (Aware):* Code Yellow represents a state of having a healthy attentiveness to our surroundings by using our physical senses together in order to provide where possible, a 360 degree peripheral awareness. In terms of self-protection, although there may be no specific threat of attack present, the mind-set should be such that a potential threat may always be possible. Code Yellow is not (and should not be) a state of paranoia, but rather a state of relaxed mindfulness that the world is a potentially unfriendly place and if "today is the day" then you are prepared to defend yourself. As Code Yellow is about taking in information from your senses in such a relaxed manner, one should be able to stay in this mind-set for long periods of time and with regular practice, the aim is to gradually make Code Yellow your everyday norm.

- *Orange (Alert):* If your 'awareness radar' picks up something that seems to you as being not quite right or out of the ordinary, then your mind-set should shift up to Code Orange, which represents a state of alert to a specific situation. Your attention shifts more towards a primary focus (whilst still maintaining a level of general awareness) in order to evaluate and then determine if a threat is actually present. As Code Orange is more specific, it is less relaxed and should therefore be used in conjunction with Code Yellow once satisfied that the primary focus is of no danger. In this way, you may shift between Code Yellow and Code Orange as is necessary.

- *Red (Act):* Code Red is the state of action, where a real threat is now confirmed and you need to do something immediately to help ensure your safety. In terms of self-protection, the two options in Code Red are either 'fight' or 'flight', with the assessment and decision process ideally pre-conditioned into a digital response in order to help protect against the evolutionary hard-wired freeze syndrome experienced in high adrenaline fuelled situations. Although ceasing all motion may once have been a life-saving tool to help prevent being 'locked on' as prey by animals higher up in the pre-historic food chain, it proves to be of real detriment in the face of today's urban predators. Simply put, Code Red occurs when the mental trigger established in Code Orange has been tripped and action now needs to be taken. That action may be as simple as to run away, to push someone back in order to make distance, re-affirming with assertive dialogue and body language, or it may be to combatively engage the threat.

As a point of interest, Cooper's Colour Codes is sometimes described using an additional fifth condition (Code Black), which represents being physically engaged with the threat and that such a situation may lead to lethal consequences. This fifth condition is more applicable for law enforcement operatives, special-forces or professional 'peace-keepers', so it is usually omitted from the civilian self-protection model in order to keep things as simple as possible.

As a concise summary of Coopers Colour Codes, please consider the following short sentences, which aim to reflect the necessary mind-set required for each state:

- *Code White:* I am switched off and ignorant to my immediate surroundings.

- *Code Yellow:* I am consciously aware of my surroundings and the people in it.

- *Code Orange:* I may have to protect myself if 'X' happens.

- *Code Red:* 'X' has happened and action is immediately necessary.

It's worth taking note of the fact that this system can only work effectively if you are initially in Code Yellow to begin with, as by definition, going about your daily activities in Code White would make you oblivious to any potential threats. In reality, most people tend to sit in-between Code White and Code Yellow. In other words, whilst managing to refrain from walking into lamp posts, falling down manholes, tripping over kerb stones or running red lights, there is still a deficit of situational awareness present that may be easily exploited. An added bonus of being in true Code Yellow will also allow you to appreciate the finer beauty of the world as you will notice so much more about your immediate environment.

There's also a lot to be said for 'listening to your gut'. Chances are that if something doesn't feel right, then it probably isn't. The *Samurai* of *Japan* called this skill *haragei* (belly art) and developed it to a level whereby one could sense specific threats or anticipate an enemy's movements before they occurred. On many levels, cultural conditioning has driven us down the road of desensitizing us to that little voice in our head, but in reality, that innate feeling where the hairs stand up on the back of your neck has served our species well for millennia. Remember, we are descendants of those early humans who all listened to their survival instincts, so although not always accurate, making your 'sixth sense' part of your awareness package would be a good choice.

An escalating situation would instantly be accompanied by the survival stress response and secretion of adrenaline. This is why your primary self-protection strategy must cater for such body changes and effects. For example, we know that the requirement to actively scan your environment when in Code Red is crucial to help counter-act the tunnel vision experienced by an adrenal release and resulting elevated heart rate. One way to accomplish this is to mindfully practice the habit of turning your head side to side upon initial disengagement from the threat (once dealt with) and escape.

Your training should also aim to develop expectation, understanding and inoculation in order to break from the startle reflex or freeze response, which is as previously discussed has been hard-wired by evolution and further re-enforced through cultural conditioning. Like a rabbit caught in the headlights of an oncoming vehicle, the days of freezing to avoid detection by predators is seldom required in the modern urban environment. Plus the educated communities we live in today have a habit of habituating current and future generations to believe that to fight is thuggish and to run away is cowardly. So it begs the question - What other option do we have? Hence the requirement for proper self-protection strategies.

The final thing I'd like to mention about situational awareness with respect to Cooper's Colour Codes is that one's awareness levels will naturally change at each given moment in time. Because of this, it must therefore be accepted that although it may be desirable to maintain Code Yellow throughout the day, from a realistic perspective, this would be impossible to achieve with every action taken.

For example, imagine walking into a building for a business meeting and being asked to sign the attendance log at reception. Whilst you may well be in Code Orange with respect to the awareness on what you are writing down, there is simply no way you can be in Code Yellow with respect to the awareness of what's behind you. Other examples may include ordering from a menu at a restaurant, answering your mobile phone or using public toilets.

As a consequence of the above, it's difficult to argue the truth that there is always the possibility of an ambush attack. Therefore, I feel that Coopers Colour Codes for self-protection are best utilized in respect to general 'readiness', as opposed to simply general 'awareness'. And although situational awareness is a skill that may be developed through experience, it can only ever serve to support your level of safety at any given moment, never guarantee it.

The OODA Loop

In order to make best use of situational awareness within our holistic self-protection framework, we should also understand a little about how our brain and body work together to turn observation into some form of action. The *OODA Loop* model fits very well with Cooper's Colour Codes, demonstrating the rational and recurring human decision making cycle of observe, orient, decide, and act. Developed by United States Air Force Colonel John Boyd based on his personal experiences as a fighter pilot, this is another model originally established by the military, but has found application in many other fields, including self-protection:

- *Observe:* To actively scan and gather information regarding the environment that affects you.

- *Orient:* Interpreting the information gathered. This may depend on the specific scenario, cultural conditioning, genetic heritage, experience, ability to analyse and rate of change of that information etc.

- *Decide:* weighing up options from the knowledge generated during the *orient* phase and then picking the most appropriate one. Decisions are based on deduction and as such, need to remain fluid and ready to change as new information comes in.

- *Act:* Carrying out the selected decision, with the feedback from implementation becoming the basis for the next round of *observe*.

Simply put, before we can make any form of calculated action, we must first observe the situation, orientate ourselves to the stimulus and then make a decision based on the information present. All of this takes time, which is why in self-protection we aim to exploit the *OODA Loop* to our advantage – a principle often seen throughout effective *kata* applications. To take advantage of the *OODA Loop*, our aim should be to operate at a faster tempo than our adversaries, lengthen their *OODA Loop* and appear unpredictable to create a degree of confusion.

Here is an example of how the *OODA Loop* can be understood in terms of self-protection. Presuming that you are already in a state of relaxed awareness (Code Yellow), then you are able to constantly OBSERVE your environment. If a potential situation becomes apparent, then you would begin to ORIENT to that particular problem in order to determine whether or not it is a threat to your safety (Code Orange). Based on the information gathered at this point, you would then DECIDE on the best way forward and

ACT in a timely fashion so as to implement your chosen resolution. Once your action has been undertaken, you would then return to OBSERVE to find out how the situation may have changed as a result of your action and then the loop would continue again as necessary.

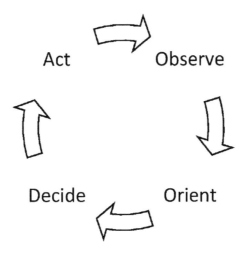

Observe: Situational Awareness

Orient: Situational Understanding

Decide: Situational Judgement

Act: Situational Influence

The main problem with having a lack of awareness to a potential threat is the fact that your aggressor will have already passed through their own *OODA Loop* and have completed *observe, orient* and *decide* before *acting* to launch an attack, which you have still yet to *observe*! The fact that you will be three steps behind means that protecting yourself against such a 'sudden' act of violence and then turning the tables to a successful counter-attack would be very difficult and in most cases impossible. Since the *OODA Loop* is a two-way street, strategies that we can adopt to help us manipulate the process in our favour should be woven into our self-protection game plan.

Examples of manipulating the *OODA Loop* include predominantly the possession of good situational awareness, general readiness and threat perception skills that help put you further along the OODA sequence and in a much better position to act quicker. Furthermore, there are methods of posturing that may be employed to draw certain attack capabilities, plus both pre-emptive and reactionary strategies designed to decisively throw the aggressor back to OBSERVE. Specific applications that feature such *OODA Loop* manipulations will be covered in further chapters.

So now having discussed the generic emphasis on *Zanshin* during the performance of *kata*, key information about increasing levels of awareness/readiness through the use of Cooper's Colour Codes, plus the importance of understanding and manipulating the *OODA Loop*, let's now take a look at how the opening salutation of *Naihanchi Kata* may be applied to address the concept of situational awareness in self-protection and prompt deeper investigation in to the subject.

Application Concept 01/01 – Mapping Peripheral Vison

The first part of the opening salutation may be used as a lesson to map peripheral vision.

Starting with your feet together with hands forming a triangle, raise your arms slowly above your head. Next, the thumbs hook and then the hands part with the arms prescribing a smooth arc around both sides of the body.

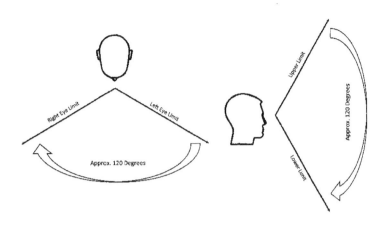

Diagram showing human field of vision of approx. 120 degrees.

As your arms raise, maintain a forward gaze by looking (but not focusing) at a point in front and allow the hands to stop just on the edge of your peripheral vision, such that if you were to move them up any further then they would disappear from sight. Then when bringing the arms around the sides of the body, keep your hands on the same threshold of your peripheral. Again, if you were to move the hands any further back then you would no longer be able to see them.

The first part of the opening salutation encourages the practitioner to expand their awareness by mapping out their entire field of vision. With the vast majority of people going about their lives with 'blinkers' on, practicing this simple application can become quite illuminating. It helps to show us just how much information our eyes may gather at any one time.

Application Concept 01/02 – Challenging Peripheral Vision

By flexing at the elbows, bring the hands up to around chest level and then rotating about the palms, return back to the original position, bringing the thumbs back out to form the triangle shape once again. As before, these movements are to be performed smoothly and should take around one second each to complete.

Once the extent of your peripheral vision has been determined by *Application 01/01*, the next sequence of the opening salutation may be used to challenge your ability to maintain this range of vision by placing an object (i.e. your connected hands) into your field and then back out again. It's important that you keep your eyes facing forward during the whole motion.

This application teaches another very important lesson about visual awareness, which is that the eyes will naturally perceive and react to movement first, before they distinguish colour and/or shape. It is instinctive for us to track movement with the eyes (imagine a spider crawling across the carpet when you're watching television), but in terms of self-protection, it is often prudent to avoid this, as many attackers will aim to exploit this natural urge through the use of deception and distraction. The classic 'pincer movement' deployed by two assailants is a great example of this, where one person engages in front, drawing your attention and taking away your peripheral attentiveness, whilst an 'assistant' moves in decisively from the flank. Another example of distraction would be someone in front looking over your shoulder to encourage you to turn you head before then attacking you. Where your eyes go, your mind naturally follows.

The second part of the opening salutation may be used as a lesson to test peripheral vision.

This part of the opening salutation prompts and encourages the practitioner to become comfortable using peripheral vision to assess the environment for potential risk, without your eyes being distracted by movement.

As your hands raise up and into your field of vision, aim to take in as much detail as possible, whilst maintaining appropriate awareness of everything else and resisting the

94

urge to look directly at them. Try to note the colour, shape, texture, even down to the creases in your skin.

Not an easy task, but a great way to exercise the ability to explore your peripheral field without the need to focus on specific objects.

Application Concept 01/03 – Maintaining Peripheral Vision

The third part of the opening salutation may be used as a lesson to maintain peripheral vision.

The third and final part of the opening salutation has the head moving from side to side, eyes remaining fixed, whilst scanning the area like a security camera. Whilst performing this movement, maintain peripheral view and avoid focusing between one object and the next. Try to preserve the feelings gained from *Application Concept 01/01* and *01/02*, simply monitoring your environment as the eyes pass smoothly from left to right. When practicing, it is often useful to repeat this head motion numerous times in order to really appreciate just how much more information you are able to take in about your surroundings when the gaze is expanded just as the *kata* encourages.

So to quickly recap, the lessons associated with situational awareness during the opening salutation of *Naihanchi Kata* are as follows. The first part (*Application Concept 01/01*) helps to encourage an expansive field of peripheral vision. The second part (*Application Concept 01/02*) challenges your ability to maintain this peripheral awareness whilst an object moves within it. The third part (*Application Concept 01/03*) aims to train the eyes to scan smoothly from left to right, taking in information without stalling or returning back to a focused or 'blinkered' state.

The above lessons are arguably some of the most important for self-protection, since they instil from the very beginning the idea that developing situational awareness is absolutely necessary for personal safety. Practicing the opening salutation in this way should also inspire you to pursue a more detailed study of other supporting soft-skills (such as target hardening, posturing, verbal de-escalation etc.) and suggests that the feeling of expanded vision may also be extended to the other physical senses in order to establish an effective 360 degree peripheral cognisance.

A good way to firmly implant the teachings on awareness given by movements of the opening salutation is to practice seeking similar sensations and feelings as you go about your daily activities. This helps bridge the gap between form and function, transferring the soft-skills explored through the practice of *Naihanchi Kata* into real-life scenarios. Although these probably sit better in *Volume Three*, I've added below ten useful exercises that you may wish to make use of:

Example 01: When walking around, aim to obtain the same feeling of expanded peripheral vision as attained during the first part of the opening salutation (*Application 01/01*). Start to take mental notes of objects, movements, colours and shapes around you and without becoming too overwhelmed, try to take in as much information as possible about your surroundings without focussing on one point.

Example 02: A great way to expand the drill above is to add some mental commentary about the information you gather, extend your awareness to other physical senses too. This is a skill often taught in advanced driving courses and promotes the feeling of being 'ahead of the game'. For instance, if you're walking down a street and see a car driving towards you, mentally note the make, model and colour. Does it have any distinguishing features? How many people are in the vehicle? What speed do you think it may be travelling at? What smells do you experience as the car drives by? Can you feel any vibrations or other tactile stimulus from your contact with the pavement? Etc.

Example 03: When at home, sit down in a quiet room for a few moments and focus on a single object. It may be a plant, a candle, an interesting ornament or picture etc. Now, start to really focus on the object and mentally note as much information as you can about it. Look at it from all angles - you'll no doubt see and appreciate things that you never have before. After a few moments, slowly bring your attention to your peripheral and relax your intense focus on the object. Absorb the object as just another piece of information within your sphere of awareness.

Example 04: For a more specific drill towards personal safety, try linking your situational awareness to threat recognition and target hardening strategies. Think about what doesn't seem right within your environment, where potential threats may reside and how these potential threats may present themselves. In addition, consider what you can/would/will do to help protect against these potential threats becoming a reality. For instance, you may notice a dimly lit pathway ahead and perceive that a potential threat may be lurking. You may then decide that the best way to protect against the realisation of such a threat would be to alter the course of your route to a safer alternative.

Example 05: Another example of developing your situational awareness/threat recognition may be in the context that you are walking across a street and see a couple of disorderly looking youths on the corner ahead. How would you react if they suddenly took interest in you and began heading in your direction? If they engaged you in conversation or began to split up as they came closer? How and when could you best initiate an escape? Which route would/could you take and why? How would you position yourself on approach if escape was not an option? How could you draw attention to your situation if you needed help? Being proactive with such questions by undertaking 'dress rehearsals' in your mind is a fantastic way to identify pre-threat cues and apply the concept of awareness to potential situations that matter. But remember to avoid becoming overly paranoid!

Example 06: A useful exercise you may wish to practice is what we call, 'find the victim'. This is about using good awareness skills to actually look for people who are in Code White or 'the victim state'. It also encourages you to actively make note of the wrong behaviour in terms of maximising personal safety. Simply place yourself in the shoes of an attacker and look for those who you believe would be easy prey. Who would you attack? The old lady carrying her handbag wide open, the sparsely dressed young woman who looks like she's had too much to drink or the loner who is stuck in a book on a quiet park bench? Be ruthless (metaphorically speaking of course) and take no prisoners, as this exercise demonstrates clearly the unfortunate reality of the world we live in, by bringing to the surface the tactics and mind-set of the violent minority we are aiming to protect ourselves against. Use the information gathered here to help strengthen your personal security protocol.

Example 07: You may wish to take the concept of situational awareness to its broadest sense and try researching the crime statistics and specific risk factors in your local area. This may reveal something that changes the way you go about your day to day life or indeed, the way you train or prepare for potential threats. For instance, if you are male in his early twenties, then you may consider the fact that according to the data in your locality, most threats to the public tend to happen say late at night by way of alcohol fuelled disputes. In contrast, a female may concern themselves with understanding local data that shows an increased risk of domestic violence. And if there is a unique rise in say knife crime where you live, then it stands to reason that the methods you employ in training should aim to match the probability of that type of encounter, which you're more likely to meet.

Example 08: In terms of a more combative drill to help tease out the lessons on situational awareness given by the opening salutation of *Naihanchi Kata*, you can try practicing the following. Have a target to strike in front (a partner with a focus mitt or a heavy bag, makiwara etc.) and ask another to move around the edge of your peripheral intermittently flashing a second target. The aim is to strike the target in front, but keeping your situational awareness broad enough to react to the second target when it's perceived within your peripheral. Different cues and scenarios can be used to enhance this 'eye opening' drill, but of note is that the main components come direct from the kata teachings.

Example 09: You could also hold a special 'situational awareness' lesson in the *dojo* (under appropriate control of course) by setting up pre-planned scenarios and having them being played out whilst the normal class is ongoing. By using staged drills, imagine if the green belt next to you suddenly drew a knife from his *dogi* and tried to attack you! Or, what would you do if an interesting discussion on *kata* began to escalate into a vicious argument and started to turn physical? How would you react if two students from the next scheduled class suddenly burst into the dojo and approached you displaying clear pre-threat cues? Again, a useful exercise that brings the concepts that come direct from the *kata* teachings into application.

Example 10: As well as identifying potential threat, holistic awareness of the situation around you also covers such aspects as attentiveness to your immediate environment, your ability to escape should fleeing to safety suddenly become a priority, plus your own persona as you interact with those around you. Use everyday activities as opportunities to study and work with these aspects, so that you may assess your personal vulnerability and become more mindful of how they may affect both the probability of realising a threat and the potential outcome(s). Life's daily happenings are the very best arena to practice and hone different facets of situational awareness, since it is naturally these exact circumstances that such tactics may need to be applied for real.

Now that we have outlined the fact that situational awareness should be the very bedrock of our self-protection protocol and detailed how the opening salutation of *Naihanchi Kata* may be used to express some key conceptual lessons pertaining to this important element, let's now take a look at what is another crucial aspect – that of range management.

CHAPTER VIII

LESSON 2: COMBATIVE RANGE

"Even after many years, kata practice is never finished, for there is always something new to be learned about executing a movement"

~ Shoshin Nagamine

The main objective in self-protection is to maximise safety. This can be best achieved by capitalising on two key components – distance and time. Simply put, the further we are from a potential threat and the more time we have to react, then our chances of realising safety are increased. Thus, it stands to reason that the level of risk will increase when distance and time become limited. In most encounters, distance and time are a luxury seldom enjoyed mainly due to the range at which we socially interact. Nonetheless, effective management of the distance available to us is critical

When I first began to practically analyse the movements of *Naihanchi Kata* using the context of civilian self-protection, it made sense to use the components of distance and time as a common reference, since these are so significant in their application. This led me to make some very interesting connections and relationships between not only the movements of the *kata* in isolation, but also how these movements are specifically grouped, sequenced and presented within the form. And as even monkeys may fall from trees, my exploration into the choreography of *Naihanchi Kata* took the viewpoint that each component within the sequence was either to follow on from or to guard against failure from the previous. This gave a common-sense based structure to my analysis of the form and what were once random jigsaw pieces then began to fall nicely into place.

We have already ascertained the huge importance of situational awareness in the previous chapter, so it wasn't surprising for me to find lessons associated with these 'soft skills' at the very start of the *kata*. In addition, we may also find important lessons within the opening salutation pertaining to the preliminary aspects of potential confrontation, well before any purely combative strategies are explored. It's almost as though the beginning of the *kata* is setting the scene so to speak and providing a useful mnemonic to those who study the form, as to the most essential aspects of avoidance and contact management.

And so, assuming that situational awareness, early threat recognition and subsequent escape has been inadequate or void (maybe due to a genuine ambush scenario, an escalating social interaction or confined space situation such as a crowded area, elevator or stairwell for instance), then it may then become necessary to more tangibly manage the potential threat presented directly in front of you. Therefore, understanding more about combative range would be next on the list of importance within the lessons given by the choreography of *Naihanchi Kata*.

The subject of combative ranges can be as simple or as complex as you choose. On one hand, you could look to understand the distinction between different fighting distances such as squaring off, kicking, punching, trapping, vertical grappling and horizontal grappling, practicing a myriad of drills to help develop a smooth transition between each. For consensual engagements, skilled vs skilled sparring or to help facilitate a more comprehensive study, this level of understanding is completely valid and beneficial. However, for self-protection, I think it would be more constructive to take a comparatively simplistic view by considering only two key ranges. These may be referred to as 'contact range' and 'non-contact range'. In other words, you're either out of range and relatively safe until your opponent moves towards you, or in range with the potential to take (and give) damage immediately. Using these two ranges incorporates a natural distinguishing boundary at around arms-length. Everything beyond this in terms of combative range is really only icing on the cake.

This border distance of arms-length is significant for a number of reasons. Firstly, it is the distance at which we tend to converse with other people during our everyday life, so from a practical viewpoint, it makes sense that classical *kata* use this range as a basis for their application. As such, we can make a confident assumption that the application strategies found in *Karate* are designed for use either at or inside this range, as opposed to the more exaggerated distances as referenced in more modern-day competitive approaches. Secondly, it's a fact that our ability to visually react to our opponent at distances inside of arms-length is severely inadequate for self-protection. We can only rely on visual reaction when the opponent is well outside of this range and moves towards us. If they are already within range to strike, then unless you are first off the mark (pre-emptive), then the reality of 'taking a shot' becomes pretty much inevitable, short of a possible flinch-based cover so long as your hands are already up and in the game.

This is also one of the reasons why developing tactile-based reaction is emphasised in traditional systems through the practice of drills such as *Kakie* or other similar 'connecting hands' exercises. Although many of these drills have been standardised and formalised to detach from the 'mess' of reality, the principles they aim to develop stand and may be extracted for use in more realistic non-consensual based scenario drills. In addition, visual reaction is processed noticeably faster when combined with touch awareness, which adds to one's ability to function more effectively at close-range.

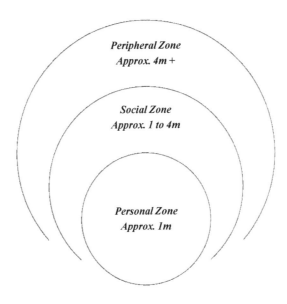

Diagram showing zones of interaction.

In developing a solid self-protection strategy, it's useful to consider three fundamental zones of interaction. These are (1) The Peripheral Zone, (2) The Social Zone and (3) The Personal Zone:

- *The Peripheral Zone* is the farthest range and extends from around 4m and beyond. There is normally minimal interaction that takes place here and there is generally plenty of time to react should anything ring your alarm bells. So unless your attacker is throwing or firing something at you then you are relatively safe from harm.

- *The Social Zone* is from between approximately 1 and 4m, where most social interactions take place. There is much less time to react here and given that distance may be closed surprisingly quickly (especially so under the veil of artifice), the social zone can offer a false sense of security.

- *The Personal Zone* is within arms-length (less than 1m) and the most dangerous in terms of self-protection. Ideally this zone should only be breached by those we trust, but unfortunately, many everyday social situations, interactions and environments may routinely force this range to be breached.

As your lack of control associated with the environment and people within it decreases, then your level of situational awareness should in turn increase to try and make up for the deficiency. And whilst the conceptual lessons in *Naihanchi Kata* primarily deal with the control and management of your personal zone, they also allude to an understanding of distance and time in general, zones of interaction and the study of how one may manipulate these components to best maximise safety and hence minimise risk from a potential threat.

Application Concept 02/01 – Establishing Combative Range

As your hands rise up in the first part of the opening salutation, your elbows should remain extended to map out the cultural and combative threshold of arm's length. As discussed, this distance is very important to control due to social interaction and lack of reaction capabilities if breached.

Try the following exercise that aims to show this in practice - Stand outside of arm's length from your partner, who should have with their hands up at around shoulder width apart. Your objective is to touch your partner's chest whilst they try to stifle your attempts by simply bringing their hands together. You should find that so long as your partner is switched on then they will be able to detect and thwart your attack in good time. Next, move a little closer so that you are just inside of arm's length from your partner and try the same exercise again. You should now find it much easier to touch them without a successful response.

Mapping out critical range of 'arms-length' and applying principle for situational control

It is much easier to visually react at distances outside of arms-length. This exercise proves that inside this critical range, it becomes almost impossible.

Within the space of what may only be a couple of inches, your partner has gone from being able to successfully defend a simulated attack, to becoming a sitting duck for an oncoming assault, even when they know it's coming! Imagine how much more difficult this would be with the addition of stress, adrenaline, a determined aggressor, plus very limited knowledge of exactly where or when it will happen. This is the main reason why a pre-emptive strategy is so crucial to your self-protection game plan.

So, this lesson in *Naihanchi Kata* prompts practitioners to understand the importance of having the hands up and in play to control personal space. Holding the hands up in front, above the waistline in an unassuming fashion helps fill the gap, establish a level of subtle dominance and provide a strong framework for any subsequent physical responses that may be demanded.

There are multiple options available from situational control. Shown above is pushing away to maintain distance, re-affirming with assertive verbal instruction and body language.

One way to apply this principle so that it becomes more natural is to practice 'talking with your hands' during normal everyday interactions. When talking to family, friends and colleagues whether at home, work or out and about, consider what would happen if the person in front of you suddenly became a violent threat? Learn how to ensure that your hands are up and 'in the game', without it looking aggressive. Experiment with naturally emphasising dialogue with hand motions that aim to fill your personal space and control the subject's centre-line.

In the *dojo*, you can also practice 'talking with your hands' and then quickly turning them into a physical barrier supported by verbal assertion when your partner simulates an attempt to close the distance. The 'hands up' position also gives you the option to launch a tactical pre-emptive strike or defensive cover should the situation turn bad. The key point in terms of the *kata* and its application, is that from this relatively unassuming control of personal space one can transition into a number of physical possibilities to help control the escalation of threat.

You can also strike proactively or cover reactively from situational control.

Many of these possible applications will be expanded upon in later chapters when we move on to look at how other parts of *Naihanchi Kata* may be used in a combative sense. For now, please keep in mind the concept of protecting your personal space and the significance of arms-length distance in terms of action/reaction. This is our fundamental platform on which our primary physical protection strategy rests.

CHAPTER IX

LESSON 3: FRAMEWORK & MOVEMENT

"Lifting weights at the gym won't make you strong."

~ Masutatsu Oyama

The human body is an amazingly malleable organism that can adapt itself to a wide variety of changing environments. This adaptation to progressive stimulus over time is essentially how growth occurs. This being said, there are a number of physical pathways, transitions and movements that are always going to be naturally stronger than others and that may provide the greatest mechanical advantage. It's important that self-protection training takes this into consideration and always aims to maximise our potential where possible. For example, there are preferred methods of striking, reacting and counter-attacking that employ universal principles to specifically help capitalise on their application. At the very least, aligning to such principles helps to give recipients of violence a fighting chance, even if the cards may be heavily stacked against them.

Three important aspects that help make the most of human framework and movement are covered within the opening salutation of *Naihanchi Kata*, which set the basis for the applications to follow. These principles work together to help the practitioner understand some of the key functional patterns that all *kata* applications should inherently possess.

Application Concept 03/01 – The Power Triangle

As the hands begin to rise up at the start of the opening salutation and come to establish combative range as in *Application 02/01*, you will notice that if viewed from above, the arms form a triangular structure with the shoulders at the base and finger tips at the apex. This can be regarded as your power triangle, which we should always point towards the enemy's centreline. A good way to apply this would be to imagine your combative applications aiming to breach the enemy's spine. This wedge shape made by the arms prescribes the 'funnelled channel' used to ensure that energy from your attacks are maximised, as well as your ability to maintain constant pressure and dominance.

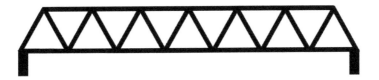

The triangle is an extremely strong structure commonly used within architecture – here for truss bridge design.

The triangle shape is used throughout karate and expressed clearly within the first part of the opening salutation of Naihanchi Kata, as well as many other movements within the form.

The triangle shape is referenced in many *karate* techniques, footwork and body movements throughout various parts of the body. This is because the triangle is an extremely strong structure. In fact, it is the only two dimensional polygon that if constructed of rigid members with hinged corners, is absolutely fixed in shape and will stay this way up to the compressive and tensile limits of those members. All others (such as a square or hexagon etc.) can easily be misshapen and the best way to strengthen such shapes is by reinforcing their internal angles through the use of gussets, which are added to make (yes, you've guessed it!) triangles.

As well as the triangle shape possessing strength, it also has the effect of focusing energy towards the apex, especially during dynamic movement using multi-dimensional pathways. However, the nature of these more advanced configurations and their deeper relevance to *karate* is out of the scope of this publication, so let's simply stick to the understanding that this triangular structure may be found throughout the choreography of *Naihanchi Kata* (upper and lower body), offering practical elements in its application.

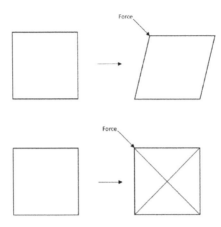

A square with hinged corners can easily be misshapen unless reinforced using gussets to make triangles.

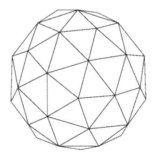

Triangles can be used to add strength to all kinds of structures.

In order to gain advantage over an opponent, it is essential that their centreline is controlled. Gross power is normally generated by swift rotation of the hips, so it stands to reason that if the enemy's core can be disrupted then so too will their ability to produce sufficient force to cause you harm. So your 'triangle of power' should always point towards your enemy's spine, whilst endeavouring to keep their 'triangle of power' pointing away from yours. This strategy is seen through the application of *karate's* classical forms and is advocated as a key concept during the opening salutation of *Naihanchi Kata*.

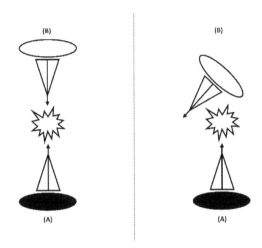

Aim for your power triangle to be pointing at your opponent, whilst theirs are facing away from you.

The power triangle works the same whether you're striking, throwing, attacking joints, restraining or simply displacing balance by forcefully encroaching into your enemy's space. As with most essential principles, there are always some exceptions to the rule, but for the most part the power triangle is an extremely valuable concept to learn, understand and ingrain into your application analysis.

Application Concept 03/02 – Envelope of Strength

The human body has a distinct envelope from which it may apply strength. As such, some positions are inherently weak, whilst others make full use of natural structure and efficient muscular activation as a platform for contextual movement. There are both generic weak and strong points along any human range of motion and even a rudimentary study of this notion can equip you to better appreciate more effective ways to move. As such, *Naihanchi Kata* offers us a simple conceptual lesson that helps us not only understand our basic envelope of strength, but to also signpost the best way to perform and apply the form's choreography.

Imagine lying down on a weight bench to perform a flat barbell chest press. If you work full range i.e. from arms fully extended to bar touching chest, then you will inevitably find areas of strength and areas of weakness within the whole movement pathway. Some of these may be due to individual issues (past injuries, lack of mobility etc.), but universally, the human body will work more efficiently within certain portions of the movement. During a chest press exercise, the weakest part of the movement is usually at the start of the 'press' when the bar is close to the chest. Here, the joint structure is less integral, the elbows are at an acute angle and the agonistic muscle groups (those doing the work) are experiencing their furthest stretch. In contrast, towards the top of the movement where muscle activation and leverage are working more efficiently, the exercise becomes easier to perform. The same is true for a pulling movement such as the biceps curl. The exercise will be more demanding from the point of full extension of the arm up to around 90 degrees, where gravity has the greatest effect. After that, the curl becomes easier to perform and indeed, more weight can be managed during the second half of the lift.

So in addition to developing physical attributes through training, the functional output of a particular movement is also dependent on contributions made from the way in which the muscles are activated coupled with how the skeletal structure is arranged, plus of course the universal effects of gravity. In terms of combative application, the prime action will normally occur in front of the body, where the opponent will most likely be. Having said all that, there may be cases where techniques must be applied on the perimeter of our body line too, so knowing more about the human envelope of strength is useful for effective application.

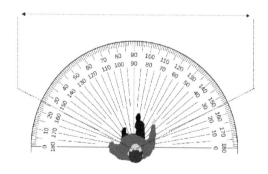

Diagram showing approximate envelope of strength.

During the opening salutation, we move our arms out from the body in a full circle from a point directly above the head towards the ground. And as we've previously discussed, this motion should map our peripheral vision. One thing to note here is that unless your eyes are located at the side of your head like that of a rabbit for instance, then your arms will normally never reach the side of your body, otherwise they disappear completely from view. To keep them within our peripheral range, both arms tend to be slightly forward of the body line. As well as your field of vision, this motion also does a great job of mapping out your envelope of strength by which ideally, every combative application should operate within.

As an example of the above principle, try holding your arms outstretched at shoulder height as in the opening salutation and have your partner apply some controlled force by pushing against them. First, experience what it's like to resist when the arms are completely to your sides (i.e. 180 degrees) and then compare that to your ability to resist the same force when your arms are positioned as per the opening salutation (on edge of peripheral vision approx. 130 degrees). You should find a marked difference between the two, showing the boundary of your structural stability and hence, your envelope of strength. This of course is based only on force applied from the front, so while some classical techniques in *karate* may at first appear to contradict this rule, you should find that their combative application will aid in justifying their most appropriate shape.

Some kata techniques that follow the triangle and envelope of strength principles as given by Naihanchi Kata.

The athletic demands of modern-day *karate* have led to many classical techniques becoming competitively aesthetic to such an extent that they may breach the envelope of strength principle as given in *Naihanchi Kata*. Whereas large square shapes, right angles, deep stances and perfect lines may be desirable in order to bring about a visually pleasing silhouette, aesthetics that are excessively prioritised over structural integrity may even risk injury through long-term dynamic repetition and excess strain on the body.

Koryu (old-school) styles that tend to lean more towards natural movement and function can be seen to more consistently follow the 'envelope of strength' principle. This tends to be safer for the body long-term, more adaptable to each individual practitioner and are generally better suited for longevity of *karate* practice. In my opinion, *Naihanchi Kata* does a fantastic job of laying the foundation for gaining function through natural structure and movement pathways that are required throughout the art.

Application Concept 03/03 – Transition Through Core & Sequential Joint Action

This third application concept in respect to developing robust framework and movement concerns point to point transitions. In particular, how the core should become the focal point for movement and also how the arms (or legs) should travel in space between one technique and the next. As such, although this lesson is expressed here within the opening salutation, it is very much prevalent in every part of the *kata*.

The opening salutation may also be expressed as a useful lesson on the basics of sequential joint action and transitional movement to and from the core, which may then be applied throughout both the kata choreography and its application.

One of the most pivotal moments in my *karate* journey was to realise the fact that the art is based on combining only a very small number of core movement pathways. It is the understanding and integration of these movement pathways, as opposed to the superficial collection of many techniques, which provides real potential to its combative application and the inherent connection between the classical forms. Coming to appreciate the true significance of this idea will require far more explanation than that of a few paragraphs, but since the fundamental basis of these core movement pathways may be found within *Naihanchi Kata*, I have chosen to provide an initial description as a starting point for readers to follow.

There are three components to this lesson that should be employed together in order to make point to point transitions within your envelope of strength most effective. Firstly, limbs should move utilising sequential delay between shoulder/hip, elbow/knee and wrist/ankle. In actual fact, this sequential action should occur throughout all joints in order to perpetuate energy from the floor, through the body and into the weapon (fist, foot, knee, elbow etc.). Thus, the first part of the opening salutation should see the arms move away from the body and then return again using this sequential feeling.

As discussed in Vol.1, sequential delay is an essential part of the body dynamics associated with *Naihanchi Kata*. At its most simple, you can separate the top and bottom halves of the body and sequence just two elements. Then you can progress to splitting up the lower half into foot, ankle and knee elements, plus the upper body into shoulder, elbow and wrist elements. Then we can start to explore how the pelvis, waist and spine may be used as a junction between both halves, in order to create a single sequential chain of elements, where the last joint to act in the one closest to the point of power transference into the target.

Using the above method, it is possible to generate substantial power from a short and potentially encumbered range. This is a valuable asset in self-protection, where distance is a luxury. Furthermore, when you come to understand that power generation is not necessarily about 'how much' you move, but rather about the efficiency and accurate timing of sequential events within the body, then the techniques found within *Naihanchi Kata* and indeed the whole art will begin to take on a new identity.

The second component is that of elbow connectivity towards the hip with shoulders nested combined with the fact that the upper limb movement pathways found in *karate* make use of a retraction towards and/or extension away from the body core. Imagine pushing or pulling something heavy - would it be more efficient to do so with elbows pointing in and toward the hips or out and away from the body? Well, the answer is obviously 'pointing in' and connected to the body. *Karate* teaches this rule consistently within its *kata*, however it's important to understand that this principle is based on a dynamic movement, not necessarily the static hold that occurs after each separate technique. Learning how to direct and guide the elbows to and from the body within each movement transition is where the potential lies. This is also expressed by the movements of *Naihanchi Kata*.

Adapting the basic form of the opening salutation to emphasize sequential action to and from the body core.

The third component is understanding the difference between square movement and circularity for both efficient and effective energy development/transfer when changing direction. Grab a pencil and piece of paper and try to draw a perfect square or rectangle (sharp 90 degree corner angles) without slowing down or stopping to change

114

direction. You should find this extremely difficult because no matter what speed you go, you'll always end up with rounded corners. The only way to achieve perfect angles, would be to utilise additional circles at each corner, so that the resulting 'inside' shape becomes what you desire.

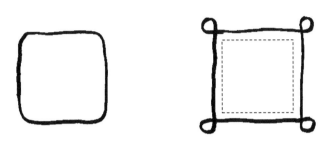

The way to hand draw a square with sharp angles without stopping would be to add circles to each corner. This is the essence of 'circularity' in martial arts.

An inefficient and rigid ('square') use of the arm to strike.

So in terms of *karate*, this means that changing direction without using circularity means that you must first slow down and stop before altering course. This is not only inefficient, but it also strips the ability to generate optimum power output and relies heavily on muscular recruitment. For instance, it's common to see *uke waza* being performed in a very square way, as the preparation movement is usually the opposite action of the technique itself e.g. up to go down, down to go up, inside to go outside and outside to go inside etc. In order to change direction however, it would be more beneficial to make use of circles as in the diagram above.

To give you an idea of how these three components extracted from *Naihanchi Kata* may be used within the context of self-protection, let's now consider a simple downward strike with the palm. From the comparison, you can see the difference between 'square' and 'circular' movement, the retraction/extension of elbow to and from body core, plus the sequential use of the arm to perform the strike (like a whip), as opposed to using the whole arm like a rigid club. It's much easier to appreciate these fundamental components in real-time, but hopefully the pictures will suffice.

A more effective way to strike using fundamental components extracted from Nahanchi Kata.

As you would expect, these components are universal to all movement pathways, so they can be employed to help aid a plethora of scenarios. It's also important to note that these are not the only body mechanic methods taught within *Naihanchi Kata* and have been explained here to provide a rudimentary understanding as to how core principles may be used to make much better use of your application, since the ability to transfer energy efficiently is of course the basis of all physical interaction with an opponent.

Please consider this example of how the principles taught within *Naihanchi Kata* may be used as you progress within a given area, as I share how my *dojo* curriculum is arranged in order to develop a student's ability to generate impact. This probably sits equally within the latter chapter on primary percussive strategy, but I feel it also shows how movement mechanics may be adapted and utilised at varying levels and within several application concepts:

Level 01:   Deliver impact using two primary motions – thrust and hook. This provides a very fundamental method of striking for self-protection that can be learned quickly and provide almost instant application benefits.

Impact Delivery Level 01: Thrust and hook line strikes.

Level 02:   Deliver impact using three secondary motions – upward, downward and backward. This adds to the two motions in Level 01 and provides all 'cardinal' angles for striking, regardless of weapon used.

Impact Delivery Level 02: Upward, downward and backward strikes.

Level 03:   Deliver impact around the clock face – requires an inherent knowledge of power generation methods and an understanding of how to apply at varying angles. Learning how to strike with sufficient force at 1 o'clock, 2 o'clock, 3 o'clock etc. is useful since it's unlikely you'll get the ideal circumstances in reality and may need to adjust angles on the fly.

Impact Delivery Level 03: Adapting about the clock face.

Impact Delivery Level 04: Striking under restriction.

Level 04:   Deliver impact under restriction – taking away range, opportunity and ability to find clear/direct strike paths. The idea is to progressively develop the ability to strike hard from any angle, from any distance and whilst facing a plethora of inhibiting challenges.

It is during the latter level and subsequent application in more free-flowing simulation drills that some of the rules previously adhered to in earlier levels may need to be broken. For example, the trajectory of your strikes may not be optimal, your shoulder may lift and elbow may flare in order to exploit the only strike path available, you may be forced to compensate with certain methods of power generation over others that have become inaccessible etc. We must become comfortable with the fact that breaking the rules is sometimes necessary to achieve the outcome required and learning to find sufficient function within the inevitable practicality gap that sits between what is 'ideal' and what may be 'applicable' at any given moment is where the real experience lies. Thus, we should use 'ideal' as a method to help us maximise what we may then work to achieve in reality. After all, self-defence by its very definition, is never ideal.

CHAPTER X

LESSON 4: POSITIONAL ADVANTAGE

"Karate has many kamae. It also has none."

~ Genwa Nakasone

Heard often in MMA circles, the phrase 'position before submission' reminds competitors of the need to ensure that a level of dominance is gained before going in 'for the kill'. This idea is essential in all forms of combat and especially so in self-protection, where gaining positional advantage aims to stack the deck in your favour and offer the best possible chance of controlling what could well be a life threatening situation. Quite often these strategies are very subtle, but they can make a huge difference to the outcome of an altercation if applied appropriately.

The notion of 'embusen' (line of performance) is an interesting component of *kata*. Indeed, one of the *Shuyo San Gensoku* (three main principles) of the *Kaisai No Genri* as described by *Seikichi Toguchi* in his book, *Advanced Techniques of Shorei-Kan Karate* and allegedly originated from *Chojun Miyagi,* states, 'Don't be deceived by the *Embusen* Rule'. *Toguchi* goes on to write…

> *"We must remember that kata is choreographed and artificial. Punching left does not mean that you fight against an enemy on your left side. Applying kata directly to kumite is a mistake."*

Toguchi is certainly not the only *Okinawan* teacher to write about the interpretation of *embusen*. Indeed, another valuable quote is from *Kenwa Mabuni* (student of both *Kanryo Higaonna* and *Anko Itosu*, later founding the *Shito Ryu* style) in his 1938 book entitled, *Kobo Kempo Karate-Do Nyumon*. In it he clearly states…

> *"The meaning of the directions in kata is not well understood and frequently mistakes are made in the interpretation of kata movements. In extreme cases, it is sometimes heard that 'this kata moves in eight directions so it is designed for fighting eight opponents' or some such nonsense."*

When you study these 'master texts', it becomes apparent that the more contemporary application of *kata* that puts emphasis on a single exponent protecting him/herself in the middle of multiple assailants (attacking with *karate* techniques at different times along choreographed *kata* angles) not only suffers from numerous pragmatic flaws, but was also viewed as being incorrect by the pioneering teachers of *karate's* past. Although it may look great for demonstrations and movies, the reality is very different indeed and such well-organised tactics would find themselves being quickly degraded into carnage. Nevertheless, the *embusen* has a very important role to play in terms of analysing the combative nature of *kata* choreography and in this chapter we will look at this idea in more depth.

Having established that position is a key element of gaining advantage in a violent altercation, we can apply this information to our analysis of *kata* techniques. Whereas the positional relationship between you and an opponent becomes very easy to discern during the practice of two-person drills, it is less obvious during the solo performance of *kata*, as no opponent exists for reference. Thus, rather than losing one of the most important aspects of combative engagement, a more practical theory suggests that the *kata* instead records these positional angles via the embusen by referencing instead, your prior location. In other words, rather than turning to meet an opponent at 45 degrees, the *Embusen* Rule suggests instead that 45 degrees is the recommended angle to shift to in relation to your opponent to help support the application of the associated technique(s). This understanding of how the *kata* records combative angles instantly shifts focus to more realistic possibilities.

Whereas the above theory fits well for many classical 'application' *kata*, core forms such as *Naihanchi* and *Sanchin*, which are limited only to side-to-side or forward and backward stepping are clearly not the same, thus may require a different explanation. This is for good reason too, as *kihongata* have a more generic premise to teach as they underpin the methodologies governing the associated style or system, rather than to impart specific or discrete applications. Although it is entirely possible, I personally don't believe that one should paint *Naihanchi Kata* with the same '*bunkai*-brush' as direct application *kata* such as *Chinto* or *Kushanku* because of the characteristic differences between them, which includes the *embusen*. Before we take a look at this idea in more depth and how such a view may affect the combative interpretation of *Naihanchi Kata*, let's first distinguish the three components of positioning that should be determined during any practical application of *kata* choreography...

- *Geographical Positioning:* This is the angular position in relative space between you and your assailant. If in front and you then shift your body to the side of the enemy, then the resulting geographical angle would be 90 degrees. If instead you shifted behind the assailant, then the geographical angle would be 180 degrees (as viewed from above).

Showing the difference between a 90 degree geographical and rotational angle from a typical face-to-face reference position.

Some examples of structural positioning in two typical clinch frames, plus aiming to best manage a far from ideal position against potential multiple enemies.

- *Rotational Positioning:* This is the angular relationship between the centrelines of you and your opponent. So rather than you shifting your body to their side, if you instead turn to the side then this would represent a rotational angle of 90 degrees. Rotational positioning is usually integral to the transitions between stances in the classical application forms, but as *Naihanchi Kata* is seen to contain only one 'stance', you will come to see that the transitions within the choreography take on a much broader role.

- *Structural Positioning:* This is the way that your body is 'set up' to gain positional advantage over your opponent. Usually governed by the placement of upper limbs, structural positioning is most often used both actively and passively to limit the assailant's options, cover or open potential strike paths and provide the best environment to carry out your physical tactics.

So, going back to the *Embusen* Rule, we can see that if the choreography indeed records a specific angle to aim for, then there is more than one way to interpret this. For example, let's consider the angle of 180 degrees, which is commonly seen in *kata* performance. As stated above, geographical positioning would be realised by shifting behind your opponent, thus offering a clear tactical advantage. In terms of pure rotational positioning, this would be achieved by turning your back to your opponent. Although at first glance this may not seem desirable in practical application, it could indicate a possible throwing technique, as this is probably one of the only times when such a movement may be viable. Thus, looking at *embusen* in this way can sometimes help us more accurately interpret the associated *kata* technique(s).

Expressing the notion of embusen by physically moving the opponent in relation to you. In this examaple, simultaneously pushing and pulling on the shoulders (tsuki and hikite) to effectively place yourself in an advantageous position behind them.

Another example showing how rotational and geographical positioning may be combined and achieved by moving the opponent in relation to you. In this case, an adapted application from Pinan Shodan Kata.

Here's a very basic application for gedan-barai with gyakuzuki that incorporates expresses the notion of embusen through a combination of all three types of positioning (geographical, rotational and structural) to create a clear combative advantage.

In addition to moving yourself in reference to an opponent, you can also obtain both geographical and rotational positioning by moving your opponent in relation to you. An example of this may be the technique of *kake-uke* (hooking reception) supplemented by a 90 degree *embusen*. Whereas the required angle may be achieved by shifting your body to the side, you may also achieve it by hooking your enemy's neck, pulling and twisting him askew. As such, and for certain postures and transitions, it may also be necessary to consider an *embusen* angle expressing a combination of both geographical and rotational positioning. In addition, that those angles are the 'end product' of movement and in application, it is the transition towards them (whether you may happen to reach them or not) that carries most value. With no real opponent present in *kata* performance and the fact that the process of *bunkai* is essentially 'reverse engineering', it pays to consider all of the above possibilities when exploring the way in which the angles (or parts of) given by the specific choreography may be applied.

It is the combined advantages of geographical, rotational and structural positioning that offer the best results in combat and this is probably why we see such a myriad of arrangements in *kata*. It was through my study into this subject that an interesting finding came to light when reading *Choki Motobu's* book, *Watashi-No Karate-Jutsu*, and in particular the images of his *kumite* practices that were clearly based on *Naihanchi Kata*, albeit with an adapted core stance with feet turned 45 degrees – a posture also seen in many other systems of traditional martial arts. To support this idea, he also stated…

> *"Twisting to the left or right from the Naifuanchin stance will give you the stance used in a real confrontation. Twisting ones way of thinking about Naifuanchin left and right, the various meanings in each movement of the kata will also become clear."*

Motobu's Naihanchi stance compared to his adapted fighting posture.

Gichin Funakoshi striking the makiwara and an old illustration showing a similar angled posture.

So in addition to advising us to open our minds to the possibilities of applying the *kata*, it seems that *Motobu* is also indicating that the main stance featured in the form may be regarded as more of a foundational posture (possibly to learn generic structural and dynamic principles – see *Volume One*) that should then be more freely adapted for use in combative application. This makes complete sense to me, as any so-called 'posture' must become transient and dynamic if it is to ever hold up during the physical chaos of self-protection.

The actual stance *Motobu Sensei* refers to is *Hachimonji-Dachi*, or 'eight-shaped stance' in reference to the *kanji* 八. He talks about this being the framework of *Naihanchi Kata* and then makes further mention of it (left and right versions) within his fighting applications and *makiwara* training etc.

Application Concept 04/01 – Positional Advantage (flanking)

The embusen of *Naihanchi Kata* clearly suggests the use of a 90 degree angle due to the unique side to side movements. However, rather than denoting the exact angle to shift to, as a core form, could it be that the sideways stepping represents another conceptual lesson on the principle of positional advantage and application of 'flanking' used in self-protection? If this is so, then the combined use of both rotational and geographical positioning begins to make more sense.

Diagram showing core kata posture with central reference vs 'adapted' posture employing geographical and rotational angles both at approx. 45 degrees, making up the classical 90 degree embusen.

By splitting the 90 degree angle into two 45 degree angles, we may breathe life into the core posture, whilst acknowledging that standing toe-to-toe with an assailant is less than ideal, as both parties have the same opportunity to inflict damage. Zoning out to 45 degrees takes you immediately away from your enemy's firing line, while at the same time ensuring that your triangle of power remains intact. Rotating the opponent too makes for ideal positioning. This generic principle introduced by *Naihanchi Kata* is prevalent within many other classical application forms, with such angles being addressed in a multitude of ways.

Employing a combination of geographical and rotational positioning to make up the 90 degree embusen.

Combining geographical and rotational positioning allows you to move outside of assailant's envelope of strength, whilst still aligning your triangle of power through centre-line.

As we are still reviewing the start of the form, let's take a look at how the movements of the opening salutation might provide some key lessons on structural positioning, both from a proactive and a reactive sense. We will then consider how rotational and geographical positioning can be used to help enhance your advantage and provide a basis for the other techniques to follow.

The opening salutation can also offer valuable lessons on gaining positional advantage.

When standing face-to-face with your opponent, effective positioning of the upper limbs should ideally place them above and inside those of your assailant's. If your hands are on top then you can pretty much guarantee that so long as it's launched decisively, your initial shot will land home before your opponent can react. The reason that your limbs should be placed inside is so that if the opponent instinctively lurches forward to tussle (a common scenario in violent confrontation) then you will more easily be able to either control the space, assume the most dominant clinch position or drive strikes directly towards the head.

Application Concept 04/02 – Positional Advantage (structural wedge)

The first part of the opening salutation teaches how to gain 'reactive' structural positioning via the concept of wedging through centreline with both hands (triangle shape), striking to the head and separating the arms in order to assume a basis for limb/body control. This tactic helps to stifle strikes and has built in redundancy such that the arms will tend to naturally fall in towards the 'funnel' created by the assailants head and arm. From this datum, you can then go to work with other applications given by the *kata*.

As a minimum, it's wise to consider that every *kata* application should provide a decisive advantage over your opponent and this particular movement is an excellent example of this idea in action.

Using the first part of the opening salutation to employ a structural wedge in order to gain positional advantage.

Application Concept 04/03 – Positional Advantage (structural hook)

The second part of the opening salutation teaches how to gain 'proactive' structural positioning by quickly hooking over the assailant's limbs, encircling and sharply snapping in a downwards motion. This instantly reverses the initiative and again, gets your hands on top and inside. In application, this should be exploited immediately with a flurry of strikes to the head area in order to assume dominant control.

Using the second part of the opening salutation to employ a structural hook in order to gain positional advantage.

From these two datum positions and initial contact with the arms, a whole host of applications from the rest of the form (or any other *kata* for that matter) may be applied. Plus, by combining the lessons with rotational and geographical positioning, many more variations can be explored that lead to different parts of the form's choreography. For instance, we already know that flanking away from your enemy's centreline is advantageous for a number of reasons. Thus, by employing the principle of *tenshin* (body-change) with the same structural manoeuvres as given above, we can create very effective positioning strategies.

The Transient Use of Stances

In addition to that of embusen, another important component of positional advantage for self-protection as found in *kata* may be expressed by the various stances used within the specific choreography. However, in order to apply these postures correctly, we must again learn to understand them in context of self-protection and the reality of such scenarios. This is even more imperative with respect to *Naihanchi Kata*, where on the surface it seems as though the 'choice' of stances are somewhat limited.

As I explained a little in *Volume One*, the potential found in *karate* stances are not so much in their static qualities, but more so in their dynamic qualities or more accurately, the transition between them. The precision of a stance is more of a structural concern, not so much a dynamic one. The only real benefit (in a dynamic sense) is that it helps to guarantee that the start point (origin) and end point (termination) are such that the transition between them is also correct. So in this sense, the main reasons to strive for accuracy in stances are to:

1. Develop good structure.

2. Develop body awareness, condition and proprioception.

3. Develop a framework for seamless transitions.

If we ignore point number 3 then it becomes very difficult for us to understand how the stances in *karate kata* may be freely applied. Think about it in terms of music. The same notes are used in every genre, but the overall piece can change so much depending on the way in which they're played, how they're combined, how fast or slow they're executed, what instruments are used etc. Therefore we can say that it's not so much the notes themselves that create the uniqueness of music (they simply provide the datum), but rather the intervals between them and how the combination of both are altered. The correct application of music, just as the correct application of *karate* stances, is inherently dynamic.

So, as alluded to in the previous volume, stances in *karate* are much more about the transient shift of structure and bodyweight in order to help accentuate a particular technique. For example, by simply changing the length of your gait and flexing/extending at the knees at different rates, one can shift bodyweight up, down, forward, back, left, right or any combination of these. With this idea in mind we can see that postures such as *Neko-Ashi Dachi* (cat foot stance) would naturally be used to support applications that require the bodyweight to be quickly shifted back and down. In contrast, *Zen-Kutsu Dachi* (front leaning stance) would naturally be used to support applications that require the bodyweight to be driven forward and down.

With the above viewpoint in mind plus the understanding we've now gained from the lessons on positional advantage, the interpretation of *Naihanchi Kata* for combative application begins to take on a whole new personality. Let's now turn our focus to the 'cross stance' or *Kosa-Dachi* – a posture seldom considered for practical relevance, but in my view, essential for the form to come alive.

Chosin Chibana performing Kosa-Dachi from Passai Kata.

Kosa-dachi is not only seen in *Naihanchi Kata*. It also appears in numerous other forms such as the *Pinan* series, *Kushanku* and *Passai*. On the surface, it looks to be a very peculiar stance, especially as crossing your legs in an altercation would appear to be practically flawed. Nonetheless, rather than us contemplating the ins and outs about why we shouldn't assume such a posture, let's instead explore why crossing the legs may be desirable from a dynamic perspective.

This 'epiphany' came to me whilst watching my wife practice her dance routine for an upcoming stage performance. I noticed that either before or after a turn/spin, her feet came closer together or her legs actually crossed over. I then asked myself, "Could this be *kosa-dachi* from *karate* in action?"

When you look at *kosa-dachi* in other classical *kata*, you will notice that the stance is very often followed or preceded by a pivot into or out from another stance. This isn't always the case, but it certainly occurs frequently enough to 'raise eyebrows'. Depending on the style and form, some of these pivots range from 180 degrees to 360 degrees. In terms of understanding the stance in *Naihanchi Kata*, this observation becomes very significant as the act of pivoting the body to face another direction is one of the common reasons why one would bring their feet together or indeed, cross their legs.

In addition, a smaller footprint can make twisting both easier and faster by reducing the moment of inertia to conserve angular momentum. This commonly occurs in activities such as figure-skating, where to speed up a spin, exponents will draw in their arms and legs. The same is also true for high divers who want to spin in the air, by drawing their body into a compact ball. Assuming *kosa-dachi* can also provide a degree of stability when compared to simply having both feet together, as the bodyweight is dropped and legs stay firmly connected.

Kosa-Dachi is normally either followed or preceded by a pivot.

If you stand with your feet shoulder-width apart (*heiko-dachi* or *shizen-dachi*) and then twist the body to face behind, then you will find that the legs will begin to wrap around each other in typical *kosa-dachi* fashion. So if twisting can generate such a stance then it stands to reason that adopting *kosa-dachi* first would also be an appropriate pre-requisite to a follow-up twist. And why would we wish to twist? Well, here are three reasons – all of which are key features of gaining positional advantage and used frequently in the combative application of *karate kata*:

- As preparation to drive bodyweight in a different direction.

- To add rotational force to an accompanying technique.

- To evade/ride/absorb/dissipate external energy.

So, by taking the above back to *Naihanchi Kata* we can see that interpreting the embusen directly, as you may do with 'application' forms, is in my view at best limiting

134

and at worst, a complete misunderstanding. Although during the choreography we step into and out of *kosa-dachi* laterally (side-to-side), this does not always have to be the case in application. The *kata* thus offers us the fundamental reference of entry/exit, but eloquently leaves the exact geographical/rotational positioning to our intended application(s). As we will explore later, the upper body movements of the *kata* are designed to offer common mechanics for a multitude of functional uses. The stances and transitions I feel, are no different.

Using Kosa-Dachi to explore outside of the form's set choreography, allowing movement in pretty much any direction.

Experiment using *kosa-dachi* in your practice of the *Naihanchi* choreography to change direction so that instead of remaining on the same latitudinal plane (180 degrees) you have the potential to move in pretty much any direction (360 degrees). It makes one wonder if the *kata* was originally designed to be this way, or indeed intended to be performed as such, and has subsequently been rationalised to fit a more defined and structured model. Nevertheless, it's always good to keep an open mind.

CHAPTER XI

LESSON 5: REACTIVE TACTICS

"Karate kata are just forms or 'templates' of sort; it is the function of their application that needs to be mastered."

~ Choki Motobu

In addition to a strong pre-emptive strategy, any holistic self-protection game plan must also contain a functional reactive approach to be employed in situations where either mistakes have occurred within your layers of protection, or if you happen to be faced with a genuine ambush attack and all your soft-skills have thus been made redundant. During seminars, I often explain to participants that physical self-protection is about 'making the best of a very bad situation' and as such, you can pretty much guarantee that *Murphy's Law* will be in force (i.e. anything that can go wrong, probably will). It's a safe bet to assume that the environment, time, opportunity, aggressor and tactics used against you will not be to your advantage.

The opening salutation may be interpreted to set up a useful default protection strategy.

Of course we know that action always beats reaction, so if avoidance and escape are not feasible options and it becomes necessary to go physical then a decisive pre-emptive attack would be next on the list. Being caught off-guard, forced into a pure reactionary state or (even worse) waiting until physically attacked before responding will place you at an immediate disadvantage. For self-protection, this is undesirable and *Naihanchi Kata* identifies this early on. Thus, how you deal with these 'emergency moments' is a vital part of training and what we'll be focussing upon within this chapter.

Human beings have startle reflexes hard-wired into them. These reflex movements are extremely fast, pre-programmed and automated protective responses to sudden and/or potentially life threatening stimuli. They serve to help protect vulnerable parts of the body such as the throat, brain-stem and eyes, and are triggered by the limbic system, commonly referred to as the paleo-mammalian brain. This part of the brain is thought to have arose early in the evolution of mammals and such inherent reflexes may be found across many species. The startle reflex is rapid and occurs before any cognitive process that would allow us to make applicable decisions. Combined with a massive shot of adrenaline, this can also cause a victim to literally freeze on the spot (like a deer caught in the headlights) – good for hiding from predators under camouflage, but not the best course of action in modern-day self-protection.

The specific mechanics of the startle reflex can vary between individuals and modern research has recognised over 30 different 'styles'. Perform an Internet image search for 'baseball bat flying into crowd' and you'll see a plethora of real-life reactions captured by camera to study. However, the general characteristics of the flinch will be familiar to most from our past experiences. The head drops or shoots back, shoulders lift, jaw tightens, arms raise (either one or both) and eyes close. These are automatically engaged to help protect the head and neck area from percussive impact and safeguard vital functions such as breathing, eyesight etc.

Because the startle reflex is something that is designed to protect us then I guess it makes sense to embrace it within our self-protection strategy. However, to attempt to control what are essentially sub-conscious neuromuscular actions in order to elicit a more prescribed 'trained response' would in my mind only serve to turn an innate process into a cognitive function, which it is not nor could ever be. Since we have already established that there is little chance to visually react in time to stimuli when at distances around or inside of arms-length, then I think it is more logical to train in a way that may 'support' these reflexes (should they happen to occur) rather than purposefully try to 'replace' them.

According to Hick's Law, the time it takes for a person to make a decision increases exponentially as a result of the increasing number of choices they have. So the more defensive options available, the longer it will take us to respond to the stimuli presented. Add to this the loss of fine motor skills due to adrenaline and we can easily see the reason why 'simple' and 'few' are vital characteristics for any good self-protection strategy and particularly, reactionary tactics. In short, having only one (ideally) or two (max) well-trained gross-motor responses, which are adaptable enough to cater for a variety of common attacks, will help enable their application to be immediate.

The notion of having and honing a single default reactionary response is very favourable in an ambush situation, as it helps prevent us from falling victim to the OBSERVE-ORIENT log-jam where it's all too common for DECIDE and ACT to become an impossibility due to the continuous barrage of oncoming attacks. Having a simple default protection measure allows us to effectively skip past the ORIENT and DECIDE phases so that we may jump from OBSERVE to ACT as swiftly as possible and with minimal cognitive processing. It also provides a common datum (familiar ground or a home base if you like) in order to launch a swift and solid counter-attack.

If such a response could be set up to work in tandem with our startle reflex, it means that it would be best to share similar generic characteristics and reference points. The closer we can make our trained response resemble the generic mechanics of our subconscious reaction, then the more efficient it will be (both physically and mentally) to enable a successful marriage. So the core mechanics of lifting the arms, raising the shoulders and dropping the head don't really change, apart from a few simplistic 'tactical' adjustments. The main point of consideration should be in respect to your mental attitude associated with any reactionary tactics. In sharp contrast to a passive or submissive response, we need to develop more of an assertive approach with a 'how dare you' mind-set if there is going to be any hope of turning the tables during an ambush situation.

We also have to consider the fact that the most dangerous and powerful aspect of an attack coming toward you is usually the point of contact, as all efforts, angles and distances have already been set up to converge at this one point in time. This means that our reactionary strategy must also contain tenshin (body shifting) in order to create positional advantage where possible. Thus, contrary to what may seem good sense, the most effective direction to shift to during a reactionary strategy is actually forward, driving either inside the arc of an angular attack or in an attempt to stifle a linear attack. This will serve to mess up the attackers 'story' (predetermined plans) by acting in a way they least expect and forcing them to re-enter the OBSERVE element of the *OODA Loop*. In contrast, moving back usually only serves to promote a submissive attitude and offer greater opportunity for further strikes to be launched your way. Unless part of a more tactical strategy, the result is normally inevitable.

As such, the four key elements of *(1) cover and support the head against impact, (2) reduce distance to stifle further strikes, (3) create angles to maximise potential and (4) launch an immediate counter attack* provide the basis for a solid reactionary strategy that will serve you much better in a violent altercation than a bunch of '*karate* blocks' ever could. This conceptual lesson happens to appear within the first two movements during the opening salutation of *Naihanchi Kata*. The very same techniques that usefully couple up to the opposing pro-active methods explored in earlier chapters. Therefore, this section of the choreography can be thought of as representing a 'starter pack' if you like, before the physicality of an altercation begins to take hold. Let's take a more detailed look at this principle in application.

Application Concept 05/01 – Reactive Tactics (wedge)

The first reactionary tactic is found within the 'arm lift' motion during the opening salutation and supports a function whereby the arms instinctively flinch out and extend as if to push away danger. The objective would be to bring your hands together and use the strong triangle structure created along with forward momentum in order to intercept, bridge the gap and stifle further impact.

With situational control in place, bring both hands together and drive forward towards the enemy's head. This application resolves naturally towards the 'funnel' created by the antagonists arm and head.

If your hands are already up and employing some form of situational control (which they should be), then it's more likely that an attack will originate from the periphery, such as a swing or hook punch, as a barrier is already set up in front. So rather than meeting the attack 'force against force', this tactic looks to cut through the line of attack and toward gaining a tactile reference suitable for an immediate counter-response.

In the heat of the moment you can do far worse than simply putting your hands together to create a strong frame and driving forwards. The prime target to aim for with your palms would be the enemy's centreline in order to cause a 'pattern interrupt' and an opportunity to turn the tables to your advantage. However, in application it is very possible that you may glance or even miss the target completely and slip into the left or right 'funnel' created by the enemy's upper arm and head. These are the prime areas that this application focusses towards, offering effective control opportunities to the head, body and limbs.

This reactionary tactic is so versatile that it may also be used as a pre-emptive attack to the head. Simply put, it quickly gets both hands up, out and in the game, creating both a level of protection and pattern interruption, as well as a home base for potential follow up options as given within the rest of the *kata* choreography.

Application Concept 05/02 – Reactive Tactics (cover)

The second reactionary tactic occurs during the second part of the opening salutation, where the elbows flex and hands lift. If we take the formal aesthetics away from this movement and focus on the structure and core movement patterns, we can see a valuable protection measure against ambush situations, which in contrast to the previous application, supports a function whereby the arms instinctively flinch in and up to cover vital areas around the head and neck to protect our main computer and control system against potential damage.

Wrap and cradle your head with your hands creating a strong frame and drive forwards, leading with the elbows. Bring your chin in, shoulders up and bite down to help protect the jaw and neck. Look through the tops of your eyes from behind the 'jail bar' type structure created by your forearms. It is designed to offer a level of protection and support the head against the 'brain shake' caused by rapid movement of the skull upon impact. Although not a pleasant experience, it is entirely possible to fight on with chipped teeth, a broken nose, lacerated eye or cracked jaw. However, it is impossible to fight on if you are knocked out, so this should always be your prime concern. Driving forward helps to stifle any further impact and leading with the elbow (like a sharp rhino horn or battering ram) offers a surprisingly effective counter-attack.

By using this tactic and making subtle adjustments with your arms/body, you can achieve an impressive defence coverage against most angles of attack to the head. Furthermore, by sinking the elbow slightly whilst raising the same side hip, it is also possible to reduce the potential of debilitating body shots. A good way to drill this range of cover is to have your partner throw light strikes either with open-hands or light gloves (nothing too cumbersome) towards various head and body targets. Practice adjusting the cover to suit whilst resisting any large movements to explore the versatility of the application. You can also practice driving forwards into an impact shield with this structure, using your elbows to strike the pad.

We must search past the classical formalities and standardisations in kata in order to find potential. Slight adaptations help bring the principle-based lessons of the kata to life and offer a greater range of protection.

As with all defensive tactics, this position is not designed for long-term use as it is inevitable that sooner or later a strike will creep through. It works by offering a few valuable milliseconds to re-group and get to work on an immediate counter-assault. Of course, it's much better than taking shots with your hands down, but it's not guaranteed to last under continuous fire – especially if multiple assailants are present for example. Using the four key reactionary principles given earlier, we must (1) cover and support the head, (2) drive forward and get inside the effective range of subsequent attacks, (3) angle and attach to a datum at either the left or right 'funnel' and (4) launch an immediate counter-attack.

Three examples of how the defensive cover may be used to help thwart various attacks – straight line, hook line and body shot.

As well as the two defensive tactics that support either extension or retraction of the limbs, *Naihanchi Kata* also provides two distinct follow-up options within the same opening salutation. These may be used interchangeably and as a minimum, offer a clear advantage to branch into other application methodologies given by further choreography. Where one is based on moving up the hierarchy of impact by increasing distance to affect more powerful strikes, detachment and potential escape, the other choses to remain close and manipulate the clinch position in an attempt to fell the opponent through the use of a seemingly unsophisticated, but very effective takedown manoeuvre.

Like all of these application methodologies, it is the principles and not necessarily the specific techniques representing them that should be understood and explored more deeply.

Kata choreography from opening salutation expressing reactionary follow-up options.

Application Concept 05/03 – Hierarchy of Impact

The first follow-up application concept uses close-quarter attacks in an attempt to cause the attacker to flinch back away from the source of pain, thereby opening up other striking possibilities that result in greater impact, plus the possibility to detach and escape. This may be employed for example when have been pinned with your back against a wall and have no other way to increase distance.

Using the 'head turn' and 'thumb hooks' from the kata to work up the hierarchy of impact.

The two methods represented in the *kata* are the eye gouge (hooking in of the thumbs) and the head butt (turning of the head left and right), which may also be used to press into the side if the enemy's face in order to help protect against the possibility of bites. Given these two methods are representative, there's no reason why other close-quarter attacks may not be implemented such as seizes, tears and bites. The combative principle given by the *kata* is to cause trauma sufficient to increase range so that the primary percussive strategy (as covered in the next chapter) may be employed.

Traditional *Karate* contains a number of close-quarter attacks and manipulations that may be used to help control the outcome of a physical altercation. These follow the simple rule that every hand that is placed on the opponent (whether to grab, push, pull, twist or turn etc.), should be employed in a ballistic way and aim to cause pain/damage.

Application Concept 05/04 – Clinch and Drive to Ground

Driving the enemy's head towards the ground and re-orientation from the two-handed neck tie.

The second follow-up application concept considers the possibility that for whatever reason, you are unable to increase range to strike, detach and escape. It involves manipulating the assailant's head from a clinch position and forcefully driving them towards the ground. This is a simple but very effective method of controlling an opponent, especially if executed after striking below the waist (groin or legs) in order to disrupt their base of support.

From a two-handed neck clinch you can push the enemy's head down by sliding the hands up towards the top of the skull. This focusses all the pressure towards the neck/cervical spine and rudimentary physics puts you in the strongest position. Once the head is down and the base of support destabilised, then it is much easier to drive your assailant towards the ground.

When clinching around the back of the enemy's neck, be sure to refrain from interlocking your fingers in case the head snaps back, keeping your forearms pinned across the enemy's chest/shoulders to help stifle attempts to generate striking torque through rotation. If you happen to encounter a problem with applying this takedown, then the first technique of *Naihanchi Kata* (after the opening salutation) suggests a possible contingency by changing the angle of force by turning and twisting the assailant's head. Again another simple but very functional felling manoeuvre. As with the snatch (and as the *kata* shows), keep your elbows connected to your core and apply the motion with your whole body.

The first technique of the *kata* also offers another option to transition from the neck tie directly into the primary percussive strategy. The sideways step, extension of one arm and accompanying retraction of the other may be applied in such a way as to roll one hand around the head and whilst maintaining pressure, shift to the opponent's flank and index before striking. All of these concepts will be covered in more depth within the next chapter.

If pushing down is problematic then a force reversal contingency is also expressed by the first 'techniques' of Naihanchi Kata, as well as a method to transition into the primary percussive strategy.

The reactionary methods given by *Naihanchi Kata* are not the typical passive block and counter, but instead are highly functional strategies based on sound physical and psychological principles. They are designed to make the best from a bad situation, reverse dominance as soon as possible and offer useful contingencies to help increase success rate should Murphy's Law keep pressing on.

CHAPTER XII

LESSON 6: PRIMARY PERCUSSIVE STRATEGY

"As Nage is for Judo, so Tsuki is for Karate"

~ Isamu Arakaki

Explored in previous chapters, we have now considered the possibility that the opening salutation of *Naihanchi Kata* may be thought of as a record of key lessons used to emphasise the importance of developing good soft-skills, effective pre-cursors and reactive strategies to potential violent altercations. Essential tactics that would otherwise leave us with no other option than to panic and respond ineffectively after either conscious or subconscious ignorance of warning signs and pre-threat cues. Remembering that the main aim of self-protection should be to maximise safety, it's important that an adequate level of control is established as quickly as possible by exercising safeguards against the inherent risks associated with the least desirable option. That being a surprise ambush assault.

A natural progression from the conceptual lessons given within the opening salutation are the next five movements of the form (commonly labelled as the open-handed strike, elbow smash, guard, low-level block and hook punch), which focus on what commonly makes up *karate's* primary physical strategy within the self-protection game plan – the use of percussive impact. Given that we are still at the beginning of the form, the lessons here delve into how one may quickly 'stack the deck' in their favour should the situation (for whatever reason) turn combative and thus, impact delivery then becomes an overriding priority.

So why does *karate* emphasise the employment of percussive impact over other physical methods of combat? Well quite simply, this tactic is by far the most clinical way of dealing with an aggressor and shutting down the threat once it becomes physical. Also, by aiming to deliver swift and shocking impact sufficient enough to render the opponent either unable or unwilling to continue posing a significant danger helps to increase the possibility of subsequent escape. The classic 'stun and run' method is an ideal example of this, followed by successive strikes should they become necessary to achieve an accumulative effect, along with simplistic ancillary skills used to clear lines of attack from limb obstructions.

By striking towards primary target-rich areas above the collar bone, the objective of the primary strategy is to end the physical altercation as quickly and effectively as possible. If carried out with full commitment and under the veil of artifice, pre-emptive percussive strikes can significantly reduce the risk of being seized, which would make escape more difficult, especially if facing multiple assailants. Indeed, the *karate* adage of *Ikken Hissatsu* (one fist, certain death) helps remind practitioners of the attitude and potential required to be behind such a strategy. Although not written to be taken literally, we have to remember that once a potentially violent encounter has turned physical, then committing anything less than 100% may only result in a more substantial risk to your safety. A better description for this may be 'stopping power/potential', which is more mental than it is physical and is why in self-protection, attitude trumps aptitude.

The first section of the kata after the opening salutation expresses numerous lessons associated with the primary percussive strategy.

Another well-known martial principle of 'Mitsu No Sen' (three kinds of initiative) may also be used to help define the ways in which one may interact with an aggressor using the two key components of distance and time. This is commonly linked to *Kendo*, but was also transferred into the *Wado Ryu* style of *karate* by its founder *Hironori Ohtsuka*. In relation to self-protection, *Sen Sen No Sen* would mean to attack pre-emptively and BEFORE your opponent initiates their attack. *Sen No Sen*, would refer to your attack being launched at THE SAME TIME as your opponent's and for the purely reactive *Go No Sen*, you would counter AFTER your opponent has attacked. Logically, these three options are really all there is in terms of responding to a physical encounter, aside from the most preferred option of not being there in the first place. However, if escape is not available and the situation deems it necessary to strike, then the most effective way to maximise safety would be a decisive and fully committed pre-emptive attack (*Sen Sen No Sen*).

Percussive impact and in particular, issues surrounding the use of pre-emptive strikes, has proven to be a subject of hot debate between traditional *karate* practitioners over the years. Especially since the execution of such tactics can initially come across as being somewhat 'brutal' and from a literal perspective, in direct contradiction to the famous *Karate-Ni-Sente-Nashi* (there is no first attack in *Karate*) philosophy. Some hold faith in the notion that 'true' *karate* practitioners would always wait for the first blow to be launched before countering. This is usually justified by proposing that all *kata* begin with a 'block' and/or suggesting that 'attacking' does not constitute true self-defence. But of course this is all subjective, based on what one may define as being an 'attack'.

As ideal or chivalrous as the above may seem, the unfortunate reality is that violence is not so forgiving. There are no prizes offered for fairness and once the situation turns physical, the dynamics are very 'digital' in nature. You can either be the one hitting or the one being hit. Therefore, I would suggest that if the theories we have on *karate* are accurate and the system was (is) indeed based on self-defence, then percussive impact should (and does) feature heavily in the methodologies given by movements within the classical forms. The idea that all *kata* begin with a 'block' is in my opinion an outdated/misinformed view, with the actual application of this notion being completely counter-productive to effective combative strategies.

The *Karate-Ni-Sente-Nashi* precept is often misunderstood as it is commonly attached to the reception of an actual physical attack. However, in many self-protection scenarios, the initial 'attack' to the victim's safety may become apparent well before the first strike is thrown. Additionally, the law (certainly here in the U.K.) acknowledges not only the fact that such a 'threat' may be multi-faceted, but also that a pre-emptive assault may be considered justifiable as self-protection so long as imminent danger is inevitable and such force was honestly deemed to be both necessary and reasonable. I am not a legal expert, but I would suggest that so long as you are not the architect of conflict, then the genuine necessity to strike pre-emptively based on intelligence gained from environment, behaviour, body language, verbal escalation and other pre-threat cues would not be opposing the law nor indeed, breaching the principle of *Karate-Ni-Sente-Nashi*. Of course having said that, readers are encouraged to be totally clear about the specific details of self-defence law within their own locality and especially so if their locality routinely changes due to their lifestyle.

While the *Ni-Sente-Nashi* maxim is often attributed to *Gichin Funakoshi*, there are also other notable masters who wrote about 'no first attack' and who explain their understanding of the concept quite clearly. Here are a few examples…

> *"Some people interpret Karate-ni-sente-nashi literally and often profess that one must not attack first, but I think that they are seriously mistaken. It is certainly not the budo spirit to train for the purpose of striking others without good reason. Therefore, the meaning of this saying is that one must not harm others for no good reason. However, when a situation can't be helped and even though one tries to avoid trouble, when an enemy is serious about causing harm, then one must fiercely stand and fight. Taking control of the enemy is crucial and one must take that control by attacking first. It is very important to remember this."*
>
> *- Choki Motobu*
>
> *"Properly understood, Karate-ni-sente-nashi indicates a mental attitude of not being inclined to fight. When faced with someone who disrupts the peace or who will do one harm, it only stands to reason that one should get the jump on the enemy and pre-empt his use of violence. Such action in no way goes against the precept of sente nashi. Karate ni sente nashi means that one must never take a bellicose attitude, looking to cause an incident; always having the virtues of calmness, prudence and humility in dealing with others."*
>
> *- Kenwa Mabuni*
>
> *"When there are no avenues of escape or if one is caught before an attempt to escape can be made, then for the first time the use of self-defence techniques should be considered. Even at times like these, do not show any intention of attacking, but first let the attacker become careless. At that time attack him concentrating one's whole strength in one blow to a vital point and in the moment of surprise, escape and seek shelter and help."*
>
> *- Gichin Funakoshi*

Common sense should tell us that it's not really a safe strategy to wait for a potentially dangerous assailant to strike first before then actively responding. The reality however is that for most rational human beings, the act of delivering percussive impact to another will encounter three substantial barriers – physical, mental and emotional. Not only must your strikes have the 'juice' to cause sufficient trauma, but you must also be fully committed to the act and be confident that your actions will be effective. The physical barriers of conviction, confidence and associated adrenal coping mechanisms may be challenged through well-designed training methodologies. Many of these we will look to explore in *Volume Three*.

But it's not only physical intensity that causes a problem. Quite often, it is the pre-conditioned mental, emotional and cultural limitations we've grown up with that causes the 'freeze' to impede us from acting first. It is these factors, including our own personal belief system that must all be deliberated as part of our training in order to adequately prepare us. These metaphysical components of self-protection should be considered just as significant as the development of strong physical skills. These may be developed through such methods as scenario training, pressure testing against varying levels of compliance, stress inoculation drills, thorough self-assessment of personal belief systems and/or deep visualisation etc.

As previously highlighted, the close-range nature of civilian self-protection means that it becomes very difficult and in most cases impossible to utilise any form of cognitive blocking manoeuvres as often employed in more long-range contemporary approaches of *karate*. At most, we have to put some faith in our evolutionary flinch-based responses that have been hard-wired into us for generations, given of course that our hands are already up and in the game to begin with. At distances inside of arms-length, it is usually the one who launches first who will land, so unless you can boast a *Jedi* Master Certificate from the lineage of *Yoda* himself, it would be prudent to embrace the notion of pre-emptive striking as an integral part of *karate* for self-protection. Anything employed later than this becomes a reactive strategy and although important to consider, is by its very definition, fundamentally flawed.

The above does not mean that we should completely disregard reactive strategies (far from it), as we still have to consider the requirement to respond against common acts of violence such as strikes, grabs, chokes, head butts, pushes etc. But this should always be based on the assumption that you may have already made an error in your awareness protocol, let your guard down, are forced to deal with a genuine ambush situation or are coping with secondary in-fight attacks. Ultimately, self-protection comes with no guarantees apart from the fact that something will probably go wrong. So the hierarchy of importance we give our protection strategies needs to be based on not only their function, but also on their probability of success. If the choice is for the taking, then dealing with an assailant before a physical attack is launched upon you is always far more favourable than having to work 'under fire'. The problem for many modern-day *karate* practitioners is that their tool-box of *kata* applications tend to ONLY consider reactive strategies and furthermore, visualise these as occurring ONLY at the initial phase of a physical encounter.

As a general rule of thumb, all percussive strikes should conform as close as possible to the following characteristics. Simply put, the more of these characteristics can be met, the greater chance the strike has of being ultimately successful:

- *Strikes should consist of strong weapons aimed towards weak targets*: This is all relative to the situation of course, since the knee may be considered a strong weapon when aimed to strike the groin, but a weak target when attacked by a stomping heel. A seemingly strong weapon such as the knuckles could end up worse off if the target area is the skull. Thus, a softer weapon such as the palm would be a more appropriate choice. It could be argued that the palm does not offer the same shock and subsequent 'brain shake' as the bone on bone collision offered by fist and jaw connection. But in its defence, the palm is a structurally stronger, requires less skill/training and a more adaptable alternative, offering less chance of injury if misaligned or insufficiently conditioned.

- *Strikes should be swift in motion and take the shortest path to the target:* Again, this is about finding the right balance for the specific situation. Increasing the distance travelled may help produce more power, but in most cases, the luxury of distance rarely exists in self-protection. So it's important to develop your striking ability so that the reliance on external distance/motion becomes less dependent. Then, in situations where extra time and distance does exist (such as when the opponent has been sufficiently controlled or subdued), then this opportunity may be exploited to aid the most desirable conclusion.

- *Strikes should carry an appropriate level of redundancy:* This means that if something goes wrong and the strike hasn't had the effect hoped for, then the situation can be recovered and an appropriate level of control still maintained. For example, a strong and well-placed forearm strike to the enemy's radial nerve against a lapel or throat seize may be very effective. However, should the strike be misplaced and the radial nerve is not sufficiently impacted, then we still need to make sure that the very action of dynamically attacking the location around the elbow joint, should cause a significant effect regardless and as a minimum, weaken the assailant's structure in order for you to exploit the initiative. The orientation of the striking surface in relation to the target is another aspect worthy of consideration here.

- *Strikes should be based on strong fundamentals:* This is about making the most of what you have and doing your best to ensure that every strike thrown is functionally effective. Although size and strength are significant factors in transferring force, the specific mechanics of traditional *karate* techniques are effective regardless of individual shape. The system makes the most of natural human structure, movement and advocates the relaxed perpetual flow of energy from floor to weapon within the body as opposed to relying on external distance or excessive muscular contraction for effect. This swift and explosive wave-like power is necessary for close-range confrontation.

- ***Strikes should be delivered unexpectedly to help maximise their effect:*** Usually, it is the strike you don't see that knocks you out because when the body is physically and psychologically unprepared for impact, the effects are greatly magnified and there is much less chance of the attack being countered. It is often the case that professional muggers will use deception to increase their chances of surprise and success. So if they can make use of that tactic then so can we! Artifice can take many forms and be applied in a variety of ways using the eyes, the hands, voice, body and technique etc. However, the objective is always the same - to strike the opponent down and ideally, when they least expect it.

- ***Strikes should be delivered with full commitment:*** A half- hearted attack can be potentially more dangerous than no attack at all, so once the decision has been made to go physical then there should be no less than 100% commitment and vehemence. Every strike should have the intent behind it to end the altercation immediately. To 'stun and run' would of course be the most clinical, safest and legally desirable outcome. You will very rarely get more than one clean shot, so it NEEDS to count!

- ***Strikes should be part of a seamless strategy for continued dominance***: As explained above, one ferocious and well-placed strike would be all that's required in an ideal world, in order to neutralise the threat and escape to safety. In the real world however, mistakes and failures occur and the chaotic nature of self-protection means that things hardly ever go to plan. Therefore, each and every strike must be considered 'one of many' and once dominance has been gained, we do not ease the pressure until assured that the threat can no longer pose a risk to our safety. Always keep in mind that just because the *kata* may show an application once, it doesn't mean that you may only apply it once! If something proves successful then the best strategy would be to keep repeating what works until the moment it's no longer effective or to the point at which you can safely make your escape. Of course, the use of excessive force is against the law, but failing to use enough force could very well become the last mistake you make.

In our *dojo* we often make use of the word K.A.R.A.T.E, which acts as a useful memory aid to remind us of the most essential components of a successful strike:

Keep it simple – natural gross motor actions are always best.

Action beats reaction – pre-emption gives you the upper hand.

Resolve, commitment and dominance – a combative asymmetrical mind-set is a must.

Appropriate weapon to target – strong and robust with high levels of redundancy.

Tactical initiative – positional advantage and the veil of deception for maximum effect.

Effective structure and dynamics – fire bullets (techniques) from a powerful gun (body).

Due to the dynamic nature of *Naihanchi Kata* and *karate* in general, we could argue that most of the movements in the form contain the potential for percussive impact. However it is my opinion that the first series of five techniques following the opening salutation are those that aim to really emphasise the lessons associated with our primary physical strategy. Rather than limiting our thinking to the direct application of the techniques themselves, by taking a step back in order to study their underlying principles, we can come to see a more holistic approach beginning to take shape that not only considers how the *kata* records information but also, how the *kata* may be used as a basis for more advanced and progressive training. Interestingly, *Choki Motobu* wrote the following comment about the *Naihanchi* elbow smash in his 1932 publication, *'Watashi no Karate-Jutsu'*:

> *"In practical application, one should not impact with the left elbow but use the clenched fist instead. In the kata, the elbow looks better, but don't forget its practical application."*

So although the techniques found in *kata* may be determined by shape, it is the concepts they aim to express that justify both their inclusion and preservation. In terms of a 'functional' use of the body, I often use the analogy of drawing pictures. It's inconsequential if you hold in your hand a pen, pencil, crayon, paint brush or a piece of charcoal. If you can't draw accurately then what comes out on paper will never reflect the subject. The same is true for *karate*. If you are unable to utilise effective body mechanics in order to generate potential, then it really doesn't matter if you employ a fist, palm heel, elbow, forearm smash, uppercut or kick – all your tools will lack the ability to do their job.

I believe that *Naihanchi Kata* at its core teaches how to become an accomplished (body) artist. The techniques themselves (or in other words, the artist's tools) are and will always be secondary to its chief aim. They merely provide a method of expressing those particular teachings within the physical choreography of the form. Can the open-handed strike and elbow smash be applied directly as given by the form? Of course they can. But they can also be applied in many other ways too and propose a more inclusive study that fits the framework of the *kata* perfectly.

Let's now take a look at the conceptual lessons on the primary physical strategy as given by the techniques within the first section of the form.

Application Concept 06/01 – Default Striking Option and Datum Setting

This first technique provides a default and versatile striking option. The primary target being the neck area using the 'funnel' created by enemy's head and shoulder.

The distinctive open-handed position found at the start of *Naihanchi Kata* may be regarded as a default shape for initial striking and threat management. From a situational control position it is easy to raise the lead arm towards the opponent to strike across the throat area. This application is very gross motor, utilizing both a large strong weapon (the forearm) against a prime target rich area that is easy to locate due to the natural 'funnel' shape created by the opponent's shoulder and head. It also offers a degree of instant control, by covering centreline and employing an active physical barrier between you and your opponent that's flexible enough to respond to a variety of tactile energies.

The other feature of this application concept, which associates with the two-handed palm structure as featured in the previous chapter on reactionary tactics, is that it provides one with a datum, or familiar territory from which to work from. This is certainly desirable in self-protection, as our physical game plan will always be much more effective if we can work to our own terms. You will see as we progress through the *kata* that this position (the very first technique of the form and a motion that is as simple as 'reaching out') may be used to connect all of the other application concepts together in order to establish a sense of familiarity with a single point of reference.

Application Concept 06/02 – Range Adaptability

The specific path that the open-handed strike takes is interesting and is in fact, how most technique in *karate* should be delivered. That is, either from the core outward or from the peripheral back toward the core.

As this strike occurs, the arm is extended sequentially from the shoulder, elbow and wrist joints in order to perpetuate the energy from the body into and out of the striking limb. The chronological order of this movement along with good body mechanics means that the transfer point into the target is not limited to the hand, but can take place at almost any point along the power chain.

Range adaptability is a very important concept for self-protection because it's very unlikely that the chaotic mess of violence will create the perfect set of circumstances for your strategy to be applied. One of the most common variables in conflict is that of opportunity and depending on the range that's given will mean that the ability to cause percussive impact needs to be flexible. Depending on the distance between you and your opponent, the time available to exploit plus the targets available to you at any given point, your weapon (means of energy transfer) may need to change swiftly and accordingly.

If you happened to be pinned tightly against a wall for example, then your preferred primary striking option may neither be appropriate nor effective. So your only option may be to reach up to your assailant's face and attack the eyes, employ a short-range head butt or even resort to more 'primal' tactics such as biting.

If these short-range tactics succeed in causing the opponent to flinch back away from the source of pain, then the opportunity may then become available for close-range elbow strikes, then forearm strikes, then back to your primary palm strikes and hammer fists etc. as those 'longer' strike paths become accessible.

Striking with the shoulder, elbow forearm, wrist, hand and fingers.

The importance of moving up and down the hierarchy of impact according to available range and opportunity is a key skill to develop within your physical protection strategy. In terms of the open-handed strike found in *Naihanchi Kata*, weapons may include the fingers, back of hand, wrist joint, forearm, elbow and shoulder etc. The movement represents a key lesson in learning how to employ the power developed by the

158

body into various striking tools and to utilize these as the situation demands. As always, this lesson may be extracted and applied in a plethora of ways, not necessarily as depicted by the specific *kata* technique.

Application Concept 06/03 – Using Both Limbs Together

It is no accident that the open-handed strike and following elbow smash technique serve to express the two gross motor pathways required for percussive impact. The open-handed strike with simultaneous pulling hand promotes the feeling of dynamically separating the limbs (ripping apart) and may be applied in a multitude of ways with impact issued to almost any part of the enemy's body in order to strike, tear, hyper-extend, rotate, constrict, control, displace balance and/or throw. The elbow smash depicts the exact opposite feeling to the open-handed strike – that of dynamically bringing together (colliding). The principles however are essentially the same as the open-handed strike and the development of both techniques together helps to emphasise the skill of *Meotode* (husband and wife hands). That is, the active and mutual use of both limbs during an altercation in order to create the best possible advantage – a critical feature within a close-range percussive strategy.

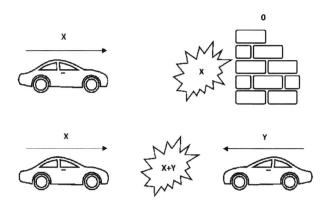

Although it's possible that a simultaneous pull (or anchor) using the non-striking limb may be used to enhance the 'collision effect' of strikes, but this does not take into account the type of collision (elastic/plastic), the specific combative aim, nor other influencing internal/external factors that may be relevant.

The term *Hikite* (withdrawing hand) is used commonly across *karate* styles to define the pulling action associated with the non-striking limb. Often criticized by practically minded martial artists as being ineffective and unrealistic, it's true that drawing back and chambering one hand against the waist is nonsensical for functional combatives. Most notably, it takes one limb out of the fight, which is tactically the same as going into war and choosing to send half of your army off the battlefield. However, it is not so much the static 'waist' (end) position we should focus upon when analysing this technique, but rather the generic movement pathway of dynamically retracting the hand from a peripheral point back towards the body core, even if in application, the movement only occurs over very short distance. Thus, it is within the transitional aspect of *hikite* (rather than the photographic snap-shot) that we find its massive potential. To quote *Gichin Funokoshi* from his 1925 book, *Rentan Goshin Karate Jutsu…*

> *"The meaning of the hikite is to grab the enemy's arm to twist and pull as much as possible, in order to break their posture."*

A functional study into the action of *hikite* reveals a useful reason as to why this technique may be so common in *karate*. Simply by assuming that something is already contained in the withdrawing hand as it drives back towards the body, *hikite* may be used to seize and pull the enemy's arm, body or head etc. to help facilitate your subsequent assault and put them into a more disadvantageous position. This in a combative sense provides the opportunity to maintain a greater level of control and dominance, index the target for improved accuracy (covered later), increase the effect of subsequent strikes through physical manipulation, plus gain vital tactile information for swifter reaction times and continuing real-time adjustment according to situational changes.

Although it's true that *hikite* may be used to help maximise the effect of subsequent strikes, the commonly held idea that it is solely designed for power generation by facilitating a more dynamic rotation of the torso by pulling one hand back to the hip is a misunderstanding. The human body is a far more complex system than what this notion tends to suggest, with the body having the natural ability to move in many ways and totally independently from the arms. The hands should ideally move as a consequence of the torso, not the other way round. Plus when striking, there are numerous other components in dynamic interplay that contribute to effective power generation than merely hip rotation. As such, it's entirely possible to strike just as hard (if not harder) without the other hand being actively pulled back at the same time. In fact, excessive rotation and pulling back one side of the body only serves to send a proportion of your body mass in the opposite direction of the intended target (in front), which of course is counter-productive.

Despite the above, we should consider that short dynamic snap-retractions or cyclical motions of the non-dominant limb can consequently occur when striking to maintain a natural state of balance and minimise restriction within the body to move freely. This reaction may even be honed and implemented to help facilitate one's technique, which is not only seen in the application of martial arts but also across many other physical/athletic pursuits. A strong tennis serve or shot put throw for instance will see the non-dominant hand move harmoniously and as a sequential consequence of the body/active hand. It is neither overly constrained, nor purposefully driven back.

So in short, the rather formalised manner that *hikite* is performed in *karate* and indeed, the position where it ends up on the hip are in my opinion expressions of an ideal dynamic action that prescribes a pathway of the hand from a peripheral point back to the body core. In combative application, this complete movement may never be fully realised due to the opponent's physical mass/movement/resistance, but there's no doubt that the active use of *hikite* to seize, pull and manipulate can serve very well to maximise the effect of one's primary striking strategy.

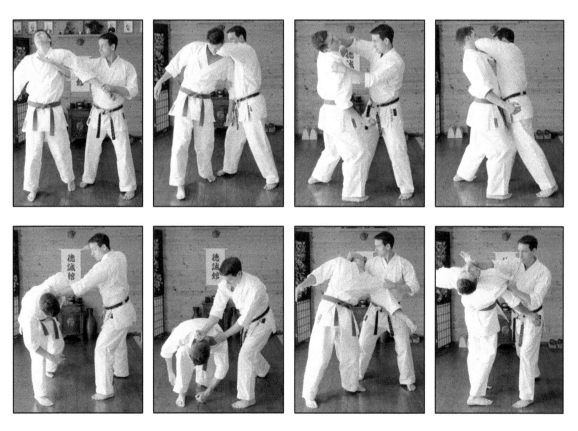

Some examples of how the separation and meeting energies found in the first two movements of Naihanchi Kata may be applied.

Despite the above, the theory and application of *hikite* as a 'pulling' mechanic is really only a part of the whole picture and it would be a misunderstanding to focus solely on the 'withdrawing' aspect of the non-striking limb. For instance, if you look at an art such as *Wing Chun* you will see that many of the associated 'secondary' limb actions have distinguishing labels that go some way to indicate their intended use. Examples such as, *Bong Sau* (Wing Hand), *Gum Sau* (Pressing Hand), *Huen Sau* (Circling Hand), *Jut Sau* (Jerking Hand), *Lap Sau* (Grabbing/Pulling Hand), *Man Sau* (Asking Hand), *Pak Sau* (Slapping Hand) and *Wu Sau* (Protective Hand) describe actions that help to express a wider potential for using the non-striking limb.

So, the concept of *hikite* in *karate* is for me, one component of the more substantial model of *Meotode* (husband and wife hands), which as previously discussed, aims to encourage the ability to have both limbs in active and complementary use during confrontation. I would also suggest that the above listed limb actions (plus more) from *Wing Chun* may be found throughout the movements of classical *karate kata*. Again, quoting from *Choki Motobu*…

> *"When facing an opponent in a combative engagement, it is important to know that the lead hand may be used to deal with both defensive and offensive issues. In other words, the lead hand can be used for both protecting and attacking concurrently."*

The fact that the open-handed strike and elbow smash from *Naihanchi Kata* utilize both limbs and that they also employ opposing motions I feel is no coincidence. What other manual task would you opt to use a single hand if the other was available to assist? Imagine trying to hammer a nail with one hand, hanging a door, drilling a hole or sawing through a plank of wood? At the very least, the non-dominant hand would always be employed to support, guide or manipulate.

Application Concept 06/04 – Ipsilateral & Contralateral Actions

The open-handed strike and elbow smash are also made up of ipsilateral (same side) and contralateral (opposite side) actions respectfully. The artistic 'jab and cross' in boxing, a front punch and reverse punch combination in sport *karate* and even the less formalised 'grab and pound' strategy found in street altercations all over the globe contain these two principal movements. The fact that the choreography of *Naihanchi Kata* contains these at the beginning of the form emphasises their importance within one's primary percussive strategy.

Ipsilateral and contralateral actions combined and used in a natural continuous sequence in order to create and maintain dominance.

Application Concept 06/05 – Indexing

Indexing (also known as a 'set up', 'controlling', 'gauge' or 'leveraging arm') is another important concept taught in modern day self-protection systems and is also a key tactic expressed throughout the application of movements found in classical *karate kata*. You only need to spend a few moments searching The Internet for video footage of real street attacks, self-protection encounters or bar brawls and you will see that the use of indexing is prevalent. This is simply due to the fact that it is both natural and highly advantageous. It is also a strategy used extensively in weapon attacks (especially puncture weapons such as knives or screwdrivers), where repetitive thrusting or clubbing styles may be employed to devastating effect. It is no wonder that the principle of indexing makes a stark appearance early on in *Naihanchi Kata*.

In a combative sense, the term 'indexing' essentially means to actively use one hand in order to make contact with the opponent for means of tactile awareness, control and deception in order to increase the success rate of subsequent strikes with the other limb. Rather than attacking the opponent 'unattached', the use of indexing works to help make your primary strategy (percussive impact delivery) much more effective.

Using an index against a moving target makes striking it much easier.

Indexing is most often applied with the lead hand as it is reached out like a tentacle in order to make contact with the opponent. The tactile stimulus here offers vital and almost instant information that far surpasses visual stimulus alone, making a physical response more likely to succeed. To understand the clear advantages that indexing can offer in a close-range altercation, you can try out the following drill.

With eyes closed and unattached, try to strike a focus mitt that's being continuously moved by your partner. It would be only luck that would cause you to hit it. Now, reach around and hold the back of the focus mitt with your non-striking limb, or touch the pad-holder's forearm and repeat the exercise. Hey presto – who needs eyes to fight! In reality, your opponent is very unlikely to stand still and make it easy for you to throw repetitive shots. So, attaching to the target with your non-striking limb offers a reference point that moves along with the opponent and provides the ability to 'tactile map' between your index and striking hand, or to another nearby target.

Of course, you would never voluntarily close your eyes in a self-protection scenario so in most applications you can expect to make the best use of both visual and tactile sensory information. However, what's to say you haven't already been hit and are disorientated, or maybe you have tears or blood in your eyes. You may have had your vision compromised by clothing or through positioning. Add the potential for weapons or multiple assailants into the mix, plus high levels of situational stress/fatigue and you can then begin to appreciate how difficult it can be to land accurate strikes that carry enough purchase to end the altercation swiftly. Thus, it becomes clear that the unregulated and sheer chaotic nature of combat makes the use of indexing essential. Here are some of the instant benefits:

- It improves accuracy and the ability to locate target areas.

- It increases the level of control, forward pressure and dominance.

- It facilitates quick adaptation to changing circumstances.

- It allows for active limb clearance and the ability to clear potential strike paths.

- It helps to manage and maintain combative ranges.

- It offers more seamless transition to auxiliary strategies such as joint attacks, clinch work, chokes & strangles, throws & take downs or anti-grappling skills.

- It can be used to distract and/or create opportunities to attack under the veil of deception.

Indexing is such a natural tactic that most antagonists will tend to employ it unconsciously. Therefore, it's also imperative that you practice drills in the *dojo* that aim to counteract or exploit an enemy's attempts to control you via indexing. Again, it's not surprising that many classical *kata* contain these methods too.

The open-handed strike in *Naihanchi Kata* also serves very well as an indexing limb, which is launched out towards the opponent in order to obtain a tactile reference point. The next movement of the *kata* then shows the striking limb (elbow smash) being driven towards the indexing hand. Again, if we remove our fixation on the weapon choice, techniques or specific choreography, we can begin to see more clearly the lesson, which the *kata* is attempting to convey.

Using an index to help facilitate strikes by adding pressure and tracking the adversary's movement.

Application Concept 06/06 – Anchoring

After the elbow smash technique, both hands are brought together and 'stacked' at one side of the waist. Following this, one hand is launched out to the opposite side of the body to make *gedan-barai* (low-level sweep). To end the sequence, a *kagi-uchi* (hooking strike) is performed at middle-level, with the non-striking limb once again driven to the waist in *hikite*.

Still within lessons concerning our primary percussive strategy, this part of *Naihanchi Kata* looks at subsequent actions of anchoring the assailant to assist your striking strategy. This naturally comes after the more desirable detached or 'indexed' striking, because it assumes a closer range (attached) scenario and as such, the reduced possibility of making a clean escape. However, the principles associated with anchoring should still be a vital part of your primary percussive strategy. In addition and as you will see later, the 'stacked' position from *Naihanchi Kata* also depicts a typical 'two-on-one' formation that is very useful for restricting limb movement, especially against weapon attack.

Using the 'stack' position for two-on-one control either on top with a high line strike, or underneath with a low line strike.

I first learned the concept of anchoring not through *karate*, but through my childhood interest in fly fishing. If you intended to take your catch home, then the fish must be dispatched quickly and humanely. This is normally achieved using a *priest*, which is a heavy blunt tool so-called from the notion of administering the last rites via a strong percussive blow to the head. I was taught that in order to cause the least amount of stress it's important to anchor the fish firmly with one hand, to make sure that the forthcoming strike hits home and does the job. Fish can be rather slippery, so correct grip and stabilisation was just as crucial as the strike itself. It wasn't until many years later that I was able to connect the same idea to self-protection and the conceptual lessons given within *Naihanchi Kata*.

Controlling the enemy's head and arm to open up potential strike paths.

Encompassing the idea of anchoring to some degree, controlling the enemy's body is another important use for the non-striking limb. In contrast to clearing strike paths, which generally refers to moving the enemy's limbs that are creating an obstruction, controlling is more about exposing potential targets themselves through the use of force. A case in point from the *kata* would be gaining control of the head before twisting it in order to expose the jaw and throat for subsequent strikes. Another example may be to pull the enemy's arms or kick their opposite leg in order to jerk the head forward and down, thus exposing effective targets to your oncoming strikes.

Creating a whiplash effect by rebounding the opponent's head back and forth from crook of elbow to palm and then striking with elbow.

One important concern to bear in mind is that when seizing to anchor or control, we must take care not to build habits that may be counter-productive to overall effect. For example, the open-handed strike and elbow smash combination is often applied as a grip around the head/neck to help facilitate the oncoming elbow attack. If this grip is too secure then the concussive effect of this 'hold and hit' strategy (which actually requires the head to be somewhat loose when struck in order for the skull to move fast and cause brain shake) is significantly reduced.

An alternative way to drill the kind of application described above would be to use the open-handed strike to effectively rebound the opponent's head to and from the crook of your elbow and palm. Then the elbow smash may then be thrown during that dynamic action. So rather than relying solely on blunt trauma, maximising movement of the head via a whiplash effect whilst still maintaining a sufficient level of control helps to increase the chances of causing disorientation or unconsciousness.

To summarise this chapter on how the first section of *Naihanchi Kata* may be used to express lessons associated with developing a primary percussive strategy, we can see a number of important concepts being expressed including:

- The use of a default striking option and datum.

- The ability to adapt striking tools and work up/down the hierarchy of impact according to range and availability.

- The active use of both limbs together.

- The sequential use of ipsilateral and contralateral actions for repetitive striking.

- The employment of an 'index' to assist striking.

- The use of control and anchoring to support the percussive strategy.

- Creating a whiplash effect by dynamically rebounding the skull.

The use of these rather simplistic but nevertheless effective application concepts, along with the ability to hit hard and with full commitment, may help set up a very solid primary strategy for physical protection. Let's now move on to take a look at what *Naihanchi Kata* advises next, should your strike paths become obstructed.

CHAPTER XIII

LESSON 7: NEGOTIATING OBSTACLES

"Knowledge of just the sequence of a form in karate is useless."

~ Gichin Funakoshi

The conceptual lessons we've covered so far in *Naihanchi Kata* are now beginning to construct a picture that's well aligned to the outlined framework for civilian self-protection explored at the beginning of the book. Firstly presenting active environmental awareness, early threat recognition and avoidance as being essential factors to help maximise safety. Following this, the *kata* then looks toward gaining an understanding of the core elements of range, framework and movement, before focussing on positional control and emergency reactionary tactics should those soft-skills fail and/or a genuine ambush attack becomes your reality. Only when these fundamentals are in place does the choreography then progress to setting up a primary percussive strategy.

The fundamental principles of negotiating obstacles are expressed within the gedan-barai and kagi-uchi combination.

As we have already established, management of the enemy's limbs is important in self-protection due to the close ranges involved and is probably the reason why 'push hands' or 'sticky hands' type drills are featured in some traditional *karate* styles, along with a number of traditional martial arts systems. Of course, there may be various motives to employ limb control, but all methods to do so generally accomplish the same outcome – *to minimise your assailant's ability to attach/control/strike whilst at the same time maximising yours.*

Limb control may be thought of as the 'bridge' between primary (detached) and secondary (attached) strategies and as you would expect, appears heavily throughout the classical forms. Although very 'formalised' within the various training methods labelled as *kakie*, *kake-te* or *muchimi-di* and the like, they nonetheless contain the same essential elements for the development of valuable attributes including tactile awareness and the ability to manipulate the enemy's energy (e.g. the *Chinese* martial principles of *float*, *sink*, *swallow* and *spit*) at the most appropriate times. As such, limb control is as much about controlling the antagonist's body and mind, as it is their arms.

It is easy to become fixated on numerous methods of limb control and overlook the actual aim to maintain or regain the ability to end the confrontation as quickly as possible. Thus, the real application of limb control should occur in a 'flash' and does not resemble the fluid and drawn out affairs featured in more formalised two-person drills, which are designed to focus on this specific skill. Indeed, the 'artificial' flow commonly associated with limb control training drills is necessary only in order to aid the ability to develop ancillary skills and offer a more time-efficient method of training. The reality of course is that if you're flowing then you're losing!

Having stated the above, two-person flow drills that help to tease out and develop some of the skills associated with limb control are nonetheless very useful, so long as their limitations are understood. As a case in point, you will see that the area of limb control will be further expanded within the forthcoming chapters covering *Bunkai Sandan*. Acknowledging those limitations, we will also include some auxiliary components to emphasise breaks in flow at different reference points, rather than being only focused on maintaining continuity. With the right mind-set, this is a valuable method of training because it allows for a more spontaneous expression of the various application lessons found within *Naihanchi Kata,* whilst retaining a controlled and generic framework for continuity. More on this idea later.

So, having established that limb control first offers the ability to counter the efforts made by an opponent to impede your ability to deliver percussive impact, it also provides a degree of control to help reduce the likelihood of grappling. Although the limb control skills found in *karate* may not be as 'sophisticated' as those from specialist trapping arts such as *Wing Chun*, *Silat* or *Kali* (just as *karate's* throwing techniques are not as refined as those found in systems like *Judo)*, they more than adequately meet the requirements for non-consensual conflict. These being (1) simplistic, (2) gross motor and

(3) easy to retain, offering a high degree of effectiveness and redundancy. For self-protection purposes, this is a balanced trade off.

Since we'll be looking at limb control in more depth within *Bunkai Sandan,* this chapter will be used to consolidate some of the key conceptual lessons of limb control found in *Naihanchi Kata* for use as an adjunct to your primary percussive strategy, in order to maintain or regain the upper hand before counter-grappling skills (as featured in the next chapter) may become necessary.

As recognised within the previous chapters on reactionary tactics and startle reflex actions, it is highly likely that if your initial pre-emptive strike or retaliation hasn't had the desired effect then your opponent may have the opportunity to intervene. Due to the dynamics of such scenarios, this response is likely to fall into one of four categories. These are: (1) *Passive Barrier*, (2) *Active Barrier*, (3) *Strike Back* and (4) *Reduce/Increase Distance*. It is the passive and active barriers that lend themselves to the application of what we could term 'reactive limb control', whereas proactive use would occur to support the employment of pre-emptive strikes.

Applications found within *Naihanchi Kata* for dealing with the above reactions and are in contrast to the mutual 'back and forth' interactions as seen in consensual engagements. They focus heavily on creating and maintaining dominance with minimum interruption, since the opponent should ideally never get the opportunity to retaliate. In addition to the clear physical skills required to make this strategy successful, we must also cultivate the proper mentality and determination in order to ruthlessly overwhelm and dictate the outcome of the confrontation. Without this state of mind, even knowledge of a thousand applications may be rendered practically useless.

Application Concept 07/01 – Passive Barrier

The opponent may simply cover up in an attempt to obstruct your strike path and reduce the level of impact upon vulnerable areas. This is usually the most common response to an overwhelming attack and a state of capitulation may present an opportunity to escape, which should always be your main priority. However, if this is not possible or viable then it's important that control be maintained with successive dominating strikes.

As we progress further through the choreography of *Naihanchi Kata*, you will come to see that numerous movements may lend themselves to passive limb control applications and as already discussed, we will cover this idea in subsequent sections. For now however, the *kata* presents two rather crude but very effective methods in order to offer a level of continuity within your primary percussive strategy by using the *gedan-*

barai and *kagi-uchi* combination. The ability to clear strike paths with the indexing limb and/or change levels to exploit openings are fundamental to maintaining control and as such, should become deeply ingrained within your application practices.

The *gedan-barai* and *kagi-uchi* combination expresses a very basic way of clearing strikes paths against an enemy's attempt to raise a limb to protect against your oncoming attacks. As soon as you become aware that limbs have clashed, then use one hand (like a hook) to rip away the obstruction before continuing to strike with the other hand. It's interesting that the *Wado Ryu* version of *Naihanchi Kata* makes use of an angled punch before pulling back to the *kagi-uchi* position, which seems to express this application concept more accurately and strengthen the notion that stylistic differences are very often nothing more than variations on a central theme.

Using the gedan-barai and kagi-uchi combination to removing a passive barrier (pulling away limb) in order to clear a strike path.

In stark contrast to the sophisticated use of multiple technique combinations, feints, draws and reaction audits used in typical skilled vs skilled contests, the general rule of thumb in non-consensual self-protection is that if something is working then it's best to keep on doing it until either the threat has been dealt with, or whatever you're doing is no longer having the desired effect. This tactic is much more simplistic, requires far less cognitive processing and is more likely to be reliable under duress. As we've just discussed, the standard gross-motor reaction to an obstruction would be to clear the strike path and continue on with your attack. However, another effective option would be to simply change the level of attack, as it will be difficult for an opponent under pressure to split their attention between two separate areas and still manage to affect sufficient cover.

Using the gedan-barai and kagi-uchi combination to counter a passive barrier by changing levels from both high to low and low to high.

Changing levels, from high to low or low to high, is another concept expressed within the *gedan-barai* and *kagi-uchi* combination. We also see this repeated in later sections of the kata with progressions such as simultaneous motions and the use of the legs to attack low, whilst the arms attack high. This shows the importance of changing levels to aid your ability to maintain dominance. We are not wasting time on the complexity of switching various weapons and targets for the sake of it, rather exploiting the notion that if the high line is occupied in terms of defence, then there's a strong possibility that the low line will be exposed and available to attack (and vice versa).

Application Concept 07/02 – Active Barrier

Using the gedan-barai and kagi-uchi combination to clear an active barrier caused by assailant gripping wrist as a response to eye attack.

An active barrier is where the assailant attempts to purposefully hinder your striking motion. This may be achieved by reaching out to push or jam against the arm, chest or shoulder. It may also be achieved by actively gripping a limb to reduce/remove the ability for you to inflict further trauma.

Although this response requires a comparatively greater degree of both skill and cognisance than the passive barrier, it is still nevertheless a possibility from a 'panicked reaction' and as such, is often addressed in *karate kata*.

Using the gedan-barai and kagi-uchi combination to clear an active barrier caused by assailant resching out to push against shoulder.

Active barriers may be risky because there's more chance of the opponent gripping and thus, hindering your ability to escape. These need to be countered quickly by clearing the offending limb away so as to regain the ability to strike unrestricted.

A similar example to the previous, this time under-hooking the arm and striking to the body.

Application Concept 07/03 – Strike Back

The opponent may lash out with a barrage of reactive strikes in an attempt to regain a position of dominance. So long as your pre-emptive attack has been powerful, persistent and committed enough then the opportunity to 'strike back' with significant force will be limited.

Any attempt by the opponent to strike back would most likely occur if a gap becomes present in your striking assault or if your assault has been employed with less than full commitment. However, it is not impossible for the opponent to retaliate in this way out of sheer desperation, so should this reaction occur then it's vital that you attempt to regain control as quickly as possible.

Using the default cover from the opening salutation to counter 'strike back', re-group and regain the percussive initiative.

No different to the skills covered in the chapter on reactionary tactics, the *kata* has already provided effective default manoeuvres in order to recover the situation if the assailant's strikes become overwhelming. So if sufficient enough to put you on the back foot then you have the option to transition immediately into the default cover position from the opening salutation. Use this as a means to re-group, regain dominance and put you firmly back onto your primary percussive strategy once again.

Application Concept 07/04 – Reduce/Increase Distance

The opponent may attempt to (1) back away from the source of impact or (2) impulsively drive forward in an attempt to reduce distance, take hold and stifle your ability to launch further strikes by encumbering body/limb movement. The latter reaction is often seen in boxing matches for instance when fighters are under pressure, with the standard response being for the referee to break and reset the bout. However in self-protection and with no referee present, there's a significant risk of going to the ground if an active clinch is not successfully managed.

The key skill to protect against range changes is the ability to maintain strong index and control capabilities with the non-striking limb, such that the opponent is unable to neither bridge nor break the gap. A critical reason as to why use of the non-striking limb is fundamental in traditional *karate*.

If distance is increased and you become unattached through the opponent backing away then the specific situation will depend on the chosen response. For instance, if a clear escape route is present and the enemy is somewhat capitulated, then it may be sensible to make a run for it. However, if no clear escape route is present and/or there is a chance for the opponent to re-group, then it may be more prudent to swiftly aim to close the gap, regain your index and continue striking. This scenario is a useful example for the use of kicks in self-protection – in order to bridge an extended gap so as to maintain an unbroken percussive response.

Dealing with someone who has closed the distance and actively taken their own attachment will be covered in more depth within the next chapter and is represented by the latter part of the *kata* choreography. In short, counter-grappling skills may need to be employed to ascertain a dominant position whereby you can then work up the hierarchy of impact towards the primary percussive strategy once again. The opportunity may also present itself to transition into secondary or tertiary strategies such as joint attacks, chokes and strangles, manipulations or felling techniques.

If range is increased then the 'hierarchy of impact' principle from Naihanchi Kata may be applied by making use of longer weapons (kicks) to bridge the gap and re-establish control.

CHAPTER XIV

LESSON 8: COUNTER GRAPPLING

"Enter, Counter & Withdraw is the rule for Torite."

~ Anko Itosu

We have now arrived at a natural junction in terms of the *Naihanchi Kata* application methodology expressed within this book. Up until the point that the opponent employs some sort of active attachment, then the primary percussive strategy, along with its ancillary skills to control range plus obtain and maintain clear strike paths should always be kept in play until the threat is dealt with and/or escape becomes possible. However, if this situation breaks down, range is further compromised and some sort of grip is affected upon you, then the secondary strategy of the *kata*, counter grappling, must be then utilised.

The principal aim of counter-grappling is to remove the attachment. The ancillary aim if the former was unfeasible is to obtain a level of control via some form of a structural frame, restrict the enemy's options and then to retaliate with skills such as short-range strikes, seizes and manipulations, joint attacks, blood or air restrictions, throws or takedowns etc. Rather than grappling for grappling's sake and becoming unnecessarily exposed to the dangers associated with this range in self-protection, the intention is always to detach and work back up the hierarchy of impact towards the primary percussive strategy.

Reacting to and countering grips is often poorly applied in *karate dojo*. As the script goes, "if someone seizes your wrist then do this" or "if someone takes hold of your lapel then perform this technique". The problem with this approach is that more often than not, these applications are taken well out of context. Of course we need to start somewhere for beginners, but let's face facts – no one is going to simply stand there, take hold of your wrists and then wait for you to respond. In reality, assailants will grab you for a reason. Sometimes it may be part of their plan or it could also be an active barrier as discussed in the previous chapter. As such, it is the reason, not the grab itself that needs to be given priority. If we become too fixated on the technicalities of what the grab is and various options on how to manipulate it, then the very advantage it aims to effect (usually a painful one) may be more easily exploited by the opponent, much to your demise.

A simple drill I often share in the *dojo* or at seminars when introducing the dynamics of dealing with grips is to partner up and ask one person to act as the assailant, whose job is to grab their 'opponent' by the wrists (or lapel etc.), in any configuration they see fit. The aim for the other person is simply to defend against those grabs with whatever skills they already know. You can pretty much guarantee that those who have not been exposed to this drill before and are accustomed to the 'usual way' will instinctively wait for a grab to be affected before attempting to break free with their chosen technique. Then they'll wait for the next grab before responding again and then so on. Each time, they may try something different to escape. This represents a mind-set typically cultivated in martial arts, where emphasis is placed on collecting a range of techniques to deal with specific attacks after they've been implemented. In this case, they're literally conditioning themselves to being grabbed!

Of course, the best way to counter the scenario above would be not to get grabbed in the first place. So instead, the drill should ideally see the 'defender' escaping the scene if possible and if not, then striking and/or manoeuvring their body and arms in such a way as to prevent themselves from being seized, only resorting to a more tangible escape, should it become necessary. This more closely maps to our self-protection game plan in terms of 'defence in depth' and as such, should be the mind-set we always make use of in training. Of course, for the sake of this chapter we have assumed that our efforts to stay detached have for whatever reason, failed.

Another issue with 'defence against grabs' is that numerous applications tend to be collected for pretty much every eventuality. A single-handed cross wrist grab, a single-handed same side grab, a two-handed wrist grab, a two-handed lapel grab, a single handed lapel grab – you get the picture. The problem with this is that in reality, you simply won't have the time nor presence of mind to sift through a large tool box of applications in order to find the most appropriate (refer to *Hick's Law* and *OODA Loop* from chapter on reactionary tactics). Preferably, you need a single principle-based strategy that will work for most common scenarios and prioritises the use of percussive impact.

Grips in all their forms are generally used to assume a level of control. That may be in order to stop you from escaping, to intimidate as part of a pre-attack interview, to impede your ability to defend or fight back, to create openings to exploit, or indeed to stifle your own attacking attempt. For instance, someone may grab both your wrists just before head butting, seize your arm to pull you off balance and into repetitive knife stabs, dive forward to clinch in order to impede your continuing percussive assault or pin you up hard against a wall to threaten before verbally laying out their demands. Whatever the situation, you can assume that any grab is going to both precede something harmful and be delivered with serious intent, so it's important that your response is both immediate and committed.

A good tactic is to limit response options to grips wherever possible. Of course, this is never going to be totally achievable as there will always be some unavoidable variables to consider, but there's no reason why a single 'principle of operation' may not be utilised in order to deal with the most common scenarios. As with the rest of this book, it's obvious that a combination of sound fundamentals, coupled with the expertise and experience to make simple adjustments where required under pressure, are the hallmarks of a solid core self-protection skill-set.

Around half way through the choreography, *Naihanchi Kata* makes use of three shapes and transitions with the upper limbs that may be applied in order to help respond quickly to a variety of common grabs. The first shape (*soto-uke*) sees one hand pull back to the waist as the other forearm drives out and across the front of the body. The second shape (*morote-uke*) sees both hands cross and then split apart. The third shape (*uraken-uchi* or *ura-zuki*) sees one hand 'hit' over the top of the other that makes a horizontal 'frame' from shoulder to shoulder.

The soto-uke, morote-uke and ura-zuki combination represents key in-fight transitions for counter-grappling.

It's interesting to note that the same three techniques given above also make up valuable extensions for close-range limb control, since in principle there is little difference between a limb grab and limb barrier in terms of the fact that both employ a physical connection, which must be managed. Thus, these should be regarded as your fundamental in-fight shapes/transitions and combined with previous lessons, they act as the secondary go-to tactic should the primary percussive strategy fall short of the mark. It's also interesting to note that this is the only combination of techniques that appear in

184

all three versions of the *Naihanchi* form (*shodan*, *nidan* and *sandan*), which may also serve to indicate their particular significance.

Indeed, you will come to see how this part of the choreography may be extracted and further explored in *Bunkai Sandan*. But for now, we will focus our attention solely on how these movements contain valuable conceptual lessons on gross motor applications against a range of common grab scenarios.

Vertical grappling or in-fighting is an important consideration for civilian-based self-protection. Given the fact that altercations will begin at distances at or inside of arms-length, some form of 'tangle' is pretty much guaranteed if initial attempts to exercise dominance using the primary percussive strategy have failed and especially so, if the opponent responds by trying to stifle further impact by driving/falling forward. Such a desperate attempt to launch in, attach and suppress further impact is a very common reaction when 'under fire'.

It is improbable that the 'clinches' you'll experience in self-protection will look or feel anything like those found in dedicated grappling systems or consensual-based wrestling bouts. There will likely be a frantic and full-energy fight for control that may only last a few seconds and more closely represent a badly tied fishing knot than a neat technical hold. Due to the inherent risks at this range plus excessive energy expenditure, it is imperative that your chief aim at this point (as already discussed) is to break free and continue striking, rather than over-investing valuable time battling for strength and control. This gives the application of grappling in *karate* a specific personality over more specialist wrestling systems and I believe that this difference is well represented in *Naihanchi Kata*.

Whereas in a sporting engagement with two skilled assailants, wrestling for optimum positioning within the clinch may well be a favourable tactic. It can offer various ways to seek submission and the opportunity to progress the fight towards the ground where a particular speciality may be exploited. In self-protection however, these tactics can be very dangerous due to potential threats from the environment, multiple adversaries and weapons. A well-controlled clinch with strong dominance can of course become a favourable position in any scenario, but that control should always include the ability to strike hard, break free and escape.

The inherent limitations in both distance and freedom to move within clinch-range will naturally impede the ability to strike with full power. That said though, there are still effective options available in such tight positions that may be employed to increase distance, progress up the hierarchy of impact and transition into strikes that will potentially have the largest effect. Again, the main feature of 'breaking away' at the earliest opportunity cannot be understated.

Felling the opponent is another valid option from the clinch and is covered within the latter portion of the *kata* choreography. However, this can be quite risky due to the fact that the opponent is also actively gripping, so it is possible to end up being dragged down to the floor. It is for this reason that the felling techniques found in *karate* are opportunistic at best and should not be actively sought or prioritised over primary methods. Again, I'll cover more on this topic within the next chapter.

Application Concept 08/01 – Dealing with Grabs

In terms of countering grabs, most situations if not avoidable or dealt with pre-emptively may be answered with a common principle-based response made up of five key components – Base / Check / Strike / Position / Detach. Please note that some of these may occur together, in different orders and in some situations, not at all.

- ***Base*** yourself and get free hand(s) in play so that it becomes more challenging for the enemy to control or strike you. This can simply be achieved by bending at the knees, dropping your weight and raising your hands in order to occupy the space between you. This should make you more stable and having the hands up provides the ability to cover against any attacks that may be already on their way.

- ***Check*** the grabbing limb in order to monitor and manipulate. The fact that you've been grabbed means that the attacker has not only tied up either one or both of their hands, but is also providing you with valuable tactile information that may be used to aid your response, especially at such close-ranges. If the grip is already attached to one or both of your limbs i.e. wrist or arm grab, then you could argue that the 'checking' part of this component has by definition already been met. Checking also provides some control capability.

- ***Strike*** at the earliest opportunity in order to dominate the situation quickly and to ensure that barriers are kept in place between you and the opponent. Specific weapons and targets will of course depend on the situation. Strikes may also be aimed at the grabbing limb(s) to either break free, cause trauma or force a response that would offer a greater level of control. For your fundamental game plan, forget fancy wrist locks, counters and aesthetic throwing techniques – the quicker you can assume or regain your primary strategy, the better.

- ***Position*** yourself where possible in order to minimize risk and offer the best tactical advantage. If someone grabs you with their left hand then it would be fair to assume that an attack may swiftly follow with their right. The best position therefore would be to flank to your right side and as far away as possible from the attacking limb. Again, as the grabbing limb is already tied up and you have connected to it, it makes sense to move towards what you have perception of and away from what you don't (i.e. danger). Always aim to create angles (*kata embusen*) that maximise your potential, whilst minimising the enemy's.

- ***Detach*** from the grip if possible so that the opponent loses their ability to control, which makes striking, fleeing to safety, dealing with multiple assailants and/or weapons more manageable. In some instances, impeding the opponent from releasing their grab by pinning or restraining may actually work to your advantage, but this should not be regarded as the prime option in terms of effectively managing the wider situation, which should culminate with situational escape if feasible.

Looking at the *soto-uke*, *morote-uke* and *ura-zuki* combination as a series of shapes and movements, we find some really interesting points to note. First of all, the fact that we're utilising both limbs together makes use of *meotode* and that both transition on the same 'beat', rather than one arm moving before another as depicted in the more contemporary (block and punch type) *karate*. Secondly, the stance assumes the requirement to provide a strong base. Thirdly, the common form in all three techniques is the *soto-uke* shape, which indicates the requirement to quickly fill the gap between the attachment (providing a physical barrier between you and the enemy). Finally, the transitions between the *soto-uke* shape and the other limb in unison prescribes three key movements that are valuable for countering most common grips, namely:

- '*Hikite*': To pull, pin or rip,

- '*Gedan-Barai*': To cross, split or separate

- '*Osae-Uke*': To press, check or clamp.

The first two motions within this part of the *kata* (*soto-uke* and *morote-uke*) use motions that operate within both horizontal and vertical planes respectively. Along with *ura-zuki*, these pulling, splitting and pressing dynamics, either separately or together, may be used to help quickly detach from a variety of limb grabs whilst also providing centreline cover/barriers. I've added a selection of examples below to help show this conceptual lesson in action. For the sake of clarity, I've omitted specific context and any striking from the applications given here, which should obviously be employed as and when appropriate. Also, the fact that I'm using still images inevitably show these

187

applications in a rather sterile way, whereas realistically they would occur in more 'dynamic' conditions.

Applying the soto-uke motion with 'pulling' dynamic against a cross-side wrist grab.

Applying the morote-uke motion with 'splitting' dynamic against a same-side wrist grab.

Applying the soto-uke motion with 'pulling' dynamic against a double low wrist grab.

Applying the ura-zuki motion with 'pressing' dynamic against a double high wrist grab.

There are many more applications to be derived from this conceptual lesson on dealing with limb grips, so I would recommend you explore these three *kata* movements more deeply in training and aim to become accustomed to aligning a few effective principles, rather than a plethora of technical escapes or locks etc. In my view, this is the most productive way to approach this subject.

Application Concept 08/02 – Framing

Already discussed in the chapter on reactionary tactics, a percussive two-handed neck tie is a typical dominant position for dealing with an extreme close-quarter situation, especially where distance has been almost entirely compromised. Both of your hands are above the assailant's with potentially unrestricted access to vital targets above the collar bone such as the eyes and throat. From here, you may create an opportunity to drive the opponent towards the floor and break free (refer to next chapter) or make enough distance in order to progress up the hierarchy of impact and resume your primary striking strategy.

Using reactive neck tie from opening salutation against a two-handed lapel grab.

This simple neck tie allows for the assailant's head (and therefore body) to be manipulated and controlled in order to swiftly gain the advantage, end the altercation and facilitate situational escape. It appears at the beginning of the *kata* because it's the 'go to' strategy should your opponent launch forward and latch on.

In addition to above, the *uraken-uchi* or *ura-zuki* shape found in *Naihanchi Kata* contains a useful lesson on framing, which is further expanded within the choreography using side-to-side twists from left to right and leg lifts/kicks. This alternative grappling frame may be used in numerous ways together with the neck tie, seizing, striking, choking and throwing options.

Generic frame from Naihanchi Kata with associated movements left and right.

This frame can be taken at any point during attachment in order to provide a little breathing space to work. The horizontal 'pressing' hand is used to check and latch on to the appendage, whilst the vertical arm is used to control the enemy's body by cutting across their centre-line. This stifles their ability to rotate and limits the potential to strike with their free hand, plus it impedes their ability to attack with the head and legs.

Using the generic frame from Naihanchi Kata against a lapel grab, removing 'base' and 'positioning' etc. for ease of explanation and to more directly resemble the standard choreography.

In this one simple yet valuable motion, you can regain a level of control enough for you to start working from. Realistically, it is impossible to completely negate all the enemy's attacks for any length of time, however a cracked tooth, broken nose or bruised rib means that you are still very much in the game and in terms of self-protection and far more desirable than being knocked clean out.

Using the generic frame from Naihanchi Kata against a throat grab, this time adding 'base' and 'positioning' etc. as the principles of the choreography suggest we utilise.

The twisting from side to side in the *kata* is an auxiliary lesson on creating angles whilst applying the clinch frame. As in the previous lesson on *embusen*, these angles may be created by moving yourself, your opponent or both. The additional leg lifts also indicate the application of kicks, sweeps and stamps etc. once the enemy's base has been weakened from such manipulation.

The above is an important consideration for grappling since by definition, kicking will temporarily place you on only one leg. Therefore the close-range in-fighting applications expressed within *Naihanchi Kata* via the *Nami-Gaeshi* (returning wave) technique are specifically for low-level targets close to the ground and are to be applied in conjunction with the counter-grappling strategy given by the upper half of the body.

A good way to practice the low-level kicking applications taken from *Nami-Gaeshi* is to take a clinch with your partner, set a timer for 20-sec intervals and then take turns at applying various techniques. Performed in a controlled fashion to begin with, this is a very effective way to investigate different applications and gain an understanding into how the upper body may be used to manipulate your partner's base to help facilitate your subsequent low-level attack. Think about not 'what' is the most appropriate way to attack, but also 'when' is it most appropriate to attack based on the connected interaction between you both and how the conceptual lessons given within *Naihanchi Kata* may be physically expressed (applied) in order to help support your efforts.

Some applications for the 'returning wave' technique as an adjunct to the generic upper-level frame and left/right twisting featured in the kata choreography.

Application Concept 08/03 – Negotiating the Clinch

The skills associated with clinch fighting can be very advanced and two experienced exponents can make this look like a combative game of chess. Indeed, whole systems have been created that deal primarily with this range. However, in keeping with the simplistic and gross motor requirements of self-protection, it pays to focus one's attention on the most fundamental principles that will raise the likelihood of being able to remain standing up, create positional advantage, detach and break into the primary percussive strategy once more.

By combining the previous two application concepts, we can use the same movements from *Naihanchi Kata* to help us find dominance within the clinch. Although in reality it's unlikely that you'll find yourself in technical holds akin to consensual skill vs skill based practices, it's often useful to use generic and controlled 50/50 frameworks to explore the various ways one may employ tactics to create an advantage. Once better understood, these tactics can then be practiced in more 'untidy' conditions.

For the sake of this chapter, I've added below an example drill that I've extracted from the anti-grappling lessons found within the *Naihanchi Kata* choreography and includes a number of useful strategies for use when in clinch range. This is of course one of many and I encourage you to discover other ways in which these lessons may be employed.

From a conventional 50/50 clinch position, first attack the face and eyes whilst your leading arm forms a structural frame across the opponent's neck (funnel) using the *soto-uke* technique. Then bring your other arm to the inside, strike again and follow through to wrap around their arm. This is an application of the *ura-zuki* shape. Next, use the *morote-uke* technique as an arm drag to clear the limb and gain the outside line before striking.

A basic clinch drill that can be practiced to express some of the anti-grappling concepts from Naihanchi Kata that highlight positional advantage, detachment and the ability to break into the primary percussive strategy.

In summary and like all other methods covered so far, the essential counter-grappling skills from *Naihanchi Kata* are made up of a simplistic principle-based strategy and conveyed by a small number of effective physical templates that may be used in a variety of common scenarios. The objective is to detach and regain your primary percussive strategy. If this is not initially possible, then employ a generic frame to limit the enemy's attacking options and buy some valuable time to get to work using restricted-range skills.

Naturally, these lessons don't cover every eventuality, but that is not their aim. The core intention of *Naihanchi Kata* in terms of combative application is to provide a baseline methodology analogous to the *Pareto Principle* that developing a 20% (fundamental) skill-set will help deal with 80% of likely situations. Further development may be then gained through more progressive analysis.

CHAPTER XV

LESSON 9: FELLING OPTIONS

"Those who think that Karate only consists of kicks and punches, and that throws are only to be found in Judo or Ju-Jutsu, show a lack of understanding."

~ Kenwa Mabuni

If a potentially violent situation turns physical then we can presume that the best outcome would be for your opponent to be lying on the ground capitulated, whilst you remain standing in order to make good your escape. There happens to be a variety of felling techniques found in *karate kata* designed to achieve this conclusion with the minimum of fuss. The most simplistic and efficient of these would be to knock your opponent down to the ground with a single clinical strike or failing that, a fully committed barrage of shots. This would help lessen the risks associated with initiating a wrestling match due to unnecessary attachment. However, *karate* also employs a number of throws and takedowns as opportunistic alternatives and as expected, *Naihanchi Kata* is by no means deficient of these.

When most people think about felling/throwing techniques, they tend to visualise specialist arts like *Judo* or *Ju-Jutsu* and indeed, exponents of these throwing systems are without doubt some of the best in the world at driving someone to the ground. Nonetheless, from the perspective of self-protection, there are a number of distinctions that must be understood between these disciplines and the specific techniques found in *karate*. Especially, if the aim of such disciplines are heavily focused upon consensual engagements, where of course *koryu karate* is not.

Although cross-overs do exist, throwing for consensual combat and throwing for self-protection are based on two different viewpoints that require two different strategies. As such, the combative applications found in *karate kata* tend to be much less sophisticated than the more 'specialist' throwing arts, relying on secondary gross motor movements that emphasise the need for the thrower to remain standing in order to protect against the potential of third parties and to facilitate escape. Take a look at the table below, which aims to show some of the distinctions between the throws and takedowns found in *karate* with those of competitive Judo. Although not an exhaustive list, it nevertheless shows how even techniques that look very similar on the surface, may be trained in different ways to meet specific goals.

Throwing in karate for self-protection	Throwing in judo for competition
Considered a support method.	*Considered a principal method.*
A small percentage of time is devoted to skill development.	*A large percentage of time is devoted to skill development.*
Techniques designed for non-consensual engagements against one or multiple assailants.	*Techniques designed for one-on-one consensual engagements.*
Applied as techniques of opportunity, if the primary strategy falls short of the mark.	*Techniques actively sought and applied as primary strategy for success.*
Engagement still active after a successful throw is applied.	*Engagement usually ceases after a successful throw is applied.*
Thrower should attempt to remain standing to avoid the risks associated with ground fighting in self-protection.	*Thrower may choose to over-commit or sacrifice balance in order for throw to be successful.*
Due to context of application, throws are mostly designed with simplistic, gross motor movements in mind.	*Throws often require a high level of technical ability due to skilled vs skilled engagements with other expert throwers.*
Techniques are to be applied in a threatening and uncontrolled environment.	*Techniques are to be applied in a challenging, but risk controlled environment.*

Table comparing characteristics between throwing for consensual and non-consensual aims.

The choreography towards the end of *Naihanchi Kata* looks at a number of combative methodologies associated with felling the opponent using throws and takedowns, dealing with what is the closest and often most dangerous range in self-protection. Close because these applications require you to actively grab, push, pull or twist your antagonist. Dangerous because attached strategies such as these decrease the chances of making a clean escape, increase the time at close proximity to the threat and the chances of being taken to the floor, which should be avoided if at all possible. As alluded to earlier, the ideal felling strategy would be via percussive impact, but if circumstances present themselves, then a decisive throw or takedown may be used to great effect. After all, one is never going to be able to hit as hard as the floor!

If not mindful to the practical requirements for self-protection, the use of protective mats in martial art training halls (although vital for safe and effective practice) can often cultivate a false sense of security. As an example, break falls, rolls and indeed any form of ground fighting will feel completely different when executed on a mat than when executed on much less forgiving concrete. If your 'opponent' happens to accidently bounce their head off the ground in a fully matted venue then I guess it'll be a sharp reminder to keep their chin tucked in next time. If this occurs outside on the pavement then it may well become the site of a death scene. Additionally, many *dojo*-based applications will see the 'thrower' drop down onto one knee to help accentuate the technique. Again, if such a tactic is performed with potency on the street then you're probably looking at a smashed patella. Good luck trying to run away after that!

As we have seen throughout the choreography and sequence of the *kata* so far, the lessons in this chapter assume that you have either made enough errors (or have been taken off guard) to end up tangled with your opponent or that during the altercation, the possibility for a successful throw or takedown has become apparent. Again to re-iterate, felling an antagonist using a throw or takedown should be a tactic exploited through opportunity, rather than one actively sought due to the inherent risks involved. Before we start to look at what these opportunities may be, let's first spend some time to gain an understanding of what a throw or takedown requires for success.

As bipeds, a frame of support is formed by our footprint on the floor. This footprint has a strong axis and a weak axis at any given moment in time during motion. For instance, let's examine a traditional horse stance. If you assume this stance when pushed or pulled side to side, then you'll be relatively stable. However, if the push and pull occurred to the front or rear, then your ability to resist will be severely limited. So generally speaking, if you were to draw a line between each foot, then this would indicate the most stable axis for that particular stance. Conversely, perpendicular to that line would indicate the weakest axis.

A stronger base of support would be four legs, like a horse for example (quadruped). Imagine for instance a coffee table on a planar surface even with only leg removed and how instable it would be if only two were providing support. The difference between a human being and an inanimate object such as a chair is that we also utilise intelligent sensory processing to help maintain our balance on two legs. If this state of balance is compromised then we tend to respond by moving a leg (or legs) to re-establish our position. All throws and takedowns in *karate* essentially work by impeding the ability for the opponent to regain their stability. This principle is also how something as simple as a raised curb, trailing cable or slippery surface can offer a swift and often painful fall.

Zen Kutsu Dachi: Resistant against forces from front, but weak against forces from side.

Shiko Dachi: Resistance against forces from side, but weak against forces from front.

Felling techiques in karate essentially aim to create and exploit the weak axis of the enemy's base.

Every movement in *karate* and indeed human locomotion has its own inherent strengths and weaknesses at any point in time. In the case of self-protection, these lines of stability/instability will be in constant change with those hard-wired instincts to maintain equilibrium. This actually makes the clean application of throwing difficult to achieve in reality without the inherent risk of sacrificing your own steadiness. As an attached strategy, there is always the possibility that the throw may fail or that you may be grabbed by the opponent, even if out of sheer desperation to remain standing, thus both ending up horizontal. To help minimize these risks, there are a few considerations that we should always look to apply.

The old adage of 'blow before throw' makes perfect sense in self-protection, as percussive impact should always take priority and the opponent should ideally be in an imbalanced and subdued state before a throw is applied. In order to create the state of imbalance required for a throw or takedown, the general rule of thumb is to force the enemy's centre of gravity (COG - *tanden* or *hara*) beyond the stable axis of their footprint. In simple terms, you must ensure that their hips are breaching the fringe of that imaginary circle drawn around their feet. This may be achieved by actively pulling/pushing/twisting their torso, manipulating their base of support, and/or taking advantage of the enemy's mistakes.

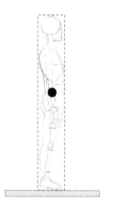 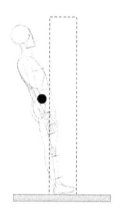 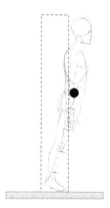

Stable posture showing base of support and centre of gravity.   *Falling back so that COG moves outside base of support.*   *Falling forward so that COG moves outside base of support.*

Breaking balance and making the most of mechanical advantage are essential principles in any kind of technique that aims to physically move the enemy's body, including joint attacks, throws and take downs. Mechanical advantage is where the load is close to the fulcrum and the effort is applied far from the fulcrum, allowing a small effort exerted over a relatively large distance to move a large load over a small distance. Conversely, mechanical disadvantage occurs when the load is far from the fulcrum and the effort is applied near the fulcrum. Here the effort applied must be greater than the load to be moved. An important aspect to consider is that we should never try to oppose strength with strength, as the stronger person will naturally always have the upper hand. But manipulating mechanical advantage can help increase our probability of success.

A rudimentary knowledge of lever systems also helps towards understanding the successful application of a throw or takedown technique. Each of the three classes of lever alters the position of effort, load and fulcrum to various effects. Class one and class two levers can produce a positive mechanical advantage greater than one – examples include a seesaw and crowbar (class one), bottle opener and wheelbarrow (class two). Class three levers can only produce a mechanical advantage less than one, such as a pair of tweezers. So in throws and take downs we aim to apply class one and class two levers incorporating as much mechanical advantage as possible.

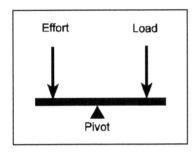
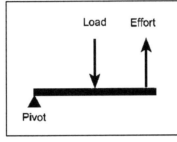
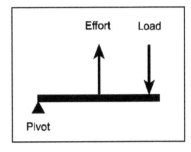

First Class Lever   *Second Class Lever*   *Third Class Lever*

All of the felling applications in *Naihanchi Kata* make use of the principles explained above. They focus on manipulating the enemy's centre of gravity away from their line of stability, impeding the ability for their base of support to be reaffirmed or destroying their base of support altogether. All of the applications assume that the opponent has already been struck or weakened to some degree and require the thrower to remain standing. A well-executed throw or takedown can of course end the altercation there and then. Poorly applied however and/or without the appropriate conditions first being met and you could be mixing a potent recipe for disaster.

I believe that the choreography of *Naihanchi Kata* inherently acknowledges the risks associated with felling techniques. Indicating the extreme close-range and attached nature of such tactics, most of these lessons tend to be expressed towards the end of the form's choreography. However, there are a couple that are highlighted towards the start of the choreography, as they provide a natural conclusion to both the primary percussive and reactive strategies. We will take a look at these first before moving on to movements featured at the concluding section of the form.

Application Concept 09/01 – Striking the Enemy Down

I've added this application concept to reiterate the fact that throws and takedowns will not be required if your primary percussive impact strategy is successful. It is very difficult to maintain an upright posture against a barrage of powerful and well-placed strikes. If applied well then the opponent is likely to either collapse or at the very least turn away from the source of impact, cover up and drop into a semi-foetal position. From here, you can rag them to the ground completely and attack the legs to hamper mobility before making good your escape.

The most 'clinical' way of felling the enemy is to strike them down.

As a side note, the stamping techniques within *Naihanchi Kata* may be seen more clearly in styles such as *Shotokan*, which have exaggerated the performance of the form somewhat to include deeper stances, longer steps and larger leg lifts. In application, it would be more prudent to attack a felled opponent with your feet than reaching down to attack with your hands. This tactic is covered numerous times within the form, indicating its valuable use.

Although essentially a primary percussive tactic, it would of course be foolhardy to expect this application concept to work in every case. For instance, the opponent may just have enough composure to stifle your strikes and instinctively dive toward you hard in an attempt to overbalance you. In this case, it's also important to know what to do in order to protect against common street-based felling techniques such as tackles, head locks with drags, bear hugs with dumps plus chokes and pulls from behind. Simply put, if you're unable to maintain your centre of gravity over your footprint of support then I'm afraid any further resistance is futile - you're going to go down. The best tactic then would be to brace for your inevitable landing and get to work on the ground. You may try to use your assailant's energy against them, aim to land on top and have swift tactics for getting back up to your feet as soon as is humanly possible.

So other than the usual complications that are expected to crop up during self-protection, the beat down represents a natural continuation of the primary percussive impact strategy and therefore, is probably the most effective way of concluding the altercation there and then. It's certainly not nice or aesthetically pleasing to the eye, but it is nevertheless very functional.

Application Concept 09/02 – The Snatch Takedown

Already covered earlier on in the form during the opening movements, the snatch takedown is also repeated during the closing salutation and can also be performed as a head manipulation to the rear of the opponent by seizing underneath the enemy's chin.

Covered originally as a useful conclusion to our default reactive strategy, this felling principle can also be used following our primary strategy in order to help the assailant on their way to the earth. It is entirely centred on rather crude 'cave-man' style movements and gross motor dynamics, which makes it perfect for self-protection.

The snatch takedown is so simple and effective that variations of the technique may be found across all martial arts and it is also considered a fundamental skill of wrestling systems such as *Greco-Roman*. A key requirement to make the snatch effective is to first ensure that the enemy's head and hips are out of vertical alignment. Therefore, causing the opponent to crunch up and cover, or to pre-empt with a low line strike will work perfectly to achieve this pike-style position. Then it's just a case of 'snatching' your assailant forcefully forward and towards the floor using *hikite* dynamics, whilst simultaneously allowing them space to fall by lunging back with your leg(s). You can also shift quickly to either side of the opponent or behind in order to gain better positioning and further disorientate. If your back is against a wall, then you can use the mechanics of the snatch to make best use of the environment as a weapon of opportunity.

The snatch takedown is best applied from the double neck tie clinch given at the start of the form.

The essence of the snatch takedown expresses exactly what an effective self-protection based felling application is all about…driving your antagonist to the floor ideally face down as swiftly as possible in order to assert control and facilitate your escape. Depending on the severity of the situation, the added bonus of this takedown also allows you to exercise a level of control over the enemy's head to ensure that they don't bite the concrete or crack their head open, causing post conflict complications and consequential legal actions.

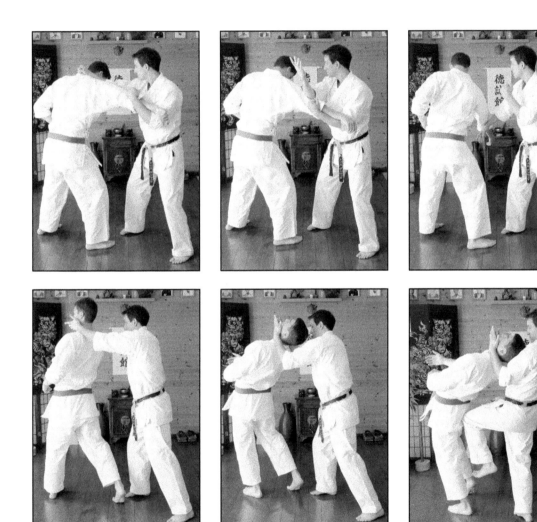

A similar idea from the end of the form (closing salutation) may be applied when behind the opponent.

The idea of snatching the assailants head may also be utilised from the front or side clinch frame as expressed in the *kata*, by using more rotational force to drive them off balance and either towards the ground or to facilitate other options.

All in all, the snatch takedown is a very versatile technique and just as every other principle-based lesson from *Naihanchi Kata*, lends itself to a multitude of application scenarios.

Two options for using the snatch from a side clinch frame.

Application Concept 09/03 – Manipulating the Head

There's an old martial arts saying that states *"where the head goes, the body will follow"*. This can be taken both in a mental sense (i.e. what you think, so shall you become) and a literal sense in that by physically controlling the enemy's head, you can also control their whole structure. The head twist takedown makes use of this concept and is another very effective way of felling an assailant with minimum fuss. It can follow on seamlessly from the primary percussive strategy and also be used to great effect within a flinch-based response to attack.

Since all impetus is governed by the brain (the central computer system), attacking the head is considered the prime target, whether striking or manoeuvring. As well as the physical control gained from twisting the head, a swift and percussive application will also have a significant disorientating effect, not to mention create the onset of panic and a real sense of vulnerability. These aspects combined with such natural and functional movements makes the principle of manipulating the head very appealing in self-protection.

Stacking the limbs towards the body and subsequent 'unravelling' feeling associated with the concluding movements of the form express the key attributes required to make a head turn throw or takedown successful. It is also best to turn the head in more than one plane to help make it even more difficult to resist. If instigated by the body, rather than the hands alone, then it becomes pretty much impossible for the small muscles around the neck to cope with the turning forces applied. It is also good practice to use the assailant's shoulder (where possible) to act as a base and pivot point for the application to operate.

The retracting motion and subsequent throwing out action of the limb in this sequence of the form may be regarded as a conceptual lesson on manipulating the assailant's head. In application, this can be a very effecive way of achieving 'them-down-now'!

Having physical hold of the enemy's head also provides the opportunity to ensure that their fall isn't life-threatening. Once the initial impact has been taken by the body, the head can either be released, pressed into the ground or cradled (indexed) for further strikes before making good your escape. Of course, this all depends on the specific situation and whether weapons or multiple assailants may be present. In short, the head twist takedown is both simple and effective.

Application Concept 09/04 – Overbalancing

Overbalancing occurs when the body's equilibrium is disrupted, either by causing the enemy's upper body to move past the base created by their feet, or by moving their base away from their upper body. Most felling techniques tend to use the concept of overbalancing to some degree, but there are applications that emphasise this concept.

There are a number of simple but effective felling techniques from the latter movements of the *Naihanchi Kata* choreography that use the concept of either impeding or manipulating the assailant's legs in order to compromise their base and with force applied to the upper body, cause a state of overbalance. These include basic leg sweeps and reaping throw variations.

The *nami-gaeshi* 'kicks' followed by arm swings both to the left and right are indicative of overbalancing techniques from within an attached clinch. These movements are done in both directions and with both sides of the body (1st and 2nd halves of the form) to represent the ambidextrous nature and requirements of these applications.

Using body rotation along with the nami-gaeshi kick and/or striking to overbalance the assailant.

Another two options for overbalancing from the Naihanchi Kata choreography.

Application Concept 09/05 – Throwing

Using the legs and hips to throw requires more skill and because of this, carries more risk. Actively turning your back to your opponent is not optimal when applied within the realm of non-consensual violence as there's just so much that can go wrong. However, it does have place should the opportunity present itself, either via your positioning or the positioning of your antagonist, especially if they are already in an unbalanced state. Throwing applications do appear throughout many of the classical *kata* and for *karate* as a holistic system, they should be given sufficient attention. As you would expect, *Naihanchi Kata* presents a fundamental option to consider.

Using the stance and rotational aspects of the kata to apply a throw using sequential action of legs, hips and arms.

BUNKAI SANDAN

Breaking the Mould

CHAPTER XVI

MOULD...WHAT MOULD?

"It is not the number of kata you know, but the substance of the kata you have acquired."

~ Gogen Yamaguchi

Our study of *Naihanchi Kata* so far has taken us on a journey into its key structural and dynamic *components* (*Bunkai Shodan*), followed by a contextual exploration of its choreography in order to provide a fundamental principle-based methodology to protect against the threat of civilian violence (*Bunkai Nidan*). The next stage in our analysis is to use the solid foundation gained to apply what we have learned in a more free-flowing and adaptable way. Not only will this provide more depth and meaning to our study, but it also relaxes the proverbial reigns that many *karate-ka* often hold excessively (and unnecessarily) taut, opens our eyes to other distinct possibilities and potentially reveal new doors to open that may have previously been hidden from view.

In Japanese martial arts there is a formula often used to express the progression of a student from beginner to master – *Shu Ha Ri* (守 破 離). Most *karate-ka* should be familiar with these three *kanji* and those who are will know that they do not only apply to martial arts, but also to almost every other developmental aspect of human life. It is also a principle that may be applied to the analysis of *karate kata*.

Back in 2012, my students and I were fortunate to take part in a private training seminar with the late *Isamu Arakaki Sensei* at his home *dojo*. I had already met him a couple of years earlier, so I was more than eager to practice *karate* with him again. As well as being able to significantly enhance my structure and power with seemingly minute adjustments (almost like magic), he also expertly displayed for us how most *karate* techniques have their roots firmly planted within the *Naihanchi Kata* choreography.

He was kind enough to invite us for food and drinks at his home that evening, where we were also able to enjoy chatting about *karate* with a number of prominent teachers from different styles. Despite only spending a short time with *Arakaki Sensei*, he nevertheless left a lasting impression on me and his teachings have had a huge impact on the way I've looked at martial arts since. Sadly, it was only a matter of weeks after returning to the UK that I received news of his passing, which only makes me further cherish the time spent in his company and wonder whether the old saying that 'once a student is ready to learn then the right teacher will appear' was in operation that day.

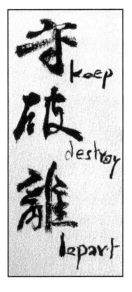

keep
destroy
depart

After training, I asked *Arakaki Sensei* to sign my note book, which I always have with me in Okinawa. He took my book, mumbled something in *Japanese* and then proceeded to walk out of the *dojo*! I wasn't sure if I'd not asked correctly or even offended him somehow – we all just stood there in silence looking at one another. After a few minutes, *Sensei* returned with a calligraphy brush and ink pot, sat down on the floor with my book, signed his name and then wrote the *kanji* for *Shu-Ha-Ri*. Of course, I'd seen these characters many times before, but what was more interesting were the *English* translations he chose to write beside them – *Keep*, *Destroy*, and *Depart*. I'd never thought to attach those specific words to these characters before (normally *Obey, Detach* and *Separate*) and indeed, listening to *Sensei's* descriptions to follow opened my mind to a more thorough understanding. Below is a summary of my own understanding of Arakaki Sensei's message.

In all quests for development, we must first act as 'keeper' to the specific form used to teach us the way without any deviation. Since without form, there can be no structure or shape for the essential principles to be transmitted. However, remaining an avid protector of form purely for the sake of antiquity will progress you little further from that which lies on the surface. In order to go beyond this first stage of learning, we must proceed to 'destroy' the specific form used to teach us with an investigative mind and comparable to the aftermath of an explosion, pick up and analyse each piece of shrapnel you've created for a deeper understanding. Finally, you should aspire to 'depart' from the form altogether in order to transcend towards a more personal identity and expression.

A caterpillar is protected within its chrysalis and undergoes a remarkable metamorphosis. Once this transforming shell has had its use, the butterfly breaks free and leaves to express her new form of life. Although now on the surface looking nothing like a caterpillar, the DNA of her original caterpillar form is forever within. Nature displays the process of *Shu-Ha-Ri* very well and I believe that this universal blueprint for development should be mindfully applied to the process of *karate kata*, so that those who practice it may learn form, break form and then eventually, transcend form. *Bunkai Sandan* is the level of analysis whereby we may begin to explore this transformational process.

I like to use the term 'breaking the mould' to describe the two ways in which I approach *Bunkai Sandan*. Firstly to break the mould created by the specific *kata* choreography and secondly, to break the mould created by one's own former analysis. Although this may seem to be a stark contradiction of previous work, it should be taken more as an acceptance that the physical limitations of the choreography, although helpful in order to express a conceptual framework, become more of a hindrance in our efforts to enrich our holistic understanding of *karate* through the process of *kata*. In this way, even one *kata* may indeed be used as a platform for a lifetime's study.

Due to the nature of *Bunkai Sandan* and the fact that it portrays more long-term exploration, it would be impossible to present the whole process within the pages of a full collection of books, let alone this single volume. However, what I have opted to do is provide some useful models that may be followed, adapted and expanded upon according to each reader's particular area of interest.

Firstly, I'd like to make use of the principles gained through *Bunkai Nidan* to explore some ways in which the lessons from *Naihanchi Kata* may be used away from the baseline model of standing upright empty-handed with a single adversary. As such, we will explore three other important realities to consider in self-protection – on the ground, multiple and weapon attack. We will also take a brief look at the tertiary physical strategy from our core self-protection game plan, discuss where such skills sit in karate and where they may be used to enhance the fundamental framework of *Naihanchi Kata*.

Next, I'd like to look at the process of seamlessly transitioning between different combative methodologies as given by *Bunkai Nidan*, away from the set choreography and as specific situations may demand. Rather than becoming a 'slave to the *kata*', this serves to break beyond the prescribed order of techniques so that your application may become freely adaptable to a wide variety of common self-protection based scenarios. This is essentially the culmination of learning and subsequent application of the principle-based framework developed within previous chapters.

Following the above, I would then like to draw attention to the concepts of 'depth' and 'breadth' in terms of more progressive combative analysis. Depth will be illustrated by taking only one or two movements from *Naihanchi Kata* and then exploring them across all potential combative ranges. In contrast, breadth will be explained by taking a single combative aspect and then applying this to the whole choreography. Once a fundamental contextual-based framework is derived from *Bunkai Nidan*, this next level serves to open your mind to other potential possibilities. This is important since of course, no one can claim a definitive answer.

Finally, I will touch upon how the movements given by the *Naihanchi Kata* choreography may be studied in a deeper sense in a way to directly connect and support application principles from other *karate kata*. Where Vol.1 proposed this idea for core structure and dynamics, I would now like to expand this in terms of functionality in application, as opposed to aesthetics, which is where much of contemporary *kata* performance now tends to sit. Seeking such a relationship between *Naihanchi Kata* and other classical forms within one's style can really help to bring to the surface *karate's* essential blueprint, regardless of the particular system practiced.

The principal aim of *Bunkai Sandan* is to develop a sense of realisation that once the fundamental methodologies have been studied, we must refrain from becoming restricted by the form's physical and inherently limiting template. Of course, the choreography initially serves a very valuable purpose, but only during the most superficial levels of study. The non-scripted and chaotic nature of civilian self-protection alone demands that we must transcend any adherence to 'formality' and learn to extract what is necessary to deal with complex and ever-changing environments. Similarly, the non-scripted and chaotic nature of life requires us to exist and thrive with comparable adaptability. In this sense, *karate* uses the *conduit of combat* as a representation to express a deeper meaning towards daily improvement.

From a combative sense, *Bunkai Sandan* starts us off on the path of adaptation, whilst still maintaining a level of compliancy from one's training partner, so that the development of specific skill-sets may be encouraged and honed. Rather than a chaotic 'free for all', a more mutual understanding of partner interaction for training purposes, which aims to help isolate and repeat certain application concepts from the *kata*. With consistent practice, the skills developed in *Bunkai Sandan* may then be taken into *Bunkai Yondan* where compliancy is gradually lessened to help develop more realistic development. This aspect of training will be covered in *Volume Three*, along with a range of supplementary training methods (*Bunkai Godan*) to support associated attribute development.

Accumulating discrete applications like an avid collector, or less mindfully seeking variances and new ways of doing things just for the sake of it will only hinder progress and unfortunately, this is where many *karate* practitioners who study 'the meaning of *kata*' tend to remain. Instead, you should take it upon yourself to delve further below the surface of *kata* and attempt to 'join the dots' in numerous ways. Then take sanctuary within the realm of commonality and make your exploration about seeking those mutual connections that bind the art of *karate* together, rather than those superficial aspects that are often considered to (artificially) separate us. It is through these principle-based relationships of movement pathways that we come to find how *Naihanchi Kata* may provide such a fascinating source of progressive development.

CHAPTER XVII

ON THE GROUND, MULTIPLES & WEAPONS

"Karate is a martial art that completely and freely uses the entire body, objects to hand, and a person's surroundings."

~ Morinobu Itoman

Three possibilities during a violent encounter that are often insufficiently acknowledged in modern-day *karate*, but yet are of serious concern are: - (1) you end up on the ground, (2) you are forced to deal with more than one individual or (3) there are weapons involved. An omission of these in contemporary *dojo* (especially where emphasis is given to a single unarmed adversary at long range) can cause a 'disconnect' to what may be considered real-world self-protection, where of course situation dictates action. At times, this has led to discerning practitioners venturing outside their current curriculum and attempting to 'fill the gaps' by borrowing techniques from other more seemingly practical systems.

Arts such as traditional *Judo, Brazilian Jiu-Jitsu* and their evolution into modern *Mixed Martial Arts,* focus on developing exponents that are very comfortable with their ground-game. However, these systems often focus heavily on consensual bouts under rule-bound contests against other skilled martial artists and with similar goals in mind. Again, as we've already discussed, this is not to say that consensual-based applications may not be useful in self-protection (many are in fact very effective), but rather that the context of such training can sometimes be at odds with non-consensual violence and indeed, *koryu karate*. Of course, borrowing from other arts to enhance and evolve your own individual approach is certainly nothing new and is one of the critical mechanisms by which both personal growth and further advancement of 'art' occurs. However, an upshot for the uninformed or non-savvy 'borrower' may be a dis-jointed hybrid with disparate principles and inherently mixed perspectives.

It is my opinion that in order to facilitate our core self-protection game plan and deal with the most common habitual acts of violence, there's no real requirement to look outside *karate*, nor even *Naihanchi Kata* for the most part, if our study in the *dojo* is principle-based and contextually driven. It's always useful to explore other martial arts for inspiration or to gain insight and additional skill in a particular aspect (or aspects) of traditional *karate*, in fact I recommend it, but I don't feel it's essential.

Let me explain further. Whilst I may not conform to the idea that *Naihanchi Kata* has been specifically designed to be applied directly on the ground, against multiples or weapons (any more than I believe it was originally intended for fighting people in a straight line or on a long thin boat), I do acknowledge the fact that the principle-based lessons given within the choreography possess a number of very valuable cross-overs. Furthermore, it makes sense that the fundamental tactics and characteristics used in effective self-protection are broad enough to cover a variety of potential situations. Especially those that constitute real statistically backed threats, rather than overly complex and heavily choreographed unrealistic routines that are often mislabelled as being 'practical'.

When training for self-protection, it always pays to assume that the fight may well go to the ground, you may be outnumbered and/or be forced to face a weapon. Why are these real possibilities? Well that's simple. Cowards and scum bags rarely work alone, footing can easily be compromised during chaos in uncontrolled/unfamiliar environments and weapons provide attackers with a huge advantage. You can simply take a look at the vast amount of security camera footage on the Internet from all over the globe to see the realities of violence in all its gruesome glory. So even if you can't confirm the existence of an accomplice or weapon, it's always much better to have prepared for that possibility. As I'm sure you'll agree, lying on the pavement being stabbed 'sewing-machine style' by a knife wielding maniac with his two friends (who you didn't see) now playing football with your skull won't exactly make the most enjoyable end to your day.

Naturally, this single chapter is far from sufficient enough to offer a comprehensive analysis of how to deal with such dangers. Rather, it has been included to show how in contrast to superficial technique-based analysis, a broader principle-based approach to *kata* application may be better utilised to offer more wide-spread means of protection. So with the above in mind, let's take look at how some of the conceptual lessons we've already covered within *Naihanchi Kata* may be adapted to suit potential risks associated with ground, multiples and weapons. Like all other aspects of self-protection, absolutely nothing is guaranteed, but stacking the deck before you 'play' is always more favourable than being forced to fold your hand mid-game.

On The Ground

Ever since *MMA* burst on to the scene in the early 1990's, it became quickly apparent that having a strong ground-game can offer a considerable combat advantage. Accomplished strikers were instantly transformed into complete beginners at the hands of those skilled enough to take the fight to the floor. Fast forward to today and ground fighting in its many forms is now considered so mainstream across the globe that even your regular 'arm chair warrior' will know some techniques simply from regular exposure to *UFC* style matches on the television. We now have pretty much an entire generation of people who have grew up with *MMA* as a conventional combative sport so it's more likely than ever that the adversary you face in a self-protection scenario will at the very least be able to pull out a couple of surprise tricks from their sleeve.

The early emphasis on horizontal grappling for effective self-protection was justified by the supposed statistic that 'nine out of ten violent street encounters end up on the ground', which at the time had the instant effect of linking competitions like *UFC* to 'real fighting'. Personally, I have huge respect and admiration for anyone who makes it a priority in their lives to train, prepare and compete in the cage. It takes a colossal amount of skill across a wide spectrum of areas, first-class athleticism, and unparalleled dedication…not to mention a huge amount of heart! However, even though *MMA* is probably one of the most (if not the most) demanding activities on the planet, it is still based on consensual rule-bound engagements and so we have to be careful when trying to make a relationship with non-consensual self-protection.

The '9 out of 10' statistic that swept through the martial arts community and what provided a very convenient marketing slogan for the effectiveness of ground-based systems such as *Brazilian Jiu-Jitsu,* seems to have been derived from either an exaggeration or misinterpretation of a study and subsequent report conducted for the *LAPD*, which looked at data from use of force reports. It concluded that 62% of incidents ended up with someone (criminal, police officer or both) on the ground.

First of all, 62% is a far cry from the 9 out of 10 statistic. Secondly, we have to bear in mind specific context. A police officer arrest will usually end up with the perpetrator on the floor being restrained and handcuffed. This skews the figures somewhat and therefore cannot be likened to civilian self-protection where the emphasis is on escape. Furthermore, although the 90% claim may well support *MMA* style matches where ground grappling is more common, it would still be wrong to compare this directly to civilian encounters. To cut a long story short, we need to consider the 90% claim as being somewhat erroneous in terms of non-consensual conflict.

Is hitting the ground a real possibility in self-protection? Yes, of course it is. But what is the probability? Well I suppose that all depends on situation, scenario and skill. For someone who has very good stand up skills, can hit swift and hard, has solid control capability at clinch-range, is working from a flat and comfortable environment and has full awareness of the potential threat, then there may only be a small probability of ending up on the ground. In contrast, for someone who has little capability, under the influence of alcohol and is caught off-guard whilst stood on a urine ridden night club toilet floor, then there is naturally going to be much more likelihood of that person hitting the deck.

As another example, going to the ground in a knife hold-up situation would certainly not be desirable for an attacker who's looking for an easy target, some quick cash and a clean getaway. However for a twenty-stone rapist who's chosen to prey on an unsuspecting eight stone college girl in a dark and secluded car park, forcing his victim to the ground would no doubt work to his advantage.

So what does the above mean in terms of civilian self-protection as a 'whole' and the art of *karate* as a means to provide effective skills to meet this aim? Well, although we should not mindlessly overemphasise the likelihood of being forced to fight on the ground, it is equally important to acknowledge the fact that the unpredictable nature of a violent encounter means that we must also be prepared for the possibility of hitting the floor.

For me, I feel that *koryu karate* understands and aligns to this way of thinking very well. Whilst the curriculum is heavily based on developing a solid primary strategy based around percussive impact, it does not forget to teach the ability to control limbs and make use of counter-grappling strategies at clinch-range to help keep you away from the ground if at all possible. Then if the worst should happen, it also provides auxiliary skills for ground fighting, albeit comparatively rudimentary when compared to specialist grappling arts (and rightly so).

Thus, the aim of ground fighting in traditional *karate* is not to seek submission, but instead to stand up as quickly as possible in order to regain the ability to deliver strong percussive impact and facilitate escape. Unlike two skilled assailants in *MMA* competition, ground fighting in self-protection should be less like a game of *Chess* and more like a game of *Speed*. With the added risk of weapons, multiple assailants and all kinds of nasties that may be lurking on the floor, the less time we spend down there the better.

You may well be very happy and comfortable rolling around with a partner for twenty minutes on the *dojo* mats, but you'll find that the presence of concrete, kerbstones, broken glass and animal excrement will have a habit of quickly changing your attitude. Add to that the adrenal rush and energy sapping intensity of a self-protection based grapple and it no longer resembles anything like the match-style wrestling as seen on television. Tapping out is simply not an option and there'll be no referee to help assure any level of safety.

So the three potential dangers of *environment*, *weapons* and *multiples* makes the chief aim of ground fighting in *karate* to assume a dominant position for control so that you may regain your feet. This 'control' should be in the form of inflicting trauma such that you can break free, stand up and escape before the situation gets any worse. Forget technical arm bars and complicated chokes. Instead opt for gouging, twisting, fish-hooking, biting, small surface strikes plus using walls and the floor as impact weapons.

Techniques tend to be banned in combat sport for two principal reasons. Firstly, because they can cause a high probability of significant injury and secondly, because utilising them would end the match for participants and paying spectators very quickly. Can you imagine how long a ground-game would last in UFC if eye gouges, fish hooks and bites were allowed and what the outcome would be for that matter? So generally anything that's on the 'banned list' in combat sport is often very effective for self-protection and it's no accident that such techniques can be found in civilian-based martial arts such as traditional *karate*.

Although the use of more 'anti-social' techniques may provide an instant and welcome advantage in extreme circumstances, they are not (as some self-protection teachers may have you believe) the holy grail of 'ground-based street combat' and should be employed to help supplement an overall strategy for dominance. A strategy that should also include developing a sufficient gross-motor technical skill-set for dealing with ground-based assault. Those who think that biting and gouging may somehow negate the requirement for ground skills have either little experience in this range or are not recognising the 'copycat' dynamic that can often play out in adrenaline fuelled physical altercations. Remember that if you can bite your opponent, then given the opportunity, your opponent may also bite you back! So before attempting to apply such tactics and passing on any bright ideas, you must be sure to have gained competence in techniques for a successive escape.

An aspect that is important to understand and consider when wrestling on the ground is where power comes from and being as efficient as possible with your efforts. It's one thing to move around with someone standing up, but a whole different ball game when gravity is working against you and being forced to face a significant weight disparity. Use the floor to your advantage where possible and be mindful that every second you spend 'riding the waves' is sapping valuable time/energy. Where holding someone strategically in a closed guard whilst you work through a series of technical options may be a winning tactic on the mat, it is of little use if your opponent thinks to reach inside his pocket for a weapon, picks up a piece of loose rubble or signals his friends to help out.

The principal ground fighting skills in self-protection based *karate* involve numerous essential methods. These include framing to defend against common takedown attempts or to gain valuable space, using the environment to your advantage, fighting a standing opponent whilst on the floor, striking from the ground, and escaping pins by employing techniques such as seizing, biting, gouging, tearing and twisting to help facilitate dominance and regain your feet as quickly as possible. So based on the above, let's look at a small selection of examples that show how we may adapt a selection of lessons found within the choreography of *Naihanchi Kata* for use on the ground.

Default Reactionary Tactics

Adapted reactionary tactics from Naihanchi Kata offer a default position when mounted to help protect head, keep opponent loaded on hips and allows elbows to be used as weapons.

Adapting two-handed neck tie and head push escape from the reactionary tactics in Naihanchi Kata.

One of the worst situations to end up in on the ground is with your enemy on top, either between your legs or mounted. Based on the fact that you've probably impacted hard against an unforgiving surface, you now have to work ferociously in order to gain a dominant position, control the threat, regain your feet and flee to safety. The conceptual lesson from *Naihanchi Kata* on reactionary tactics coupled with pseudo stance formations (i.e. active use of legs) may be used to effect a useful default position in order to cover up, buy valuable time and launch a counter response.

Framing

Using the clinch frame from Naihanchi Kata to help defend against an attempted tackle.

Just as we've explored the concept of framing being useful in reactionary tactics and vertical grappling scenarios, it can also be used to great effect when defending against takedowns or indeed, escaping a horizontal position. Thus, the fundamental clinch-frame shape found within *Naihanchi Kata* has a multitude of applications, all centred on the same core principles as previously discussed.

In the first example, framing is incorporated with a semi-sprawl and used to defend against an attempted tackle. By combining upper body and leg movement to ensure a strong base, then using the forearm as a structural wedge and to deliver a solid incidental shot to the neck area, you can provide a better possibility of fouling your enemy's attempt, whilst you position yourself outside their envelope of strength. From here, you can follow up by using your enemy's position/energy to either drive then towards the ground, or to angle off and strike etc.

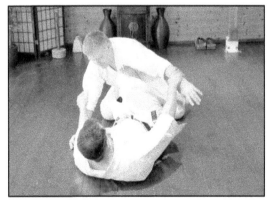 

Using the clinch frame from Naihanchi Kata to help maintain space whilst escaping from a side pin.

The second example looks at the use of framing to create or maintain space in order to break free from a side pin. Again, the arms are used as barriers so that you can move underneath them. This is essentially the same concept as in a vertical scuffle, but the main aim is now to get back to your feet, facilitate strikes and/or apply pressure such that you can escape.

A closer look at the clinch frame, where the arms and leg are used to wedge against the opponent's neck and hip. This provides a strong structural base in order to create the critical distance required to attempt an escape.

Meotode

As we already know, *meotode* is extremely effective at close-range, so it should come as no surprise that the same concept can also be used to great effect in grappling situations. The simultaneous push/pull mechanic may be employed to strike, twist, tear and manipulate target areas, spin and flip. The non-striking limb may also be used to index and control the head or clear limbs in order to open up strike paths, just as if you were standing.

Even using a simple *tsuki* dynamic against the enemy's leg can provide a useful equaliser if downed, or affect a devastating ankle/knee joint attack. As you can see, the example below uses the hands, but you could also use the elbow, shoulder or legs too.

Some examaples of how the principle of tsuki and hikite may be applied in a ground fighting context.

Using the Environment

Use of the environment around you is a significant consideration that runs throughout the whole physical self-protection game plan and especially so when ground fighting. Here, the environment may be used to your advantage (as a weapon of opportunity for example) or on the other hand it could quite literally become your downfall.

Albeit in extreme cases only, the ground may be used to maximise percussive impact delivery. With nowhere to go, all the energy is absorbed by the target.

Whilst not nice to consider and undoubtedly sitting at the most extreme end of the scale, driving parts of your enemy's anatomy into the ground or an adjacent wall may be the only option in order to provide the opportunity you need to escape a life-threatening situation. Additionally, a target restrained against a hard immovable object cannot 'soften oncoming blows' by moving away from the impact. Instead, the hard surface can provide a means to anchor the target and cause more damage by having the target absorb a greater amount of energy. Again, we can adapt applications from *Naihanchi Kata* to make use of the environment when fighting on the ground.

Dealing with Multiples

Dealing with multiple assailants is a big issue. Although Hollywood may have made five to one conflicts seem a piece of cake and provide instant hero status, in reality we have to acknowledge the fact that any more than one opponent is extremely dangerous no matter how skilled you happen to be. Any more than two assailants and the odds of getting home in one piece are going to be pretty bad. Add to this a weapon and/or a ground struggle and it could very well become the worst (and possibly last) day of your life.

I have a friend who was set on outside his home by four unruly kids half his size and half his age, just for interrupting their senseless attempt to damage his car. He spent the next few days in hospital drinking through a straw, the following six months in rehabilitation and even longer battling to cope with the fear of setting foot outside his own door.

Attackers will tend to work in packs as it's the safest option for them, especially if the attack is secondary to gaining a resource such as your cash, car or jewellery etc. Physical clashes with the sole intent to cause harm are no different and it is not uncommon for third parties to get involved simply because they can. An antagonists' wife armed with a broken wine glass, heels and a strong dose of resentment can become a weapon wielding nightmare. Plus you can pretty much guarantee that in social environments, friends you didn't even see will tend to show up and enthusiastically 'put the boot in' at the most unfortunate time. Even complete strangers walking past can get involved and quickly become your worst enemy believing you to be the aggressor, or for no apparent reason other than the fact that you may happen to provide some testosterone fuelled entertainment. Such is the harsh reality of human nature and unfortunate realism of the world we live in.

A single adversary who (for whatever reason) simply wants to beat on you, will in most cases already have their 'story' firmly planted in mind - a story which inevitably ends with your demise. However, if you turn out to be an entirely different animal to what they originally predicted then they may also have a 'wing-man' as peripheral back-up ready and willing to finish the job. Premeditated assaults are likely to involve more than one attacker, so whatever the situation may be and however it happens to materialize, you should always assume the possibility of multiple assailants.

So how can we best act to help protect against multiple assailants? Well firstly, the core strategies of 'awareness & avoidance', 'fighting to escape', 'pre-emption' and 'use of percussive impact' still stand true regardless of the situation. Not avoiding when you could, staying any longer than you need to or attaching to an opponent unnecessarily would be foolhardy decisions to make. Third parties don't wait their turn like they do in the movies or on the demonstration mat. They take only a split second to orientate, decide and act. Thus, speed and mobility is key, so any tactic that stifles your ability to exert these characteristics should be promptly abandoned.

Although actively seeking to take physical control of one adversary may be advantageous in certain situations in order to temporarily inhibit the actions of a third party, you should always aim to swiftly break any form of physical attachment forced upon you. The aim of any grappling scenario in self-protection should primarily be to disengage swiftly so that mobility and the facility to strike unrestricted may be exploited where possible. Fixating your attention on a single adversary leaves you vulnerable to attack from another and you can pretty much guarantee that this potential weakness will be exploited wherever possible. Therefore, the idea of taking control of the 'situation', rather than an 'individual' is crucial in self-protection and becomes even more relevant when in the presence of multiple assailants.

By taking a closer look at the conceptual lessons expressed in *Naihanchi Kata* we can extract some very useful tactics for dealing with the threat of multiple assailants. Let's take a look at some examples.

Positional Advantage

As we've established, delivering percussive impact in collaboration with good mobility is a must have skill when it comes to multiple assailants, as we can't afford to be tied up in a time-consuming wrestling match. So the principle of 'stun and run' makes lots of sense. However, before all of this happens, an emphasis on the skills surrounding peripheral awareness must take precedence. Even just acknowledging the fact that multiple assailants are possible should prompt an anticipatory effort to consider how best to gain positional advantage through situational control.

For instance, if walking along the street and a stranger approaches you from the front to engage in dialogue then it would make sense to use the conceptual lesson of embusen in a proactive way to re-orientate to a position that would allow you to see the wider environment around (and ideally behind) you. The classic 'pincer movement' is used to great effect by attackers because the victim's brain is 'engaged' by one, whilst their blind spot is 'capitalized on' by another. Thus, a natural-looking shift of positional angle hidden with dialogue may just be enough to discourage this type of assault from happening in the first place. If not, then at the very least you'll stand a better chance of seeing it coming and protecting yourself if things turn physical.

Aligning Adversaries

Moving one opponent to create a temporary shield using lessons from the opening salutation and applying the concept of embusen.

Another important aspect to consider when facing multiple assailants may be extracted from the specific lessons given by *Naihanchi Kata* on the envelope of strength, power triangle and subsequent positional dominance. In the case of having to deal with two assailants, the ideal would be to engage one followed by the other, rather than engaging both together. We can look to achieve this by lining up multiple adversaries to offer a valuable window of opportunity and subsequently, a better chance of success. For example, the 90 degree angle given in *Naihanchi Kata* may be applied by pre-emptively

234

shifting to the side of one opponent before striking them so that the second opponent must not only re-orient (*OODA Loop*), but also physically negotiate around the first before being able to meaningfully participate. This would be more advantageous than launching a pre-emptive assault 'square on', which may be returned with quick retaliation by both assailants, forcing you into a two-on-one situation.

As well as moving our own body to facilitate a better position, we can also move the enemy's body to provide the same temporary shield. As explained earlier in the book, during the reverse engineering process of *kata* movements we have to consider the fact that the application of *embusen* may be obtained in a variety of ways, since the actual interaction of person-to-person conflict cannot be accurately recorded within a solo representation. So, we may choose to actively seize hold, control and shift one opponent to a position that again makes it more difficult for a second opponent to engage.

If the initial engagement can be as ferocious as possible supported by assertive posturing and verbal dissuasion etc. then there may be a chance that the second adversary will capitulate and offer a chance to escape. However, if the second adversary still has aggressive tendencies and is within range then you may need to engage. Either way and at the very least, your chances of survival have improved.

Protecting Others

Another aspect of dealing with multiples would be if you were required to protect other person. Within the realm of 'self-defence', this is a potentially more common scenario than what most martial arts classes would prepare you for and not only a requisite for aspiring bodyguards. Protecting others may for instance include using verbal tactics to help cool down a family dispute, offering some useful risk mitigation tactics to a work colleague who is travelling with you on business, acting as a physical barrier between a potential antagonist and a friend, ensuring that when on holiday your family take a quick trial run through the best fire escape route after check-in at the hotel, or choosing to come to the vital aid of a complete stranger who's under attack. Although we may argue that escape is always the ideal option when facing any threat, if this is not possible due to situation/environment, or that the act of fleeing would mean leaving behind someone (especially someone you care about) at significant risk from harm, then protection of a third-party may well become an overriding priority.

Although the term 'self-defence' is widely known and legally recognised, I guess it is not exactly the most accurate label when we consider that its scope includes the protection of others. In fact, there are so many possibilities from life's everyday interactions that may escalate and require the protection of a colleague, friend or family member that overlooking this aspect from your training would mean missing an important jigsaw piece. And although the specific details of corresponding tactics may be out of the scope of this book, it is nevertheless worth investing just a couple of paragraphs so that the notion of 'dealing with multiples' is holistically covered.

The challenges associated with protection of a third party are numerous. However if we consider these at a principle level then we can see that no matter whether we're dealing with multiple opponents, the protection of a third-party or both, the core concepts of awareness and subsequent threat recognition, avoidance and situational management remain essential in order to help prevent the realisation of violence. If violence cannot be avoided then equally essential become some of the physical tactics as given within *Naihanchi Kata*, especially those on gaining positional advantage and percussive impact delivery.

Tactics for protecting others may include early threat recognition to avoid or make timely escape and verbal de-escalation to help pacify potential situations before they can be fuelled into a physical problem. Failing that, then strategies for becoming an effective barrier between the individual you are protecting and the threat may take precedence. Specifically, how the person being protected 'attaches' to you is important so that not only do know where they are at any given moment (since they will be located behind you), but also so that they don't impede your ability to move, engage with the threat if necessary and initiate swift escape.

Another tactic to consider would be how to give clear, simple and assertive instruction so that the person being protected is able to understand and comply, despite the adrenal dump you'll both be inevitably experiencing. Depending on the situation, you may also have some ego-based aggression to deal with if the person you are trying to protect is in a particularly infuriated state. Additionally, body language and verbal interaction with the threat when striving to insistently reinforce the gap between you is equally important. How you physically engage should all else fail plus the best strategy for subsequent escape are also critical concerns, given the fact that there's not only yourself, but also another person to clear from immediate danger. Consequently to this, the actual ability of the person being protected to escape is a critical component. If weak, injured, disabled or have already been engaged by the threat, then a clean escape becomes much more difficult to accomplish.

Above are just a few considerations to prompt some thought and although *Naihanchi Kata* may or may not have been designed based on specific tactics for the purpose of protecting others, there are certainly conceptual lessons from the choreography and identified within this book that may be employed to help increase the chances of coping with such a dire situation. It is also worth noting that if early practitioners of the indigenous arts of *Ryukyu* (to be later infused with other influences and developed into the system of *karate* we know today) were active in precarious roles such as bodyguards to the Royal Family, civilian peace keepers and tax collectors etc., it doesn't take a stretch of the imagination to consider that the notion of protecting others (in addition to oneself) may well have been offered high priority on the historic 'skills list'. And as a civilian self-defence system, I think that such possibilities must be considered for a comprehensive understanding of *karate* today.

Weapon Attack

Just like multiple assailants or ground fighting, being forced to deal with a weapon attack is very severe and unfortunately, much of the information concerning self-protection available on this subject is at best unrealistic and at worst life threatening. As with any potential confrontation, escape is always the preferred option, especially so if a weapon is present. You should never actively engage a weapon wielding enemy unless out of sheer desperation and when in collaboration with a third party, stand up clinch or ground struggle, it can become a living nightmare. Whether or not you'll have the composure, determination or ability to fight on will have a huge effect on determining the outcome. So again, as in all aspects of self-protection, attitude trumps aptitude.

It's often said that if someone attacks you with a knife then you're going to get cut regardless of what you do. However, whether or not that statement is true doesn't mean that one should simply give up or indeed, omit practicing methods that may offer at least a remote chance of surviving such situations? Yes, it may be almost impossible to stop but surely doing anything is better than doing nothing when fighting for your life. The same is true for all weapon attacks and in order to increase that chance of survival, tactics should aim to (1) keep you conscious for as long as possible, (2) reduce or divert damage from vital areas and (3) maintain absolute aggression. Short answer, there is no definitive solution for effective weapon defence.

Contrary to what many martial artists tend to teach, knife wielding attackers don't try to stab you with semi-compliant, over-exaggerated and robotic-type movements. Real knife attacks are sickening to witness and resemble either a slashing frenzy and/or successive sewing machine style stabs. Furthermore, the attacker's non-weapon wielding hand can also be in play to grab, rag, strike or expose vulnerable areas - anything that would help facilitate their obvious advantage. Most likely, they'll also attempt to use dialogue and deception to get in range and once engaged, won't even stop to come up for air. If anyone has made the decision to attack you with a knife (or any other weapon for that matter) then their mind-set is that of causing you serious harm, so you can guarantee that their tactics will be equally as callous.

Of course, the weapons available to *Okinawan* people when *karate* was first developed may differ from what the violent few among us have access to today. However, most can still be categorized into four main groups worthy of consideration. These are (1) impact, (2) edged/pointed (3) flexible and (4) projectile. In modern society these usually boil down to either the use of a (1) bludgeon, (2) knife, (3) garrotte/flexible cosh or (4) gun. Obviously, the tactics you'd use for protecting yourself against a gun may differ from those to protect against a knife or indeed a baseball bat. You need to take into account the way in which each weapon may be utilized, the potential damage they can inflict and how easily they may be put to use. However, all weapons have one thing in common and that is, a person wielding them. All weapons are rendered far less dangerous without user intent and once either momentum-based risk or effective range/line of fire is stifled. This is where our self-protection skills need to focus upon and in this respect, counter-weapons training can borrow some of the essential principles from that of empty-hands.

Weapons may be used by an attacker in two main ways. Firstly, they can be used to help accentuate the severity of a threat in order to elicit a submissive response to gain some sort of resource such as sex, money, valuables, access, information or drugs etc. In such cases, the weapon will most likely be on display and primed for action. A knife to the throat or a gun to the back of the head accentuated by aggressive, repetitive dialogue and physical intimidation are the staple characteristics of such a 'hold-up' strategy.

Secondly, weapons may be used in their capacity to cause harm. In this case it may be unlikely that you'll see the weapon before it is in play and doing you damage unless you can make some sense of pre-threat cues that may indicate potential concealment and thus, pre-empt a potential draw. For instance, the observation of specific body language, posture, hand positions and/or movement can help provide essential clues that a weapon may be present or is about to be accessed.

The two modes of operation detailed above are not always so clear cut, as one scenario may flow into another depending on the specific conflict dynamics. For instance, aimlessly struggling or arguing during a hold-up may cause the attacker to panic and as a desperate attempt to re-impose dominance, use the weapon in its destructive capacity.

No matter what kind of weapon is or may be present, there are five potential scenarios that you need to think about in training:

- Threat recognition on initial approach, subsequent avoidance and escape,

- Making use of an equaliser,

- Fouling a weapon draw from successful observation of pre-threat cues,

- Dealing with a weapon hold-up situation,

- Protecting against an active weapon in use.

Although guns are not impossible to obtain here in the UK, strict firearm laws mean that the two easily obtainable weapons that one is potentially likely to face are edged/pointed (knife, screwdriver, box cutter, broken bottle etc.) and impact (baseball bat, stick, brick, ashtray etc.). These apply whether armed intentionally, or are a weapon of opportunity. When we talk about protecting against 'destructive use' of these tools then we're generally looking at dealing with either a peripheral swing/slashing type attack, or a direct thrust/stabbing type attack.

These attacks can be likened to similar empty-handed acts of physical violence, which means that it's entirely possible to make use of the same core game plan of self-protection to generate a valid counter-strategy. Equating to the line of attack is a valuable tactic in developing effective self-protection skills and this idea is also reflected within the teachings of *Naihanchi Kata*. Let's take a closer look how the conceptual lessons already covered may be of some use.

The main difference is that with weapon attack, the damage is likely to be much more severe if contact (especially repetitive contact) is made. Thus, we have two significant issues to manage – control of the weapon to stifle its ability to cause damage and domination of the person wielding it to terminate the altercation. Fixate too much on controlling the subject and you'll have been stabbed multiple times before you're even aware of it. Fixate too much on controlling the weapon and you'll still have a determined attacker in your face with the intent to cause great harm. There's nothing stopping the attacker from punching, kicking and grappling just as ferociously with or without a weapon in hand!

We must also acknowledge the fact that it is very difficult to control any limb, let alone one that's wielding a weapon. Most 'typical' martial arts demonstrations of knife defence are shown where the attacker is compliantly thrusting and 'locking' the weapon out in position. This is very unlikely to occur in reality, unless of course the blade has been stuck firmly in between two of your ribs! You are much more likely to see wild slashing furies and fast retracting stabs at varying angles.

Of course, in the ideal world, a martial artist can look all heroic with the fanciful application of nice looking joint locks and throws against knives, but back on *Planet*

Reality, the odds are going to be severely stacked against you. The same is true for a bludgeon attack. The weapon will most likely be repetitively swung or if less cumbersome, retracted back quickly for successive blows until the job is done. If the situation has got to this stage then unfortunately there are only two outcomes – you either stop the onslaught or perish trying.

General Awareness and Pre-Threat Cues

As discussed earlier, the opening salutation of *Naihanchi Kata* suggests a continuous daily exercise of good awareness and associated threat recognition skills and these make up the core from which all solid counter-weapons training is based. Imagine standing alone at a train platform and noticing someone approaching in your peripheral. You glance their way and realise that one of their hands is concealed from view. This may of course be completely innocent, but it may also indicate that they have something in their hand that they don't want you to see. You have two options – either disregard it as being another one of your 'paranoid' episodes or take action by simply repositioning in order to provide a better viewpoint and route for escape/protection should it be required. A small investment of effort that potentially carries a somewhat greater reward.

Understanding and learning to react to realistic pre-threat cues is another useful skill to practice. You'll have a far greater chance intercepting the intent to draw a weapon than waiting until the weapon is out and 'in-play'. Get into the habit of always assuming that a potential assailant on approach will be armed, actively scanning for both hands and in particular both thumbs. If a weapon is concealed within the palm then the thumb will be naturally employed to grip the tool and as such, artificially hidden from view. Other cues to look out for include a hand or hands being concealed within clothing, motion of the arms when walking, reaching into pockets or around the waist line etc.

Improvised Weapons

As already mentioned, UK Law states that if you carry an object that was made, adapted or intended for the purpose of causing injury (even for self-protection) then this would be classed as an offensive weapon. Obviously, criminals couldn't care less about this rule so that can put law-abiding citizens at a significant disadvantage if ever faced with a weapon attack. However, the law does acknowledge that everyday items may be used as weapons of opportunity if deemed both reasonable and necessary. So if someone is about to attack you with a machete or baseball bat and escape is not an option, then the use of an object for use as a barrier, equaliser or force multiplier etc. may well be more favourable than relying solely on empty-handed tactics.

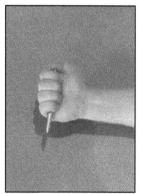 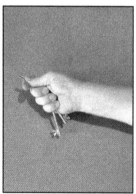 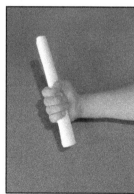 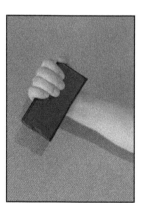

Everyday objects carried on your person such as a pen, bunch of keys, mobile phone or even a handful of paperwork may be employed as weapons of opportunity.

Increasing distance and/or creating barriers is always the first priority, so using objects like tables, counters or walls or fending off with a chair, pool cue, umbrella or even a ruck sack can help maintain distance from the threat and put you in a much better position for survival. If this is not an option then other items such as an ashtray, rock, pen, key, flashlight, belt, coins or even a rolled up magazine can be employed to help enhance your ability to distract, disorientate and/or deliver impact. Having to hand an equaliser may also serve to discourage the assailant from carrying out their plan.

The best way to prepare for the use of improvised weapons is to mentally 'arm' yourself on a daily basis. Take time to evaluate how you could possibly use everyday items on your person and practice the use of these within a controlled environment. Consider the combative application of *Naihanchi Kata* with these 'weapons' in hand and use such strategies in your *dojo* training. It is one thing to say, "Just pick up the nearest object" and something completely different to do so functionally and under duress. To make the notion of improvised weapons useful, it stands to reason that it must be practiced along with empty hand skills.

If you happen to practice a classical weapon art such as *kobudo* then it's worth spending time exploring how the motions used to wield those traditional tools may be adapted to suit more contemporary improvised weapons. Although *kobudo* may on the surface seem obsolete in its direct application, this is far from true when considered against the more holistic approach to training that *Naihanchi Kata* suggests.

I think it's interesting that many weapon arts around the world consider their tools as extensions of their body and empty-handed skills. This proves that despite a few technical issues that may be unique to certain weapon designs, the emphasis is on developing effective movement pathways. *Naihanchi Kata* stresses the same importance on effective movement and so in application, it matters little whether or not your hammer fist strike has an improvised weapon within your grip – it's no less *Naihanchi Kata*! Plus given the close relationship between *karate* and *kobudo*, it makes one wonder how many classical *kata* may have been originally designed for use with a tool in hand, or can be easily adapted to become being equally functional in either configuration?

Fouling the Draw

Failing avoidance and escape or being able to make use of some sort of equaliser, fouling the draw is always going to be your best chance of ending an altercation quickly and before the weapon comes into active play. If a stranger is walking towards you and you can't see one of their hands then you need to ask yourself why? If you happen to pick up such early pre-threat cues then you may have the opportunity to assertively insist that they maintain distance and show their hands. At least from this range you will have more time to react should the situation then escalate.

If already at conversation range, the situation is breaking down and you notice a potential play to access a weapon then it's much safer to counter this immediately than wait for the weapon to come into action. Again, the core concepts within *Naihanchi Kata* can be used here to intercept and pin the drawing hand against the enemy's body, gain a more advantageous position, whilst striking hard and repetitively with whatever tools you have available. If the fouling attempt isn't completely successful and the weapon is subsequently drawn then at least you have positively engaged, plus your hands are close enough to try and suppress further weapon movement.

Using conceptual lessons from Naihanchi Kata in an attempt to jam a right-handed weapon draw in order to control, strike with available tools and make good your escape.

Using conceptual lessons from Naihanchi Kata to foul a right-handed weapon draw by using attacker's body as a temporary barrier to control, strike and then escape.

Another way to foul a draw, especially if a potential escape route has already been identified, would be to swiftly shift your body away from the enemy's 'weapon hand' using their own body as a temporary shield. Similar to the principles for dealing with multiple assailants, imagine that the weapon is a second attacker. From here you can index for control, strike and flee using the opportunity created by forcing your enemy to reorient. Either of the two tactics above (attached or unattached) come with inherent advantages and disadvantages and like all other self-protection strategies, are based on making the best of a really bad state of affairs, hence situationally dependant.

Weapon Hold-Up

If a stranger has managed to get close enough, present a weapon and issue a demand then it could be argued that a significant failure had occurred within your awareness protocol. However, we can't always rely on our awareness to protect against weapon hold-ups and there are a number of situations where a threat could slip under the radar. For example, if someone you already know or trust suddenly turns aggressive, or you're in a confined space such as an elevator, stairwell or toilet. It's worth bearing in mind though that if someone can get close enough to push a knife against your face, then they could have also stabbed you.

Although the attackers demands are priority for them in a hold-up scenario, causing you harm may also be on the agenda. Insisting that you enter a vehicle or walk with them to somewhere secluded could well be the beginning of your demise. Plus of course, there's nothing stopping someone from 'finishing the job' once they have your money, belongings or have been sexually gratified. If your attacker asks you to change location then it's generally always a better option to fight back there and then. If it's simply a case of giving up your wallet or handbag, then that's always much better than risking something much worse. Remember that material items can always be replaced and sentimental items become redundant if you're not around to appreciate them.

Whether or not to physically retaliate against a weapon hold-up will always be a personal choice and dependent on the specific situation. However, if you do choose the physical option then your response must be immediate and fully committed. Anything less could cost you your life. Given the fact that you will also be experiencing a massive adrenaline dump, this would be no easy task and therefore requires both a swift and simplistic principle-based framework for any chance of success.

Again, *Naihanchi Kata* has a conceptual strategy to support this by adapting the lessons on dealing with grips and making use of the suitable acronym H-O-L-D:

- **H**ands: Use deception to get your hands as near as possible to the weapon. For instance, if the weapon is against your throat then put your hands up and plead with the attacker to 'take it easy'. The closer you can be before retaliating means the less time your attacker will have to react and thwart your attempt.

- **O**rient: Ideally under the veil of artifice, act swiftly and shift the weapon from the line of assault. Depending on the situation, this may be achieved by using your hand(s) only, or if possible, both your body and hands to help increase the likelihood of your attempt being successful.

- **L**atch: Without delay, latch on to the weapon limb to impede its movement and buy some valuable milliseconds in order to retaliate. Once seized, aim to maintain control over the weapon limb until the threat has been neutralised.

- **D**estroy: Using whatever effective strikes you have at your disposal, quickly attack and keep on attacking until the point at which you can make good your escape.

Applying the acronym 'H-O-L-D' against a weapon hold-up scenario, using two-on-one 'stack', head butt and elbow strike from Naihanchi Kata.

Dealing with Swings and Slashes

Just as we may protect against wild swinging hook line strikes by driving forward and utilizing the default cover position from the opening salutation of *Naihanchi Kata*, the same strategy may also be employed to create an initiative against a swinging/slashing weapon attack. Positioning yourself inside the destructive arc of the weapon is generally more advantageous than stepping back, which would open you up for successive strikes.

Dealing with swings and slashes using the reactive tactics, clinch frame and two-on-one stack taken from Naihanchi Kata.

Using the outside of your arms to protect your body helps keep you 'in the fight' and if you do happen to take some damage (which may well be likely), then the risk of it being immediately life-threatening is somewhat reduced. Crime statistics have shown that many preliminary injuries from weapon attack do actually occur to the upper limbs, which just goes to show how quickly we can elicit the flinch response. However, we must aim to keep the insides of our arms away from the weapon, especially edged weapons, since wounds to these areas are more likely to cause rapid blood loss.

As soon as distance has been closed, it's vital that the weapon wielding limb is seized and controlled to prevent succeeding attacks. This can be achieved using the default clinch frame or stacked position from *Naihanchi Kata*, by wrapping the arms tightly and securing it close to the body. The intention is to stifle further weapon movement and offer a window of opportunity to go offensive. The fact that your body is in the way and that you have made good use of angles means that it will be more challenging for the attacker to switch the weapon from one hand to the other.

Once the weapon wielding limb has been secured then it's imperative that you go to work immediately, delivering consecutive high impact strikes to vulnerable areas. Options from *Naihanchi Kata* include the forearm, elbow and head to the high-line, or kicks and knees to the legs and groin. Keep attacking ferociously until your assailant is down and it's safe for you to disengage and escape. Don't fixate on the weapon with the sole intention to disarm, but rather focus on removing the ability for the enemy to continue posing a threat.

When responding to a slashing or swinging type attack, you may end up either on the inside or outside line, so it's important that the initial flinch-based cover is identical regardless as *Naihanchi Kata* instils. If you happen to find yourself on the outside line, then the same principles apply – get inside the destructive arc, inhibit the potential for further weapon movement and then strike back hard with everything you've got.

Dealing with Stabs and Thrusts

A stabbing or thrusting attack is difficult to deal with due to the swift retraction and 'reload' of the weapon. It is also quite likely that the aggressor will aim to distract or grab you with their other hand before revving up the 'sewing machine'. If distance has already been closed and your enemy has some level of attached control then you could be stabbed multiple times within the blink of an eye and from various angles – likely before you're able to take responsive action! Even in a realistic but safe scenario training environment with practice weapons, a determined attacker trying to stab you repeatedly with quick succession and staging murderous intent can be a terrifying experience.

Adapting lessons taken from Naihanchi Kata to obtain a two-on-one control against a weapon, incorporating either a take down or joint attack with subsequent dropping strikes.

Again, the overarching principles of operation must be the same. In the heat of the moment it will be difficult (if not impossible) to maintain the frame of mind necessary in order to discern between different attack angles and respond accordingly. Again, any dynamic fending manoeuvres should make use of the back of the arms, as the opening salutation and first movement of *Naihanchi Kata* clearly suggest. But even in the case that you successfully defend one or two blows, it's unlikely that this pattern will persist. Therefore, as with the slashing attack, attempts must be made to secure the weapon wielding limb as soon as possible and if this is achieved, then clamp hard and go percussive.

As previous, fend using reactionary tactics from lesson five and swiftly seize the weapon wielding limb with the 'two-on-one' anchoring control given in lesson six. Drive forward and away from the non-weapon wielding limb to stifle inevitable retraction and successive stabbing attempts, plus protect against oncoming attacks with the other hand. Immediately unleash strikes with whatever tools are available, joint attacks and/or take down manoeuvres from lesson nine.

If the opponent grabs or makes use of a leveraging arm then the lessons from Naihanchi Kata may be used to shift to the outside line (embusen), pin and attack the grabbing arm. If the opponent continues to attack then you are in a much better positon to employ the strategies as previously covered.

If the opponent makes use of an index or leveraging arm to control your movement then attempts to stifle weapon movement instantly become even more unlikely. In this case, it's imperative that you focus your energy on dealing with the attachment and position yourself as far away as possible from the knife. Again, using the lessons from *Naihanchi Kata*, you can use *tenshin* (body movement) to shift to the outside line, pin and attack the grabbing arm. If you are still unable to prevent the opponent from continuing their attack then you are at least in a better position to employ the strategies as previously covered to stifle and strike.

Felling Techniques

As we've seen, the beauty of the core felling techniques within *Naihanchi Kata* is that they're brutally simple, ballistic in application, adaptable to varying circumstances and as a result, are geared up perfectly for the requirements of self-protection.

To reiterate, throws and takedowns are not necessarily applications you should actively seek to prioritise above those pertaining to the primary strategy of delivering percussive impact, but if the opportunity presents itself then they can become extremely effective follow-ups to your essential counter-weapon strategy.

Felling techniques from Naihanchi Kata may be used as effective follow-ups to your counter-weapon strategy.

The prime risk with this of course is ending up being dragged down to the floor with your opponent and with a weapon still in play, this reality can turn out to be disastrous. However, if the subject is well-controlled and adequately subdued, then the use of felling techniques can be valuable. For example, if within the default clinch framework on the inside line, then the snatch takedown can work well. If on the outside line then you may opt to seize the head and twist them to the floor, or over-balance them whilst keeping the weapon wielding limb trapped against the body.

In conclusion, this chapter has hopefully provided some insight into how the conceptual lessons expressed by the choreography of *Naihanchi Kata* may be adapted for dealing with dire situations that may involve a weapon, more than one assailant, the protection of a third-party and/or being forced to fight on the ground. None of these scenarios (or any scenarios for that matter) are stipulated within the core self-protection game plan and the same is true for *Naihanchi Kata*. Thus, the key feature of this chapter is not so much the specific applications I've used as examples, but rather the understanding that we should approach the notion of *karate* for self-protection according to a common principle-based methodology.

The above idea will be further expanded upon within subsequent chapters on *Bunkai Sandan*, as we start to build up a malleable and progressive application protocol for the key conceptual lessons as covered previous.

CHAPTER XVIII

MANIPULATIONS, RESTRICTIONS & RESTRAINT

"Nothing is more harmful in the world than a martial art that is not effective in self-protection"

~ Choki Motobu

This chapter will explore some aspects of traditional *karate* that are often controversial in their application within the field of self-protection. Typically these are *kyusho/chibudi* (vital point manipulation) and torite/tuidi (seizing hands) strategies for advanced grappling, joint attacks, blood/air restrictions or to affect varying levels of pain compliance and restraint. The application of such practices obviously require more progressive levels of training than the 'core combative' requirements as presented in *Bunkai Nidan* plus a far greater investment of time and development of proficiency to become sufficiently confident in their application. Nevertheless, these aspects appear repeatedly within classical *kata* and are valid considerations for a more comprehensive auxiliary skill-set. For that reason, I wanted to add this brief chapter just to share my own standpoint on these facets of old-school *karate*.

The unpredictable nature of civilian self-protection means accepting that situations may unfold that simply do not warrant the employment of percussive impact strategies and instead, would benefit from exercising potentially less injurious methods of control. However, it's also very important that we maintain clear distinction between what are the most 'essential' skills compared to those that are for want of a better term, 'nice to have'. This is why I believe that aspects such as manipulations, restrictions, pain compliance and restraint etc. should be considered part of a tertiary strategy, to be used to enhance your ability, rather than replace or take priority over one's core capabilities.

In short, you have no real business practicing fine motor strategies or advanced skill development unless you can first implement fundamental abilities for self-protection. Most importantly, the ability to hit with impact consistently and repetitively and from almost any given angle/distance, along with the physical and mental aptitude to gain/retain dominance at the earliest opportunity to abolish the threat and provide a safe means of escape. Even then you could argue that if your goal was purely self-protection, then more complex progression may actually be counterproductive in contrast to spending time to further hone the reliable skills you have already gained.

There are two general schools of thought regarding the practicality of these more intricate skills. Those who believe they are functional, and those who don't. Both of these viewpoints of course are consistently backed up by testimonials and experiences, training histories, real world examples and personal preference. I tend to sit in-between both of these camps and prefer a more conservative balance between what may be possible and what may be probable, given the specific context that old-school *karate* aligns itself to. Based on this perspective, my training tends to lean towards making use of aspects such as *chibudi* and *tuidi* as opportunistic 'strategy enhancers', rather than segregating them into completely distinct training methodologies.

It's not that these skills won't work in self-protection, only that their use within the game plan must be established without taking precedence away from the principle-based skills development of the fundamental framework. Evidently and with enough proficiency, it's true that many ancillary aspects of *karate* can be used with brutal effectiveness in self-protection, however they also tend to require an enhanced dose of both talent and dedication.

For instance, try telling *Terry O'Neil* that head-height kicking has no place in self-protection, persuading *Taika Seiyu Oyata* that vital point striking is ineffective, debating with *Masaji Taira* that sophisticated limb-control doesn't work for real, or pointing out to someone like *Tetsuhiro Hokama* that pain compliance and restraint has little effectiveness. I'm sure that each of these extremely competent exponents could support their arguments with masterful demonstrations and plenty of related stories to the contrary!

I suppose we could contend that the issue is not simply a question of whether or not something may work in self-protection, but more so, whether the time investment required to make it work consistently and under pressure has been considered in collaboration with other more efficient and effective application practices. Since the physical application of self-protection should always be born from simplicity, I think it's important for practical-based *karate* practitioners to prioritise and study to become proficient at those fundamentals before considering the inclusion of more inherently complex skills. It's like spending most of your time in the gym pumping out hundreds of strict isolation exercises without first building a solid strength-based foundation using large compound movements like bench presses and deadlifts.

For the jigsaw pieces that make up the art of *karate*, each are components that make up a greater whole. So it stands to reason that the more pieces we are conscious of, the more complete our picture of *karate* may become. Each aspect has its natural place for application, as well as its inherent limitations. Expertise in the application of *karate* therefore comes from being able to understand and accept the flaws associated with each piece, where exactly they fit into the whole picture and how much they contribute to your individual aims for practice.

Like many other martial arts, certain aspects of *karate* may be at risk of becoming stigmatised when disproportionate emphasis is placed on them above more foundational components. This is certainly true for aspects such as vital point manipulation. For example, there is no doubt that having an understanding of the weaker areas of the human anatomy would be advantageous in a combative environment. If you are to deliver strikes, then it stands to reason that they should be aimed towards specific targets that would offer the best chance of success, as opposed to simply flailing your arms around and hoping for the best. To me, this is the practical application of *kyusho* in a nutshell and does not require bespoke specialisations or complex theory often represented in the likes of movies and more worryingly, on some social media platforms being portrayed as realistic strategies for self-protection.

Thus, a thorough knowledge of vital point manipulation is very much a support strategy that should never replace the requirement to be able to strike with stopping force or at the cost of capability within other fundamental areas of the core self-protection game plan. Rather, it aims to help enhance these abilities. As such, vital points may also be used with great effect in order to augment combative applications including chokes and strangles, throws and takedowns, joint attacks and grappling etc.

Personally and no doubt due to my own lack of experience in this area, I would much prefer to identify anatomical targets by western terminology, rather than using the meridian theory of *Traditional Chinese Medicine*. Those that are listed in such texts as *Karate-Do Kyohan* or the original thirty six vital points found in *The Bubishi* are interesting to study and especially so in respect to their western nomenclature.

For self-protection, I favour the notion of referencing large target rich areas, rather than specific weak points, due to the sheer difficulty in achieving the level of accuracy required in a live altercation. Unless you are a highly accomplished expert, vital point striking is generally difficult to apply with consistency and it has been proven time and time again that the effects from such manipulation can vary greatly, especially if the opponent is enraged, intoxicated and/or obsessively intent on causing you harm. Reports of attackers/victims being shot, stabbed and receiving broken bones, yet still continue their efforts are not uncommon. In these cases, I feel that the goal of delivering sufficient/repetitive impact to any target area above the enemy's collar bone against an aggressive and non-compliant opponent is challenge enough.

Similar to vital point manipulation, seizing methods for the objective of grappling or pain compliance are part of a tertiary strategy that is principally opportunistic in application. The definition and application of these strategies require one to be 'attached' to the opponent for an extended period of time, eliminating the chances of escape and thus, increasing the inherent risk. Having said that, these tactics may of course be desirable in certain circumstances and as such, all directly contribute to the holistic self-protection methodologies we learn from *karate kata*. For instance, you may be dealing with an emotionally fuelled family argument that's happened to escalate too far or other more 'social' situations whereby a level of control through physical restraint is required. Moreover, being useful in physical arrest situations for peacekeepers, it doesn't take a stretch of the imagination to understand how in the past, such applications may have been advantageous and thus embraced by the old *Ryukyu Kingdom Peichin* specifically for law enforcement and security purposes.

Some more examples of using tertiary skills such as manipulations, restrictions and restraint to help enhance applications from the Naihanchi Kata choreography.

Today, *karate* practitioners are very lucky to have access to a wealth of information and knowledge passed on through the solo choreography of many classical *kata*. As a result, it's uplifting to see that in recent years, *karate* is being resurrected and propagated by more people to be much broader than just a system of 'blocks, kicks and punches' and that more attention is given to auxiliary combative elements that may be found within the art. As such, it's also exciting to envisage where this progress may lead us in the consistently evolving exploration undertaken by today's pragmatic *karate* proponents and researchers from around the globe.

To summarise, I would suggest that despite their intricacies, it's obvious that aspects such as *Chibudi* and *Tuidi* have been ingrained to varying degrees within the movements of classical *karate kata,* including *Naihanchi.* These tend to be used as tertiary methods to help support the ability for the practitioner to enhance fundamental self-protection strategies, as opposed to replacing them. For the particular scope of this book though, we require only a rudimentary understanding of such aspects and where they may best sit to support the core application framework that provides the basis for *Bunkai Nidan.*

CHAPTER XIX

FREE-FLOWING APPLICATION

"Kata is not fixed or immovable. Like water, it is ever changing and fits itself to the shape of the vessel containing it."

~ Kenwa Mabuni.

Just as the three primary colours of red, yellow and blue may be combined and mixed to form a myriad of other colours for painting various pictures, the distinct conceptual analysis used for *Bunkai Nidan* means that we may also achieve something similar order to convey a more 'complete picture' of *Naihanchi Kata,* dependent on the specific situation we may face at any given time. For instance, we know that although pre-emptive percussive impact forms a key component of our primary strategy, this would become unfeasible if we happen to encounter a genuine ambush attack. Likewise, the application of our percussive strategy could also fall short of its mark for a number of reasons, meaning that we must be able to swiftly transition into other tactics that may be more appropriate to gain or regain control.

Now that we have laid the core conceptual framework in *Bunkai Nidan*, let's now look at taking one step further towards the ability to move freely around the lessons depicted by the *kata* choreography as the situation may demand. As already mentioned, it's important that we never become a 'slave to the *kata*', but rather use its teachings to inspire more fluid application practices. The objective being to 'paint the most fitting picture' (application) based on the specific blend of primary colours (principles) required to deal with the scenario at hand. By treating the conceptual lessons given by *Naihanchi Kata* as a series of 'golden rules', they may be used to help guide both rich and relevant application-based training practices. The ability to move freely around this framework as and when required is critical to its function and is what in my opinion brings the *kata* to life.

The examples given here are just a small representation of how the lessons from *Bunkai Nidan* may be applied. Due to the symmetry and commonality featured within the form's choreography you will see considerable repetition. This is desirable and a key characteristic of the form's principle-based methodology, i.e. a small number of solutions given by the *kata* to cater for a somewhat greater number of questions. Also, I trust you will appreciate how difficult it is to portray dynamic applications such as these with posed photographs, but hopefully this will not in any way diminish the value of this chapter.

Subordinate only to the effective use of target hardening principles to discourage a would-be assailant from even considering you as a potential victim, exercising mindful avoidance has to be the next desirable outcome when applying self-protection. Here, situational awareness (lesson one) and subsequent threat recognition has alerted a potential problem up ahead. This may be circumvented simply by changing route or at least by crossing the road to increase distance. This may also provide positive confirmation of intent should the potential threat choose to follow. Simply put, avoid all conflict if you can!

All 'cold-call' interactions that are unavoidable should always be met with caution. Awareness and situational control protocols should be raised to Code Orange due to elevation of risk. Here, an individual approaches engaging in conversation and raises their hands. A combination of applications (lessons one, two, three and four) may be used to raise attentiveness, gain a level of control and re-orient position to check what's behind, all whilst scoping for possible escape routes. Hands should be raised, base staggered and use of dialogue appropriate to the situation. This is especially important if you think a pre-attack interview may be taking place.

If avoidance and de-escalation tactics have either failed or were not feasible options, plus you feel that the threat of physical violence is imminent, then a pre-emptive 'stun and run' tactic may be the most reasonable and necessary action to take. From a situational control position (lesson two), verbal and/or physical artifice may be used gain positional advantage (lesson four) and launch a powerful pre-emptive strike (lesson six) under the veil of deception. Here, the enemy's clothing (hood) has been used to create an advantage and facilitate application. Subsequent indexing should always be employed by default, but if this proves unnecessary then use the window of opportunity created to make good your escape.

In this example, the pre-emptive strike (lesson six) has not had the desired effect and the index employed has relayed tactile information that the enemy still poses a threat to safety. This should prompt the requirement to immediately follow up with successive strikes and forward offensive pressure until the assailant capitulates and an opportunity to make your escape becomes available.

In this situation, the pre-emptive strike (lesson six) has not had the desired effect, subsequent strikes are required, but the enemy has raised their hands to cover the head (flinch response) in an attempt to protect against further impact. Once this is realised via tactile and visual information, quickly transition to the *gedan barai* and *kagi uchi* section of the *kata* in order to negotiate this obstacle (lesson seven), clear a new strike path and resume your primary strategy once again (lesson six) until escape becomes possible. Also demonstrated here is the ability to change levels with a low kick before moving back to the high line, just so that both key principles from lesson seven may be covered by this single example.

Where distance is being closed, a percussive clinch frame (lesson eight) may be used pre-emptively, whilst shifting to the outside line (lesson four) and attacking towards the 'funnel' created by the assailant's head and shoulder. The forearm being used to lay across the chest for a level of control. Changing levels with low-line attack (lesson seven) is then employed to bring the enemy's head forward and into a head turn throw (lesson nine). Tertiary options such as incidental strikes when gripping, plus eye/soft tissue attacks and manipulations are also used here for added effectiveness. Escape when possible to do so.

This scenario sees the assailant instinctively drive forward following an unsuccessful pre-emptive strike (lesson six), in an effort to stifle further impact. In response, use a staggered base and reactive neck tie (lesson five) to brace, gain positional advantage (lesson four) and index the head. This enables tactile location of facial targets such as the eyes or to facilitate an unrestricted bite. These tertiary tactics are used to cause the enemy to pull away from the source of pain, creating distance. This makes it possible to work back up the hierarchy with close-range strikes such as the head and elbow. A clinch frame is then employed (lesson eight) to facilitate a low-line knee strike followed by a suitable felling option (lesson nine) in order to make good your escape.

Ideally, any efforts made by the antagonist to attach should be dealt with decisively upon their attempt and before requiring any form of grappling-based reaction. However, we have assumed for this example that during elevated verbal interaction, mid-engagement or when attempting to escape, the enemy has managed to seize hold of your wrists to gain control. Once realised, transition into fundamental counter-grappling skills (lesson eight) in order to base, check, strike, position and detach from the grip. Immediately take up the primary percussive strategy once more (lesson six) until you are able to escape.

A reactive response to an ambush attack should make use of the flinch-based cover (lesson five) in order to create barriers, support the head and neck from percussive impact, move inside the effective range of oncoming strikes and hopefully buy a moment of time to regroup. As soon as possible, drive forward and aim to strike the antagonist in the neck using the generic clinch frame (lesson eight). Another option may be to find the two-handed neck tie, with forearms across the front of the antagonist's body to limit further striking capabilities. Subsequent high line strikes may be used before impacting low to disrupt the enemy's base and following up swiftly with a snatch take down (lesson nine) and appropriate finish before escaping.

    In this scenario, the antagonist has managed to seize your throat and pin you up against the wall in preparation to strike. Again, it is assumed that previous protection measures from the core game plan have either failed or were not feasible options. Immediately transition into counter-grappling (lesson eight) by dropping your chin and attach to the gripping limb for both tactile reference and to help reduce the force applied against your neck. At the same time, shift to a position away from the enemy's free arm and strike hard to the head/neck area. Use the generic clinch frame to strike low before driving the opponent into the wall (using environment/weapons of opportunity). Follow up with primary percussive strategy as necessary until the opportunity arises to escape.

As already discussed, it is useful to consider the use of everyday items as potential weapons of opportunity and how these may be best used to accentuate the fundamental skill-base taught within the *Naihanchi Kata* choreography. In this example, a mobile phone is used to aid the primary percussive strategy (lesson six) by making only a slight adjustment of the grip and wrapping a thumb over the top to secure. This response also incorporates the generic clinch frame (lesson eight), positional footwork and forward offensive pressure with percussive strikes until the assailant capitulates and you can make good your escape.

Upon verbal interaction, you happen to register a number of pre-threat cues that indicate imminent physical threat. Before launching a pre-emptive tactic, you then notice the antagonist reach inside his pocket. All signals point to a weapon draw, requiring a swift response before the tool becomes 'in-play' and at its most dangerous. Here, the drawing hand is forcefully pinned using reactionary tactics (lesson five) and followed instantly with percussive strikes (lesson six) with whatever tools are available (head and/or knees for example). If the weapon is successfully drawn, then quickly aim to achieve a 'two-on-one' control to stifle movement using the 'stack' position (lesson six) and get to work with subsequent strikes, joint attacks and/or take downs.

Facing two assailants with a weapon in play is probably one of the most dangerous and frightening scenarios. In this example the enemy on the left is holding an impact weapon and you notice him rearing back to swing. Immediately employ reactionary tactics (lesson five) to cover and get inside the effective range of the weapon. Tie up the weapon limb with the generic clinch frame (lesson eight) and attack with forearm to the head/neck area whilst shifting position to align both antagonists (lesson four). This may help provide a moment of time to carry on attacking the first enemy, whilst using him as a make-shift shield against the second. Make use of extreme aggression (actions and voice etc.) to dominate and try to discourage the second attacker from continuing.

So long as you are still conscious after being knocked to the ground, then using situational control (lesson four) and reactionary cover principles (lesson five), aim to cover up, position your head away from the assailant and fill the gap between with your legs. If the enemy tries to move around you then re-orient to make sure that your legs are always facing him, kicking out hard and fast should the distance close. The aim is to make enough space in order to get up or keep attacking the enemy's base until you can. Attacking with the legs follows the same primary percussive strategy (lesson six) including the application of indexing, cycling, range adaptability and making use of both limbs together.

In this example, the assailant drives forward to restrict your ability to strike and before you can affect a strong base, successfully wraps your legs and pushes you towards the ground. Immediately tuck your chin in to your chest and brace for impact, whilst raising your hands up as soon as possible to index the head. These are all adaptations from the principles on reactionary tactics (lesson five) with added enhancements from tertiary skills. Providing you remain cognisant after the fall, proceed to attack the eyes/face to create a little space. Fill that space with the generic clinch frame (lesson eight) as a strong structure to work under and check the assailants hip with your foot (an alternative application for *name-gaeshi*). Push away and work up the hierarchy of impact, kicking hard with your feet to knock the enemy backwards and offer an opportunity to escape.

CHAPTER XX

DEPTH & BREADTH

"In the past, it was expected that about three years were required to learn a single kata"

~ Gichin Funakoshi

Reverse engineering combative applications from classical *kata* needs to be undertaken with an open-mind. One must be willing to look at extremes, search from a wide variety of angles with an 'empty cup' and just like the gold miners of the Wild West, sift through masses of river silt until you come across the odd nugget. This investigative process is not at all wasteful and although it would certainly be interesting to know for certain the historical meaning of *karate kata*, the fact that we don't encourages us to explore below the surface and in numerous ways. In my opinion, this offers far more potential for growth than if we were to already have the definitive answer.

One mould we must seek to continually break is that which is built from our prior experience and understanding. In my early years of martial arts training and when I first began to question the meaning of *kata*, I started to look outside for answers that I thought *karate* didn't possess. At this point in my journey, *karate* was exclusively punching, blocking and kicking with a few extra 'tricks' that were normally taught under the title of 'self-defence'. So as well as gaining some experience in traditional weaponry, I also took some *Wing Chun* classes to help fill the trapping void, *Ju-Jutsu* to help fill the joint lock and grappling void, *Aikido* to fill the throwing void, *Taiji* and *Chi Gung* to help fill the energy/body awareness void etc. Indeed, cross training over the years has given me some very valuable experience and most importantly, has helped me realise that the answers I was looking for were in fact all within *karate*, I just needed to break the mould created by my current understanding and look at the art with a different set of eyes.

Although cross training in martial arts can be very beneficial and a good example of how one may challenge the mould of their current understanding, if not careful it may also lead you down the path of being a 'jack of all trades', but master of none. This is why I would always recommend choosing one art to invest heavily in and explore thoroughly. Of course I'm naturally biased towards *karate* and it will depend entirely on individual aims, but I believe that all martial systems (if taught well and in enough depth) hold equal value. I don't consider cross training essential for everyone, particularly if you are blessed with a teacher who possesses a holistic understanding of their art. However, in order for you to undertake a more comprehensive study of *kata bunkai* and uncover possibilities that maybe even your teacher hasn't yet considered, then you do need to learn how to take a step back to appreciate a bigger picture. As such, I always learn a great deal from my students, who all look at *kata* in different ways and with different eyes to find new and stimulating possibilities.

In this chapter, I'd like to take a look at how considering two particular extremes for *kata* analysis may help you break the mould of prior understanding and provide impetus for continuous evolution. The two key words for these methods are 'depth' and 'breadth'. In short, we need to seek answers both across the whole surface (breadth) and more profoundly within comparatively small portions (depth). Both by using the question, what if? Thus, I will spend the next few pages explaining these two methods and offer some examples from *Naihanchi Kata* to help demonstrate how you may apply this process to your own undertaking of *Bunkai Sandan*.

Depth

Investigating 'depth' for the perspective of this book would be to take a very small slice of the pie and explore everything that's inside. In the case of our progress so far in *Naihanchi Kata*, you may look to take any of the conceptual lessons from *Bunkai Nidan* and use it as a basis for more comprehensive development.

As an example, the core framework of applications given include some rudimentary and opportunistic felling methods for self-protection. Using the principles given by these applications, you may choose to undertake a more thorough study of the throws and take downs in *karate*. Where may you find other felling techniques within the classical forms? Do these highlight any common patterns or strategies within general *kata* choreography? What about other martial art systems that specialise in throws and takedowns – do any of these show similar principles and if dissimilar, then could this new way of looking at felling techniques open more doors within the *kata*?

Let's look at another example of 'depth', by taking a single shape/transition from the *Naihanchi Kata* choreography and disregarding the original 'label' we've applied to meet the *Bunkai Nidan* framework. What if this movement is actually a strike? What if it is a joint attack, throw or choke? What if it is applied on the ground, against a leg instead of an arm or maybe with a weapon in hand?

Next, you may want to take a look at the movements prior to and after the technique in question. How does this affect the way you may now see its interpretations? Does this fresh way of looking at the prescribed chorographical make-up of the *kata* open up any other possibilities?

Above are just a few ideas to help illustrate the concept of a more in-depth exploration of *kata* using the foundational datum already set. As I'm sure you can imagine, this level of study is a long road and also a path that should continually adapt according to new levels of experience. This makes not only the function of the *kata* come alive, but also your personal understanding of it. Thus, this 'process' of *kata* acts as a vehicle for us to evolve a more personal expression of *karate* throughout our lifetime.

Looking in depth at one technique from the Naihanchi Kata choreography and investigating its possibilities across a whole range of potential combative applications.

Breadth

Investigating 'breadth' for the perspective of this book would be based around having a single application concept in mind and then attempting to align it to every part of the choreography. In doing so, you purposely take on a contrasting mind set to the previous in order to investigate other possibilities and in doing so, further expand your understanding.

So in the case of *Naihanchi Kata*, one example may be to choose the *Bunkai Nidan* aspect of percussive impact and then ask yourself, what if the whole *kata* was in fact only a record of striking methods? If you were to seek percussive impact and its associated support strategies within every movement of the choreography then what would those applications look like? Does every movement fit this ideal or are some more difficult to apply? Are those that are difficult indicate an error in thinking, or maybe a lack of experience within this particular field? If numerous applications are found, do these have any strategic links or is there any integrated methodology that may be associated with your findings?

This kind of analysis may be used throughout a range of combative aspects such as throws and takedowns, chokes and strangles, joint attacks, grappling methods and as I have detailed below, limb control.

Looking across the breadth of the Naihanchi Kata choreography to investigate possible striking applications.

Limb Control Drills

I have taken this method of breadth analysis and applied it to *Naihanchi Kata* in order to generate a series of limb control drills that we use to teach a number of more advanced principles that sit over and above those fundamental lessons as given by *Bunkai Nidan*. The idea of these is to help students become more attuned to tactile sensitivity, explore different ideas associated with limb control and as a result, enhance their skill-level within this particular area. Since the effective range of *kata* is within the threshold of arms-length, these drills also provide us with a method to seamlessly stitch application methods together and when combined with the traditional *kakie* (joining hands) type energy, artificially draw out the quality of flow in order to create a rich and valuable learning tool from which not only *Naihanchi Kata*, but all our *kata* may be more comprehensively scrutinised. This shows the potential of what the process of *Bunkai Sandan* has to offer, so another useful example for this chapter, let's consider further the idea of these drills.

Traditionally, the practice of two-person combat orientated drills would have been the way in which knowledge and understanding were originally transmitted in *karate*, with *kata* of course being the culmination of those lessons into an efficient solo mnemonic. You don't need to look far in to reality-based martial arts to see that this is the preferred approach. Today, enthusiastic *karate* practitioners, having been left with classical *kata* as their historical reference, must conscientiously aim to reverse engineer their combative meaning from educated assumptions based on context, related knowledge and prior experience, tried and tested methods, key historic sources and of course, plenty of good sense.

The general characteristics of two-person training drills are that they are (1) repetitive, (2) flowing and (3) incremental, so that they can 'tease out' certain qualities and ingrain these using consistent repetitive practice. In short, they offer a time-efficient way of instilling specific skills and attributes, but like any other training method, they are not without their disadvantages.

In recent years, the practice of two-person drills has become more popular, and rightly so I think. They are a great addition to *dojo* training and if practiced correctly, can really help to express the application of *kata* in a more integrated and cohesive fashion. However the very nature of such training drills (as in all training drills) invariably contain compromises. Although a desirable skill to acquire, the very act of 'flowing' means that by definition, the application you have just transitioned from hasn't had the desired effect! So if you're flowing back and forth with multiple applications then there is the real risk of impressing failure without ever developing the skills required to break flow and see something through to its required conclusion. This is why it's very important that along with flow drill practice, I also advocate the inclusion of associated *exit drills* at various stages so that this vital ability may also be taken into account.

Another issue with two-person flow drills is the fact that they can become quite addictive and gratifying to practice. So much so that quite often, the main combative aim(s) of the drills are given a 'back seat' to the focussed development of tactile-based reaction and subsequent movement. However, for self-protection, we must always remember that the objective of tactics within the secondary tool box is to regain the ability to employ unrestricted percussive impact (our primary strategy). In reality, this should make the application of 'flow' occur within the blink of an eye. During practice however, we may choose to purposefully and artificially draw out this requirement in order to instil particular skills.

Manipulating the advantages and drawbacks of every aspect of your training is an important ability to develop. No single training method will ever have all the answers so learning how to combine the 'jigsaw pieces' so as to create the most accurate picture overall is extremely useful. If this methodology is understood then the incorporation of *kata*-based flow drills into your regular *dojo* practice can be both a meaningful and relevant method of study. In this chapter we will look at how we can take the conceptual lesson of limb control from *Bunkai Nidan* and expand it further for a more comprehensive analysis.

In my *dojo,* we develop our understanding of *Naihanchi Kata* progressively and along this journey, make use of a series of limb control drills that are used to provide a basis for more advanced free-flowing practice. Once competent, these drills are then incorporated into a specific framework that resembles a type of *muchimi-di* (sticky hands) exercise and through the use of common connection points, they allow for a whole host of *kata* applications to be practiced at close (tactile) range, incorporating varying levels of continuity and compliance as we require.

In short, by using these limb control exercises as a template of sorts, it then becomes possible to more freely express many aspects of *kata* analysis and combative application. The flowing nature of such drills also develops the ability to transition between various combative principles as and when the time is right to do so, rather than always practicing from a static and comparatively artificial interface. As a by-product, it also very conveniently works to preserve the 'tradition' that *Naihanchi Kata* should sit at the core of *Shuri*-based *karate* practices. Unsurprisingly, it happens to fit very conveniently and all came about by considering breadth analysis upon the choreography against the single conceptual lesson of limb control.

A full explanation of our *Naihanchi* limb control drills would easily take up a full volume (not to mention the associated break out methods that sit beside them) so I will present below only a couple of examples in order for readers to grasp the basic idea. Also due to their emphasis on fluidity, these drills are also very difficult to express with written word and still images, so maybe this would be a suitable topic for more in-depth video presentation at a later date. For now though, the examples below should suffice to help show some of the results available by the process used to generate them (*Bunkai Sandan*). After all, it is the process that is by far more valuable.

Please note that the arrangement and mentality used within the standard version of these drills is that of one person maintaining dominant pressure throughout whilst the other simply uses their arms to offer barriers that need to be negotiated in order to create new strike paths. So in other words, they take the generic basis of limb control from the conceptual lesson as given in *Bunkai Nidan*, and express that idea in a continuous drill format. I much prefer this asymmetrical arrangement rather than the more contemporary back and forth flow (which may also be practiced if desired), because it instils from the very beginning the notion of consistently dominating the opponent with forward offensive pressure – a critical mentality within our self-protection game plan. It also offers the opportunity for the 'defender' to learn how to instinctively identify and cover open strike paths as they appear, which is another useful skill to hone.

To begin with, each drill is conducted with both partners facing each other in *Naihanchi Dachi* and cross arms using the initial open-handed strike position from the *kata*. Like all aspects of these exercises, this preliminary standard may be discarded once the drills have been committed to memory and more free-flowing practice can then take place. The *Naihanchi Dachi* posture should thus be relaxed and made more malleable, whilst aiming to transfer related structural and dynamic principles from the more static counterpart (as discussed in *Volume One*).

Let's start by taking a look at the common reference exercise that we use as a basis for each drill.

Naihanchi Limb Control: Reference Drill

Naihanchi Limb Control Reference Drill

Both partners begin facing each other in *Naihanchi Dachi* and cross arms using the initial open-handed strike position from the *kata*. The attacker's job is to pull down the barrier presented in front and immediately return with a successive strike to the throat area, mimicking the same conceptual lesson from *Bunkai Nidan*. In reality, the aim would be to pin both the assailant's arms so that the strike can be launched unrestricted. However for the sake of 'flow', we assume that this cannot be achieved and is thus countered. The same movement is repeated over and over again, alternating left and right sides before changing roles.

The main principle of this drill is two-fold. Firstly, it serves to remind practitioners of the conceptual lesson given in *Naihanchi Kata* on limb control - clear barriers and strike with gross motor attacks with high impact potential to primary target zones above the collar bone. Secondly, it functions as a means to transition from left to right lead and offers a common reference that may be used throughout any subsequent drills we practice.

Using the reference drill as the core movement pattern, we would then progress onto a variety of prescribed drills that aim to further develop the principle of limb control using classical movements as derived from the *Naihanchi Kata* Choreography. Although I appreciate that these may be difficult to follow via still photographs, I have nevertheless added a couple of examples below for the sake of completeness and to help exemplify the developmental process.

Naihanchi Limb Control Drill Example No.1

This drill is a slight advancement from the reference drill and looks at changing levels (part of *Lesson 7* within *Bunkai Nidan*) by using the downward sweep and outside receipt from the *kata*. And as with all of these exercises, the end of the reference drill becomes the start of the next application.

After the attempted strike to the high-line, return the same hand back and attack to the low-line. In turn, your partner (sensing the change in levels) meets and checks the attack. The dominant partner then returns another strike back to the high-line before switching sides.

This drill is practiced by alternating left and right leads using the reference drills to switch sides or indeed, switch roles.

Naihanchi Limb Control: Example No.2

Naihanchi Limb Control Drill Example No.2

This next example is more complex than the previous, but positively adds to the mix a number of auxiliary methodologies including breaking rhythm, attacking limbs, wedging with the arm to negotiate around barriers and striking around the peripheral with a hook-line attack.

The drill starts off with what *Filipino* martial arts systems would refer to as a 'limb destruction' technique. In *karate* terms, we are simply using the transition of the '*osae*' element of the *ura-zuki* technique to break rhythm and attack the nerve on the inside of the assailant's elbow joint. Use that moment to flow into a back fist strike, which is then checked by your partner.

Then immediately lift up the other hand to form a wedge or bridge, to enable smooth transition into an elbow attack. This application features the same body mechanics as given within the *uchi-uke* or *kagi-uchi* movements within the *kata*.

From the elbow attack, pass from the outside to inside line. It's vital when utilising this method that you fill space immediately so as to protect against retaliation. In this case, attack with a second back fist strike, causing your partner to check once again.

Use the energy from this defence to roll the elbow over and drop down onto the limb to clear from the high line. This application concept was covered within the chapter on counter-grappling.

Finally whilst maintaining an indexed connection with one hand, sneak the other hand around the peripheral for a hooking palm slap. This peripheral attack is met by a flinch cover from your partner (application concept from the *kata*), which initiates the transition into the drill once more from the opposite side.

Common Reference Points

Once all the standard *Naihanchi* limb control drills have been committed to memory and you have become natural and smooth in their application, then the next stage would be to explore the pre-determined commonalities that have been put in place to prompt a seamless transition between one drill and another, or to connect freely between various drill sections or components. Aligning to common reference points or similar *kimochi* (feelings) will begin to open up these drills to more accurately represent what they are trying to achieve.

To get you started on this exploration, begin by making better use of the original reference drill to switch sides at will, progress through each drill in turn without a break, or stitch different combinations of drills together. The reference drill is the generic commonality throughout the exercises and thus, may be used at any point.

Once you're comfortable with finding commonality with the reference drill, the next progression would be to seek other commonalities and learn to use them to transition between different components from each of the standard drills. This is effectively a training method that advances from the fundamental lesson given in *Bunkai Nidan*, to better understand that limb control is essentially based on a discrete number of 'connections' that the arms may make when they clash. The next stage would then be to learn how to break flow and conclude by incorporating a range of exit drills.

Breaking the Loop

It is important to supplement this kind of training with various 'exit' or 'finishing' techniques to ensure that the conceptual lesson and mind-set of 'stop opponent and escape' is sufficiently ingrained. As such, these 'exit drills' are designed to purposefully break flow and at the very least, provide a dominant advantage to end the engagement. In actuality, this is what all functional *kata* application should aim to offer as a bare minimum and why the development of *kata*-based flow drills are inherently flawed in order to practice in a repetitive and time efficient fashion.

Exit drills can come in all shapes and sizes dependent on the situation presented, but like all aspects of practical *kata bunkai*, simplicity and effectiveness should be prioritised above all else. You may choose to break into striking, attack the enemy's outstretched limb, exploit a loss of balance by throwing, or manage a decrease of range by dominating a clinch. Whatever the method, the critical emphasis is to break flow at the most appropriate time. Here are just a few examples of how this idea may be utilised as part of your flow drill practice:

- *Sequential Exit Drills* – for each flow drill in turn, practice exiting at each and every stage of movement. This makes certain that all the drills are backed up with the mind-set of breaking flow. Once flow has been broken, reset and begin again, breaking next time at a different point.

- *Focused Exit Drills* – for each point of exit, practice a particular skill-set applicable to your current study. For instance, if you're working on developing joint attacks, then you can practice the ability to find such applications within the limb connections found across the drills. You can also take this a stage further by focusing entirely on elbow attacks, wrist attacks or shoulder attacks. Of course, this notion may also be applied to other combative aspects such as striking, throwing and grappling etc.

- *Alternating Exit Drills* – Take turns with your partner to switch roles and perform consecutive exit drills as appropriate. Practice exiting from both a dominant and dominated position.

- *Kata Application Exit Drills* – When exiting, use the opportunity to practice specific *kata* applications to their conclusion. You may choose to free flow between *kata* movements, explore how a single application may be used at various points of reference or amalgamate multiple applications together. You may decide to apply only one specific *kata*, or related lessons given by numerous *kata*.

- *Exit Drill Failures* – Look also at the possibility that an exit drill may fail and how this may drive you to re-engage and return to the flow drill. This is a great challenge to see whether your flow drills are working properly to aid spontaneity, since the whole requirement for 'flow' should be as a response to failure. An example may be that you first attempt to exit with an elbow joint attack, but this is then countered by your partner, thus requiring a 'flow' back into the drill in order to try a different exit.

Employing exit drills such as those described above will work to highlight the true potential within the *Naihanchi* limb control exercises shared here in this chapter. Their malleable framework and characteristics means that their only real limit is held within the minds of those practicing them. Therefore, I would encourage readers not to simply copy these drills 'parrot fashion' (as this was never my intention when creating them), but instead use them as inspiration to uncover your own personal adaptations. *Naihanchi Kata* is more than rich enough to accommodate many different interpretations.

Combining Ideas

In the final part of this chapter, I'd like to look at how, by having a particular situation in mind, we may apply a combination of 'depth' and 'breadth' analysis to our *kata*, along with the foundational lessons gained from *Bunkai Nidan* already covered in previous in order to seek possible solutions.

Quite possibly, the solutions you find during such a course may or may not be deemed effective, they may or may not be historically accurate and they may or may not end up becoming part of your holistic skill-set. However, personal experience has shown to me time and time again that this process of exploring *kata* choreography freely and with a more open mind can be hugely rewarding on a number of levels. And even if the ensuing findings turn out for the most part to be practically useless, it's likely that the experience gained from the route taken to find them will have been more that worth it.

To isolate and hopefully illustrate this idea more clearly, let's consider the 'problem' of a typical standing head-lock. This is considered by many sources to be a common act of physical violence, witnessed across a wide range of civilian encounters. We will look to apply some practical analysis by asking questions against the contextual framework of *Bunkai Nidan* and turning to the physical choreography of *Naihanchi Kata* for possible answers…

The typical standing head-lock is a common act of physical violence.

1. ***When is the best possible time to counter this attack?***

   Well, it would be much better avoided if possible, so situational awareness and subsequent 'soft skills' to recognise and evade potential threats (lesson one) would take priority.

   If aware, but not able to avoid, then situational control with de-escalation (combining lessons two, three and four) would be next on the list.

   If all of the above were to fail and an attack is felt to be imminent, then a pre-emptive assault (lesson six) may become necessary.

2. ***How would you make it difficult for the attacker?***

   If 'defence in depth' from Step No.1 has failed then there may still be a possibility of making it difficult for the attacker to actually apply the head-lock. This may be achieved by employing principles from counter-grappling (lesson eight), including the adoption of a strong base and posture, with hips underneath and close to the assailant's, making it more challenging for you to be bent forward.

   Further effectiveness may be gained by adapting the generic clinch frame in order to brace hard against the enemy's face.

Step No.2: Using posture from Naihanchi Kata plus the principle of 'framing' to make applying the head-lock difficult.

Step No.3: Reducing pressure on neck and obtaining basic impact protection of vital areas.

3. *What if the technique is applied?*

If all else fails and you find yourself in a head-lock then the main concerns are (1) pressure around the neck, (2) being punched in the face and (3) being taken to the ground. Pressure on the neck may be reduced along with basic impact protection of vital areas by tucking your chin and twisting your head towards the assailant's body. You can also pull down on the assailant's forearm towards your hip in typical *hikite* fashion.

Step No.4: Using reactionary tactics from Naihanchi Kata to intercept attempted strikes.

Step No.4: making use of the generic clinch frame from lesson 8 to momentarily secure position.

4. *What happens if the enemy tries to strike?*

As the assailant retracts their arm to strike, you can employ the principles covered in reactionary tactics (lesson 5), by bringing your hands up and out to intercept.

You can then attempt to momentarily secure in place if possible with the generic clinch frame (lesson eight). Both of these applications are consistent with the principle-based lesson plan as given within *Naihanchi Kata*.

5. *How can you strike?*

As we've discussed, percussive impact is of paramount importance in self-protection and using principles from the primary physical strategy (lesson six), we can explore ways in which to attack from this vulnerable position.

Two effective options would be to attack the groin or if the assailant's head is forward, their face/throat. These options may be backed up with tertiary manipulations, such as seizing, ripping and tearing etc.

Of course, an aggressive mind-set plays a huge part here. Repetitive percussive attacks and painful manipulations backed up with a 'get off me now' attitude and supported by vocal vehemence may be just enough to help enable your escape.

Step No.5: Employing percussive strikes with tertiary manipulations.

6. *How can you escape?*

By adapting the felling principle of manipulating the head (lesson nine) along with tertiary skills, you can reach around to attack under the assailant's nose (philtrum) and lever their head back. At the very least, this will offer more distance to work up the hierarchy of impact and/or take the assailant to the floor.

If you can pull your head out from the grip and obtain an index, then you can resume your primary percussive strategy (lesson six) to help facilitate escape.

Step No.6: Escaping with a combination of adaptations from Naihanchi Kata lessons on felling and striking.

7. *What if the assailant drives you to the ground*?

Being taken to the ground from the head-lock was the third concern given in Step No. 3. For this situation, you can use a structural frame (lesson eight) to help reduce force of grip and to manipulate opponent's head (lesson nine).

By gaining some leverage, you may then be able to create sufficient space in order to reverse the pin and achieve a more dominant position. As usual, the aim for self-defence would be to detach and stand up as quickly as possible.

Remember that percussive impact and tertiary skills may be employed throughout as in the previous step. For example, you can attack the philtrum and exploit any extra distance offered by the frame to strike the enemy's exposed throat. With gravity back on your side, striking can also be employed from top position.

Step No.7: Escaping a headlock on the ground using a structural frame concept from Naihanchi Kata to reduce force of grip and manipulate head, offering enough leverage to reverse the pin and gain a top positon.

8. ***Can the same process and principles be applied to other head-locks?***

Following is an example of a possible counter against a rear choke, which is another common act of violence.

Like the standing head-lock, these are very difficult to escape from once fully applied, so you are being forced to make the best out of a bad situation given that your defence in depth protocol has either failed or wasn't available.

Step No.8: Can the same principles be applied to a rear choke?

Of course in reality, specific conditions and difficulties, may require a different strategy, but nevertheless, it is possible for us to use the same (or similar) principles as previous in order to construct a possible escape and counter...

Try to obtain a stable base, dip your chin, lean forward and pull the choking arm down to help reduce pressure against your neck. Slip to the side in order to create some space to attack and strike towards the groin. Using body weight and with a strong two-on-one grip, lever hard against the opponent's shoulder in an attempt to break free. Then immediately index/strike, working up the hierarchy of impact with your primary percussive strategy.

In my view, a principle-based process of analysis based on contextual aims and adaptation to circumstance constitutes a more 'fit for purpose' application of *kata*.

Step No.8: Using similar principles to counter a rear choke.

In summary, it is clear that combining the core lessons from *Bunkai Nidan*, along with an open-minded depth and breadth analysis can lead to a deep exploration of *Naihanchi Kata*. Furthermore, this is only the combative analysis - Who knows whether or not this *kata* had (has) other contextual aims to consider? Of course, we may never know the original purpose of *Naihanchi Kata*, but I am confident that it sits very well as a fundamental principle-based platform for *karate*. Venturing 'outside the box' as suggested in this chapter may be a step too far for some, but I feel that the experience to be gained from such a substantial exploration will positively serves one's holistic development as a *karate* practitioner.

For me, *Bunkai Sandan* effectively turns the downside of not having the definitive answer for *kata* in to a stepping stone for more comprehensive development. Plus, by 'breaking the moulds' of both the specific choreography and your former understanding, the process of investigating *kata* in this way can be used as a valuable tool for your ongoing growth in martial arts.

Working various movements from Naihanchi Kata on a useful training device that includes two spring-loaded dummy arms for solo practice.

CHAPTER XXI

THE WIND THAT BLOWS THE SEED

"Kata must be correct, unlimited and most of all, alive. It can never be just 'form'. It is essential to train for the 'living' form."

~ Hironori Ohtsuka.

Today, the purpose of *kata* may be different from one *karate-ka* to another and may depend heavily on the specific mind-set of each practitioner. Some may practice and use *kata* to win trophies, some may perform *kata* sequences as a meditative means to combat their stressful lifestyle and some may find *kata* to be a valuable addition to their health/fitness regime. Others may enjoy *kata* for a combination of the above reasons plus many more. For me, the fact that classical *kata* may be used in so many ways to benefit diverse aspects of our lives is a positive testament to the true beauty of *karate* and if real value is to be found, then the practice of *kata* can always be considered a worthwhile investment.

For practical *karate* practitioners who view the art as a method of effective civilian-based self-protection, then the original purpose of *kata* as a way to record, preserve and disseminate combative methods would naturally tend to take priority. For this purpose and to stimulate a holistic study, one must explore deeper than an unrelated collection of applications or 'tricks' toward a more integrated approach, which in my opinion should also include the specific way in which *kata* is performed and repeated in order to instil particular characteristics. Specifically, the movements that make up the solo representation help to ingrain important structural and dynamic elements (see *Volume One*), plus other essential attributes that support the successful implementation of their combative application. In other words, even the way in which you perform *kata* and how that method changes as you grow can have combative relevance and serves to connect different forms together as an entire cohesive system or 'style'.

Indeed, if all other *kata* 'came from' core forms such as *Naihanchi* or *Sanchin* then there would be little reason for them to exist. What I've found from my own study and as I've tried to share with readers within this book is that *Naihanchi* provides a strong fundamental principle-based platform for the rest of the *kata* (and therefore, the art) to sit. In my opinion, *Naihanchi* works very well to achieve this, whether or not it was the original purpose. So in this short chapter, I'd like to culminate the section on *Bunkai Sandan* to address the idea of performing *kata* in order to support 'function', as opposed to performing *kata* purely for 'aesthetics'. Whichever camp you may sit in, this issue needs to be personally addressed regardless so that the specific training method(s) you choose to follow may be more accurately aligned to your goals. In progression to this idea and the reason I've chosen to write about this here, I'd also like to look at a couple of examples where *Naihanchi Kata* may be connected through functional movement and used to help influence other solo form representations within *karate*. In particular, this understanding has helped me greatly in 'joining the dots' between *kata* movements and in more recent years, has succeeded to drive a much more unified approach to my study.

Firstly, it is important to mention that for a more holistic use of *Naihanchi Kata,* then it makes sense that the fundamental structural and dynamic rules you follow to ensure its effective application must remain consistent throughout. In other words, if you happen to perform cohesive structural elements within *Naihanchi Kata* and then come to find that these are broken when it comes to the stylistic way you perform other *kata*, then this could never yield a fully integrated study, no matter how well you can combatively apply those movements. For the classical view to be true that *Naihanchi Kata* should be the very core of our *karate*, then we must aim to seek its essence within the rest of our art.

I feel that the solo performance of *kata* should be a long-term developmental process aimed to cultivate the relevant *kimochi* (feelings) associated with their specific choreography. This means that the way *kata* is performed should naturally change according to personal experience, ability and current training emphasis. If the performance of your *kata* has remained the same for years, then I would suggest that you question the value you're gaining from such stagnant repetition. Quite often, the way I perform *kata* can change on a daily basis and even between repetitions, depending on what attributes I'm currently seeking to develop. Sometimes it feels like I've made progress and other times it feels like I'm still a mere beginner. But, by aligning the performance of *kata* to how it feels rather than how it looks and by coming to understand the similarities associated with their essential mechanics, we can then aim to re-create similar feelings elsewhere in training. In my opinion, this is the key to making the actual solo performance of *kata* an integral part of the *bunkai* process, making it far more valuable than a mere aide-mémoire of combative applications.

Developing *kimochi* spans much more than solo performance and is also key to gaining a strong appreciation of the spontaneous application of *kata* according to specific self-protection based scenarios. Since there are only so many ways one can 'connect' to another and the fact that the application of *kata* is designed to operate within such close-range parameters, equating to these core references, rather than a host of specific attacks for example, becomes a more valuable association to explore. As such, you should aim to seek commonalities within different forms and also what particular feelings may be attributed to different *kata*.

Based on the above it is entirely possible to hone the ability to inherently feel when specific combative attributes/principles of certain *kata* may be best applied. For instance, certain situations may warrant the combative 'sensation' given by a particular *kata*. If you happen to practice the five *Pinangata*, then this would be a great place to start, as each has its own distinct feeling and consequent application methodology. This practical use of *kimochi* may then be used to transcend a mere surface-level application study and appreciate that the choreography of the form is a template of examples that encourage a significantly deeper study. In terms of application, it means that the conceptual lessons from *kata* may be more freely accessed and employed as the situation demands, whether or not the choreography happens to be directly applied or whether in fact, the said application visually resembles any particular part of the *kata* at all!

Examples of how Naihanchi Kata may relate structurally to movements from other classical forms.

Naihanchi Kata serves to offer a selection of characteristic 'feelings' that happen to be common across many other classical forms. By seeking connections rather than their superficial differences, you will find that progression in *karate* is not about the continuous collection of techniques, but rather an unrelenting effort to internalise the essential movement pathways associated with the arts physical expression of core principles. In this sense, *karate* becomes a relatively condensed system, with functional expertise coming from the simplicity and malleability of applying less, rather than feeding the addiction to increasingly add more. When we study in accordance with the above in mind, then the term *'kihon'* begins to take on a whole new meaning.

In a similar way and as we've seen within this book series so far, *Naihanchi Kata* serves to disseminate many of the most essential elements of *karate* and the foundational strategies for effective self-protection. The integral analysis of *Bunkai Sandan* should then aspire to find these core building blocks within the rest of the art. Just like the DNA in all living organisms, the *kihon* expressed through core forms such as *Naihanchi Kata* contain the intrinsic instructions for the continuation and developmental function of *karate*.

As an example, let's consider the conceptual lesson from *Naihanchi Kata* on *Envelope of Strength*, which outlines the limits of our structural stability, outside of which we become structurally weak and in some circumstances, prone to injury. Applying integral analysis to this concept would be to conform to this rule in all the other *kata* you practice. In this way, the specific *kimochi* encouraged by this lesson within *Naihanchi Kata* may be felt and utilised throughout the whole system. If you find a part of your *karate* that breaks the rules, then ask yourself why and explore deeper.

Another example would be the various framework positions offered by *Naihanchi Kata* that again, should be sought elsewhere within the performance of other forms. By making only superficial adaptations to the *ura-zuki* position for instance, provides us with the technique of *shuto-uke/uchi* (knife-hand reception/strike). The feeling of upper arm stability developed from the *kagi-uchi* (hooking strike) technique has a direct transfer effect into all *tsuki* (thrust) techniques. The way in which the elbows are controlled during transitions and their connection to the body as maintained within the *soto-uke*, *morote-uke* and *ura-zuki* combination technique has direct relevance to the essential *kihon-waza* (fundamental techniques) in *karate*.

The above cases are only a snippet of what I could have included. The important point to consider when exploring *Naihanchi Kata* for integral analysis is that the *kimochi* or specific feelings (either structural or dynamic) associated with its choreography may be used to guide our ability to find tangible connections in other *kata* and indeed, their practical application. Unifying the way we look at *kata* using this principle of integration can help greatly towards finding a cohesive and holistic agenda, not only for a single *kata*, but across the entire art.

CONCLUSION

"Apply the way of karate to all things and therein lies its beauty"

~ Gichin Funakoshi

Although specialists will forever debate on nuances within their particular field of expertise, any good teacher of civilian based self-protection will agree that a prime characteristic of the skills required to meet such an objective would be that of simplicity. As we've already discussed, in a violent and adrenaline fuelled confrontation, solutions that require complexity above that of digital decision making, default positioning and gross motor actions are by their very nature flawed and as such, carry a much greater risk of deteriorating under pressure. Thus, the core combative framework necessary to cultivate the highest probability of success in a self-protection situation must be based on exercising efficiency wherever possible.

Successful reverse engineering of *kata* choreography requires both purpose and perspective. It is my opinion that for *Naihanchi Kata* to be considered the core of *Shuri*-based *karate* systems, as is traditionally put forward, we must aim to find within its movements a definitive relationship to an overarching strategy for self-protection, plus an understanding of those efficient human movement pathways that are universal to the art. Once we determine our purpose and perspective, then we can work to identify a suitable and integrated framework for our analysis to be founded. So rather than sailing away without course nor destination, our exploration may always be driven along an established route that is set (where possible) by level-headed preparation, supported by whatever body of historical/developmental information we are fortunate to possess.

This second volume is a modest attempt to present a written summary of how I applied the above process in my own personal study. Whether or not any of the content here is deemed to be 'historically accurate', I hope you may nevertheless be inspired to approach the subject of *kata bunkai* with a pragmatic and open mind. For me, the methodologies outlined in this book have allowed me to practice, use and teach the combative strategies I believe are held within *Naihanchi Kata* in a cohesive way. A way that seamlessly connects with other *karate* jigsaw pieces to form a much more organised and comprehensive picture of the art. As such, this volume stands merely as a checkpoint to record my findings to date and share them with those who care to listen.

As *karate* pioneers of our past have alluded to, *Naihanchi Kata* contains a wealth of information and if studied via a principle-based formula, the combative teachings given within what seems to be a rather limited choreography can be brought to the surface and extracted further to produce a myriad of practical applications, designed to support a whole host of self-protection based scenarios. Furthermore, the specific order of its choreography possesses some significance and teaches vital lessons on game plan priorities and tactics against potential failures should they become apparent.

My intention for the third and final instalment of this book series is to develop the lessons from previous volumes into more progressive live drilling strategies and then to supplement *Naihanchi Kata* study with a host of associated attribute development practices. This will hopefully serve to complete the circle and bring together a holistic and functional process that may be tweaked as individually required and incorporated directly into pretty much any self-protection or self-developmental based *karate* system.

As an additional bonus, *Volume Three* will also briefly touch on *karate's* multi-framework training protocol to provide guidance on how the fundamental self-protection focussed model may be used as a conduit for a better understanding of some of the deeper aspects of practice, a way to stimulate personal growth and longevity, as a blueprint for developmental achievement in many of life's progressive challenges, plus a way to support the daily strive to become a better person. In this way, we can successfully (and I suppose paradoxically) make use of the practicality of *karate* to find contentment and at the same time, actively resist from having the risk of violence govern our existence. After all, the consequences of being forced to exercise physical combat are seldom positive and as genuine *karate-ka*, it is always our duty to promote peace.

I'd like to take this opportunity to offer you my sincere gratitude for taking the time to read this book, supporting my work and playing a part in allowing me to continue sharing my passion with others. I hope you've enjoyed this 'checkpoint' and find the content to be of some interest and service to your ongoing martial arts journey.

Until next time…

まだまだ

"Karate is placing virtue before vice, values before vanity and principles before personality."

~ Sokon Matsumura

ABOUT THE AUTHOR

Chris Denwood has been a dedicated practitioner of traditional *karate* since childhood and specialises in exploring the art's core principles for civilian self-protection, personal development and life integration. He is the Founder and Chief Instructor of *E.S.K.K*® *Martial Arts & Fitness* and teaches regularly from his home in the North West of England.

A member of the *Martial Arts Combat Hall of Fame*, Chris is a respected author and magazine columnist, with his articles, books and video tutorials being shared across countries around the world. He also teaches seminars internationally and has travelled numerous times to *Okinawa*, the birthplace of *karate*, in order to study with senior masters and pay respects to the art's historic lineage.

As an adjunct to his martial training, Chris is also a nationally qualified fitness instructor, advanced level kettlebell lifting coach and second degree *Reiki* practitioner. These interests, alongside many years of research in martial arts have allowed him to pursue a holistic expression of traditional *karate*, away from some of the more conventional views associated with the art.

It is Chris's deep passion for *karate* that provides fuel for him to continually expand. He endeavours to teach from the heart, actively seeking to encourage the enrichment of one's life through austere training, healthy living and honest self-expression - allowing for the traditional study of *karate* to shape a practical way of life in today's modern society.

For more information about Chris and to contact him direct, please visit:

http://www.chrisdenwood.com